CW01260921

Toni Morrison and Literary Tradition

Also Available From Bloomsbury

Bret Easton Ellis: American Psycho, Glamorama, Lunar Park,
edited by Naomi Mandel

Chuck Palahniuk: Fight Club, Invisible Monsters, Choke,
edited by Francisco Collado-Rodriguez

Cormac McCarthy: All the Pretty Horses, No Country for Old Men, The Road,
edited by Sara Spurgeon

Don Dellio: Mao II, Underworld, Falling Man,
edited by Stacey Olster

Louise Erdrich: Tracks, The Last Report on the Miracles at Little No Horse, The Plague of Doves, edited by Deborah L. Madsen

Margaret Atwood: The Robber Bride, The Blind Assassin, Oryx and Crake,
edited by J. Brooks Bouson

Philip Roth: American Pastoral, The Human Stain, The Plot Against America,
edited by Debra Shostak

Toni Morrison: Paradise, Love, A Mercy, edited by Lucille P. Fultz

Toni Morrison and Literary Tradition

The Invention of an Aesthetic

Justine Baillie

BLOOMSBURY
LONDON · NEW DELHI · NEW YORK · SYDNEY

Bloomsbury Academic
An imprint of Bloomsbury Publishing Plc

50 Bedford Square	1385 Broadway
London	New York
WC1B 3DP	NY 10018
UK	USA

www.bloomsbury.com

Bloomsbury is a registered trade mark of Bloomsbury Publishing Plc

First published 2013

© Justine Baillie, 2013

All rights reserved. No part of this publication may be reproduced or transmitted in any form or by any means, electronic or mechanical, including photocopying, recording, or any information storage or retrieval system, without prior permission in writing from the publishers.

Justine Baillie has asserted her right under the Copyright, Designs and Patents Act, 1988, to be identified as Author of this work.

No responsibility for loss caused to any individual or organization acting on or refraining from action as a result of the material in this publication can be accepted by Bloomsbury Academic or the author.

British Library Cataloguing-in-Publication Data
A catalogue record for this book is available from the British Library.

ISBN: HB: 978-1-4411-8310-1
ePub: 978-1-4411-4551-2
ePDF: 978-1-4411-8446-7

Library of Congress Cataloging-in-Publication Data
A catalog record for this book is available from the Library of Congress.

Typeset by Newgen Imaging Systems Pvt Ltd, Chennai, India
Printed and bound by CPI Group (UK) Ltd, Croydon, CR0 4YY

Contents

Acknowledgements	vi
Abbreviations	vii
Introduction: 'The Changing Same'	1
1 Historical and Literary Context: The Harlem Renaissance	13
2 Ideology, Identity and the Community: *The Bluest Eye* (1970) and *Sula* (1973)	43
3 Intertextuality and Gender Politics: *Song of Solomon* (1977) and *Tar Baby* (1981)	93
4 Repetition, Memory and the End of Race: *Beloved* (1987), *Jazz* (1992) and *Paradise* (1998)	137
5 Reading and Writing: *Love* (2003), *A Mercy* (2008), *Home* (2012)	181
Bibliography	207
Index	225

Acknowledgements

I would like to thank School of Humanities and Social Sciences colleagues at the University of Greenwich for their support. I am indebted to former colleagues at Goldsmiths, University of London, especially Professor Helen Carr. Thanks also to Robert Spaven and Pauline, Jim and Sarah Baillie.

Abbreviations

BE	Toni Morrison. (1970), *The Bluest Eye* (1990 edn). London: Picador.
S	Toni Morrison. (1973), *Sula* (1991 edn). London: Picador.
SS	Toni Morrison. (1977), *Song of Solomon* (1998 edn). London: Vintage.
TB	Toni Morrison. (1981), *Tar Baby* (1991 edn). London: Picador.
B	Toni Morrison. (1987), *Beloved* (1988 edn). London: Picador.
J	Toni Morrison. (1992), *Jazz*. London: Picador.
P	Toni Morrison. (1998), *Paradise* (1999 edn). London: Vintage.
L	Toni Morrison. (2003), *Love*. London: Chatto & Windus.
M	Toni Morrison. (2008), *A Mercy*. London: Chatto & Windus.
H	Toni Morrison. (2012), *Home*. London: Chatto & Windus.

Introduction: 'The Changing Same'

In a body of work spanning five decades Toni Morrison has engaged in a project for the recovery and reconstruction of African-American history. This has involved the creation of a literary aesthetic through which she exposes hegemonic and ideological uses of language and knowledge in the construction and obfuscation of American history. Morrison's confrontation with history has necessitated the development of oppositional forms of language that function to negate the damage inflicted by racially and ideologically specific language. It is a political project that privileges the specificity of African-American knowledge and linguistic forms and articulates the history from within which these forms are created. The linguistic strategies employed by Morrison are informed not only by African-American experience in white American culture, but they also contribute to the deconstruction and reconstruction of that experience. In doing this, Morrison avoids chronological delineations of history and presents instead a non-linear historicity, a cosmology of time and repetition that itself finds reflection in the structure of her aesthetic as each novel takes up and extends the themes of the preceding work in continuous, intertextual dialogue. They are all of course engaged with the historical period to which they refer, but Morrison's novels also exist in dialogue with the social and political milieu in which they were written.

I argue that Morrison's aesthetic must be understood in relation to the historical, political and cultural contexts in which it, and the traditions upon which she draws, have been created and developed. This involves an analysis of Morrison's engagement with intellectual, philosophical and literary developments in African-American and American writing and politics and their influence upon her fiction. I consider the ways in which vernacular and American literary forms are synthesized by Morrison in the construction of an alternative and oppositional narrative of black American history, a diasporic history of black American engagement with the west.

The changing same

It is in this context of intertextuality, hybridity and synthesis that this introduction draws on poet, playwright and political activist LeRoi Jones's (Amiri Baraka) conceptualization of 'the changing same'. In his book *Black Music*, 'the changing same' is used by Jones to identify black musical creation as the imaginative response to the cultural, political and economic hegemony of the west (Jones, 1968, pp. 180–211). For Jones, although African-American musical expression has taken many forms, from the spirituals of slavery, rural and urban blues and jazz, it nonetheless retains, in all of its forms, what he calls, following Ralph Ellison, 'the blues impulse' as expressive of black experience in the west. Paul Gilroy, in *Between Camps*, has adopted Jones's concept of 'the changing same' in order to articulate the potential of a 'diaspora politics' that transcends the modern nation-state. For Gilroy, 'the changing same' is not 'some invariant essence', rather it is a fluid, political and poetic expression of diasporic existence.

> [I]t is ceaselessly reprocessed. It is maintained and modified in what becomes a determinedly nontraditional tradition, for this is not tradition as closed or simple repetition. Invariably promiscuous, diaspora and the politics of commemoration it specifies challenge us to apprehend mutable forms that can redefine the idea of culture through a reconciliation with movement and complex, dynamic variation. (Gilroy, 2000, pp. 129–30)

The value of Gilroy's reformulation of the 'changing same' lies in the recognition of cultural traditions as variable, non-static and irreducible expressions of diasporic identity and politics. This approach allows for a multiplicity of black experience that retains, as its core, the first traumas of the diaspora and yet does not reify black culture as racial essence. As we shall see, Morrison's aesthetic evolves in indeterminate variation and avoids simple, positive affirmations of an authentic blackness originating in over-determinations of the folk sensibility. In effect, Jones's blues impulse as the privileging of lower-class African-American sensibility has become the mode of expression for a much wider diasporic experience that may still privilege the vernacular and racial memory, but without essentializations of race. Morrison's treatments of class, gender and geographical dislocation problematizes received and fixed notions of African-American identity.

Jones's work is also a useful starting point for an analysis of Toni Morrison's fiction as its publication coincides with the beginning of Morrison's creative life as a novelist and also, more importantly, because Jones's reflections on the importance, in African-American music, of remembering the past for the reconstruction of the future, and on the collective expression of black experience, are also constant concerns of Morrison's work. Morrison has indeed said that she wishes to express, in the form of the novel, 'something' that has only ever been expressed in music (Morrison intv. with McKay, 1994, p. 152). This 'something' may be more clearly defined if we attempt to understand Morrison's aesthetic as a literary articulation of the musical 'blues impulse'. Jones discusses the development of a black American musical tradition in terms of its oppositional relationship to the white world and the impetus for change and improvisation that this relationship engenders. This has meant the continuous re-invention of black musical forms in response to enslavement and migration from the rural South to the urban centres of North America, and central to this blues impulse is the articulation of a racial memory that has its origins in pre-slavery Africa (Jones, 1968, p. 183). Morrison similarly draws upon a specific cultural heritage in the construction of her aesthetic, a heritage already containing those elements most expressive of African-American history and experience. She does not, however, attempt to emulate music in her writing but rather evokes what was once expressed in African-American music, which by the 1980s, for Morrison, had been co-opted and assimilated and was no longer exclusively black. Music, as a subversive, political performance, became subsumed by commodity economics and thus, Morrison argues in 'Rootedness: The Ancestor as Foundation', needed to be replaced by a new form of political language, best expressed in the novel.

> For a long time, the art form that was healing for Black people was music. That music is no longer *exclusively* ours; we don't have exclusive rights to it. Other people sing it and play it; it is the mode of contemporary music everywhere. So another form has to take that place, and it seems to me that the novel is needed by African Americans now in a way that it was not needed before. (Morrison's italics, 1984, p. 58)

For Morrison, the novel must retain the healing function of music and the oral, collective, and oppositional elements expressive of black experience in America. Orality and the tradition of storytelling are transferred into the novel form and this, for Morrison, is an important political act, narrative being, for her, in her Nobel Lecture, 'one of the principal ways in which we absorb knowledge' (Morrison, 1993, p. 7).[1]

Like Walter Benjamin's 'storyteller', Morrison is a writer who draws on communal memory and history to convey 'something useful' in a non-prescriptive and indeterminate aesthetic in which 'counsel is less an answer to a question than a proposal concerning the continuation of a story which is just unfolding' (Benjamin, 1936, p. 86). The 'unspeakable' (*B*, p. 199 and Morrison, 1989, pp. 201–30) experience of a diasporic trauma originating in modernity, Benjamin's 'secular productive forces of history', is articulated by Morrison for a community that has been left 'not richer, but poorer in communicable experience' (Benjamin, 1936, pp. 84, 86). To communicate the unspeakable through storytelling is for Morrison an act of recovery from the psychological trauma of slavery and a means to articulate possibilities for the future. From the ruins of modernity, Morrison, through the interpretation of a traumatic past, makes it 'possible to see a new beauty in what is vanishing', a beauty that can be brought to bear on the future in the communal retelling and revision of stories (Benjamin, 1936, p. 86).

To do this means reconstructing history and exposing the oppressive power of a dominant language and ideology. In choosing the novel form, Morrison must necessarily engage not only with a black literary tradition but also create her fictions in dialogue with the western narrative canon. As with her musical counterparts, this is the blues aesthetic as synthesis, as a hybrid of two traditions that, again like jazz, in even its most European, classical forms, 'still makes reference to a central body of cultural experience' (Jones, 1968, p. 181). Through a process of appropriation, mastery and inversion, Morrison improvises on European and American literary forms and employs them to foreground stories yet untold. She engages closely with romance narrative forms, Greek myths or the *Bildungsroman* and takes from them what is needed, as 'found objects', to be reshaped and decoded in order to recover the presence of blackness in the narrative of American nation building (Morrison intv. with Gilroy, 1993a, p. 181).[1]

It is the political impulse of this dialogue that leads me, in Chapter 3, to a consideration of Gilles Deleuze and Félix Guattari's theoretical delineations of

---

[1] Morrison explains that she is trying to use, in the form of the novel, 'the strategies of art' that are in African-American music. 'The power of the word is not music, but in terms of aesthetics, the music is the mirror that gives me the necessary clarity . . . The major things black art has to have are these: it must have the ability to use found objects, the appearance of using found things, and it must look effortless. I have wanted to develop a way of writing that was irrevocably black' (Morrison intv. with Gilroy, 1993a, p. 181).

a 'minor literature' as the collective enunciation of the margin. In Deleuze and Guattari's conception of a minor literature a dominant language is subsumed and reconstructed in the creation of a 'minor' language appropriate for the expression of a communal sensibility that offers new epistemological and narrative possibilities. I shall use their work on language and minority literature to elucidate Morrison's efforts to move beyond language in its defining and confining 'major', or dominant, mode. Vernacular theories of African-American literature, particularly those of Henry Louis Gates and Houston Baker provide an account of the specifically cultural and formal linguistic practices from which Morrison constructs her aesthetic. Their examinations of the formal properties of the 'black' text – signifying, call and response, the importance of orality – all of which I will refer to in later chapters, enable the identification of those art forms upon which Morrison draws to create an 'irrevocably black' aesthetic (Morrison intv. with Gilroy, 1993a, p. 181). African-American literary theory has now moved beyond the need to affirm the authenticity of African-American literature through the valorization of vernacular forms, but it is in the context of their significance as incursions into both the canon and the academy that they are introduced here.

Vernacular theories of literary criticism

Henry Louis Gates has carried out a vitally important recovery of black literary texts and vernacular traditions and has successfully contributed to efforts to establish the importance of African-American literature in literary studies. In 'Criticism in the Jungle', Gates identifies a black tradition in an attempt to provide the foundation for a literary canon, but he avoids reading black literature as the illumination of the sociological and economic problems faced by black communities, preferring instead the analysis of linguistic structures and a non-contextual, close reading of the text that does not attempt to validate particular ideological and cultural positions. In this critical project, Gates's methodology is drawn from formalism, structuralism and post-structuralism.

> The black literary tradition now demands, for sustenance and for growth, the sorts of reading which it is the especial province of the literary critic to render; and these sorts of reading will all share a fundamental concern with the nature and functions of figurative language as manifested in specific texts. No matter to what ends we put our readings, we can never lose sight of the fact that a text

is not a fixed 'thing' but a rhetorical structure which functions in response to a complex set of rules. It can never be related satisfactorily to a reality outside itself merely in a one-to-one relation. (Gates, 1984, p. 5)

The value of this move lies in its anti-essentialism and in the privileging of close and sophisticated textual analysis. Gates does not deny that the political and historical struggles to create are integral to the imaginative form of black texts, but within his ahistorical method he undermines this acknowledgement; the abstraction of literature from its context for analytical purposes can have the effect of denying literature its political, material and social construction. Houston Baker, in *Blues, Ideology, and Afro-American Literature*, summarizes these problems in his own theoretical perspective which also, through the use of the 'blues matrix', foregrounds the vernacular origin of African-American literature.

> The critic who attempted to pattern his work on Gates's model would find himself confronted by a theory of language, literature, and culture that suggests that 'literary' meanings are conceived in a nonsocial, noninstitutional manner by the 'point of consciousness' of a language and maintained and transmitted without an agent, within a closed circle of 'intertextuality'. (Baker, 1984, p. 101)

Baker's own critical stance takes the form of a structuralist, holistic, cultural-anthropological approach, and he argues that 'works of Afro-American expressive culture cannot be understood unless they are contextualized within the independent systems of Afro-American culture' (Baker, 1984, p. 109). Baker's study is notable in terms of his move towards dismantling hierarchies established by the dominant discourse and he expands the discussion of vernacular culture in order to consider the importance of the 'blues matrix', not only within African-American culture itself, but also as a trope that can effectively illuminate American culture in general: 'My project is a minute beginning in the labor of writing/righting American history and literary history' (Baker, 1984, p. 200). Baker defines the blues impulse alluded to by LeRoi Jones and suggests its relevance for the analysis of African-American literary texts and traditions:

> The blues are a synthesis (albeit one always synthesizing rather than one already hypostatized). Combining work songs, group seculars, field hollers, sacred harmonies, proverbial wisdom, folk philosophy, political commentary, ribald humour, elegiac lament, and much more, they constitute an amalgam that seems always to have been in motion in America – always becoming, shaping, transforming, displacing the peculiar experiences of Africans in the New World. (Baker, 1984, p. 5)

In both Gates and Baker's theoretical formulations the vernacular is posited as the source of African-American creativity and this undoubtedly constitutes an important and strategic development in African-American literary criticism as they reveal the unique oral qualities of texts in ways that resist assimilationist or negative cultural readings. The move to establish the racial authenticity of African-American writing by emphasizing its vernacular folk origins is, however, problematic in its denial of black identities that may not, in fact, be lower-class, Southern and poor. Moreover, as Martin Favor points out:

> Emphasizing the unique nature of African American literature, isolating the important singularity that allows us to categorize a work as black or African American, is important, progressive work. Yet returning ultimately to folk culture, or some derivation of it, may also prove problematic because such a strategy never quite destabilizes notions of 'race' and differences that can be, and have been, used in the service of political and cultural oppression. (Favor, 1999, p. 6)

In later chapters, I argue that Morrison does indeed destabilize conceptualizations of folk experience as the single, authentic source of identity. There are tensions and contradictions in Gates's work as he adopts a liberal position from which he particularizes African-American culture and vernacular forms but simultaneously abandons the politics of black presence. Nevertheless, in terms of developing an effective critical theory, there are constructive elements in Gates's desire to appropriate cautiously, where relevant, the language and critical tools of the western tradition at the same time as privileging and developing black theories of criticism (Gates, 1986a, pp. 14–15).[2]

In response to Gates's call for a 'turn to the black tradition itself to develop theories of criticism indigenous to our literatures' (Gates, 1986a, p. 13), this book considers Morrison's aesthetic within a framework of the vernacular and of her literary and political heritage, but also employs the critical tools of western literary and philosophical enquiry to argue that Morrison's texts constitute a radical incursion into American literature and politics. Although Gates's work on the vernacular and the African-American literary tradition is a useful beginning, my concern with the formal properties of her work is facilitated by an exploration of the historical, literary and political contexts from which Morrison's aesthetic

---

[2] Gates advocates using western 'theories and methods insofar as they are relevant to the study of our own literatures', but is also aware that any 'attempt to appropriate our own discourses by using Western critical theory uncritically is to substitute one mode of neocolonialism for another' (Gates, 1986a, pp. 14–15).

arises. I am also concerned to identify the political and social forces that inform Morrison's narrative choices and in turn reveal the significance of such choices for the development of an African-American aesthetic.

In 'Unspeakable Things Unspoken' Morrison re-evaluates both the white and African-American literary canons and offers three proposals for an effective critical theory of American and African-American literature. First, 'one that is based on its culture, its history and the artistic strategies the works employ to negotiate the world it inhabits' (Morrison, 1989, p. 210). Secondly she urges literary critics to examine the ways in which an African-American presence in America has shaped white American literature and, thirdly, to analyse the qualities that make a work 'black', which for Morrison are most forcefully expressed through the cultural particularity of African-American language that is 'unpoliced, seditious, confrontational, manipulative, inventive, disruptive, masked and unmasking' (Morrison, 1989, p. 210). Morrison's cultural and historical perspective and an understanding of the strategies of African-American writers inform my own analysis of her novels in the subsequent chapters of this book.

In Chapters 3 and 4, I offer a reading of the work of Gilles Deleuze and Félix Guattari as a useful means of examining Morrison's novels. As well as drawing on their work on a 'minor' literature, I argue that Deleuze and Guattari overcome many of the limitations of European theory with a critique of traditional psychoanalysis and linguistics that is appropriate for an examination of the African-American aesthetic. For example, they criticize the linearity of western knowledge and reject the Lacanian concept of desire as rooted in lack, regarding desire, instead, as a capitalist construct that is inappropriate for the site of colonial struggle. This kind of approach, which they term 'materialist psychiatry', suggests a more realistic framework for understanding the realities of African-American experience. Deleuze and Guattari are primarily philosophers whose work embraces a radical study of aesthetics, political theory, psychoanalysis and linguistics. Their writing contributes to an understanding of both the operations of colonial discourse and the geo-politics of domination, and functions as a critique of 'traditional' linguistics. In relation to Toni Morrison, what is particularly liberating is their disavowal of preceding treatments of language by linguists who rely on the existence of linguistic constants or universals, a standard stable language against which all fluctuations must be measured. As I will consider the importance of Morrison's novels in the context of her place in African-American literary and intellectual traditions, these ideas, taken together, suggest an approach that avoids conventional and less politicized interpretations in which this tradition, as a 'sub-canon', can only exist in constant relation to the major canon.

In Chapter 4, I examine the implications of Morrison's contention that language itself is not oppressive but rather that oppressive force lies in the political and ideological functions of its deployment and interpretation. Morrison insists on a political response through the indeterminacy of her texts; an indeterminacy that devolves responsibility for interpretation onto the reader. I consider her aesthetic as one in which the reader's contribution is vital for the construction of narratives. In this sense, Morrison conceives her texts as dialogical, communal acts that engage the reader in a political act of interpretation and as such her work constitutes a radical incursion into the novel form itself. Through this process of appropriation and possession, Morrison is in effect engaged in a project for the transformation of the politics of language.

This project involves Morrison in a dialogue with her literary precursors and their efforts to establish a distinctive voice with which to negotiate the ideological and oppressive use of language. Chapter 1 explores the historical context, tensions and traditions from which Morrison's work and specific use of language arises. I have taken as an appropriate starting point the literature of the Harlem Renaissance and, focusing on the political and philosophical work of early twentieth-century African-American intellectuals, W.E.B. Du Bois and Alain Locke, have examined the tensions within the movement's efforts to establish a relevant aesthetic language, its relationship with white modernism and its place in current debates about modernity. The desire to establish a black literary identity necessitated engagements with minstrelsy, dialect and the idiom of the folk in general, and the themes and linguistic strategies of the 1920s and 1930s have informed and inspired black literary descendants. Morrison's novels develop Du Bois's early concerns with double consciousness and the psychological conflict it engenders. Her work also privileges African-American art forms, orality and musical expression in the creation of a distinct and politicized aesthetic. Chapter 2 examines Morrison's first two novels, *The Bluest Eye* (1970) and *Sula* (1973), in the context of her dialogue with the Black Aesthetic movement of the 1960s and its positive agenda of celebration and affirmation. Morrison problematizes 'black is beautiful' ideologies while retaining the overtly political aesthetic impetus of the movement. I also use Mikhail Bakhtin's work to explicate the materialist, dialogical, and political operation of Morrison's language in *The Bluest Eye*, an oppositional narrative that draws upon western forms and yet privileges African-American vernacular as a counter balance to the use of language as a vehicle for ideologies of beauty and scientific racism.

In *The Bluest Eye* and *Sula* Morrison engages with both the historical periods in which they are set and with debates current at the time she was writing. In *Sula* she is concerned with migration in the 1920s and yet Morrison's treatments of gender, community and the development of a black middle class in America are very much informed by debates about these same issues in the 1970s. In Chapter 3, I move on to *Song of Solomon* (1977) and *Tar Baby* (1981) and continue with Morrison's engagement with the debates of the 1970s, but here the focus is on masculinity and feminism as Morrison shifts from the direct, contestatory narrative of *The Bluest Eye* to a closer consideration of the internal dynamics of the African-American community itself. I argue that *Song of Solomon* constitutes an intervention into the contested terrain of African-American masculinity in the late 1970s and that Morrison undercuts the romance narrative and the form of the *Bildungsroman* in her engagement with American literary forms that extends to William Faulkner's Southern gothic narratives. The discussion of *Tar Baby* begins with an analysis of Deleuze and Guattari's linguistic theories that are then used to examine how Morrison takes her place as a 'minor' writer expressing a marginal sensibility from within the canon. Her only novel with a contemporary setting, *Tar Baby* complicates and feminizes *Song of Solomon*'s masculine quest as Morrison's indeterminate narrative explores the tensions between the assertion of a female identity for the 1980s and the preservation of a cultural heritage. In the penultimate chapter I discuss Morrison's *Beloved* (1987), *Jazz* (1992) and *Paradise* (1998), as a trilogy. *Beloved* returns us to the past and slavery and marks the beginning of a deeper engagement with history, memory and trauma. I approach *Beloved* from a psychoanalytical perspective as the return of the repressed experience of slavery; in Deleuzian terms, the atemporal repetition of individual and collective trauma may be overcome in a collectively authored text that allows for the release of repressed desire. This project continues in *Jazz*, where Morrison draws on musical structures and expression to articulate ways in which history's repetitions may be disrupted. As *Jazz* is concerned with confronting and assimilating the past, so *Paradise* considers the dangers of enshrining the past in ways that obstruct a true engagement with history. In *Paradise* Morrison is concerned to move beyond race and she attempts to construct a de-raced, non-racially specific language as an opening for a psychologically secure space, the paradise of her title. The final chapter is concerned with Morrison's return to class issues in *Love* (2003) and the possibilities to be found in her twenty-first century reworking of James Baldwin's understanding that love has possibilities for the transcendence of race, class and gender divisions. I approach *A Mercy* (2008) in relation to Morrison's interpretation of America's pre-racialized origins and her engagement with America's founding texts. *Home* (2012), reclaims community and family as significant for psychological and emotional recovery from the traumas of war, migration and racism.

To trace the trajectory of Morrison's aesthetic over ten novels is to follow the movement of African-American epistemology from the protest and affirmation of the 1970s, through the ambivalence of identity and representation in the 1980s, and to twenty-first-century efforts to transcend racial distinction and difference. Each chapter in this book offers a consideration of the development of Toni Morrison's aesthetic in terms of these developments in African-American literature and theory. I want to convey how this diversity has evolved in response to the original trauma of black experience in America as a 'changing same', a fluid and variable tradition of appropriation, improvisation and linguistic subversion.

Morrison's negotiation of the ideological functions of language is a continuation of earlier attempts by African-American writers to establish forms of artistic expression appropriate for the articulation of African-American experiences and identity. The Harlem Renaissance writers, as we shall see in the first chapter, were very much aware of how African-American idiom and dialect had been appropriated and debased in the production of stereotypes by the nineteenth-century tradition of minstrelsy. Their efforts to elevate and affirm the status of African-American artistic and cultural expression to the level of the western canon while retaining their own identity and group consciousness necessarily became a political project centred upon the operation and deployment of language. It is to a consideration of this project that I now turn.

1

Historical and Literary Context: The Harlem Renaissance

This chapter establishes a historical, literary and intellectual context within which Morrison's aesthetic can be situated, beginning with W.E.B. Du Bois's efforts to forge political gain from the affirmation of black cultural and intellectual endeavour in the early years of the twentieth century. I trace his, and Alain Locke's, influence on the Harlem Renaissance and its ambivalent relationship with early twentieth-century primitivist modernism, as Locke attempted to direct the new movement from a racist minstrel tradition. The tensions between Du Bois and Locke's efforts to orchestrate a 'New Negro' identity and the desire of younger writers such as Langston Hughes and Zora Neale Hurston to express a lower-class African-American sensibility are also considered here. I end with a discussion of the Harlem writers' relationship with a folk discourse which, in the formulations of Du Bois and Locke, was shaped by the desire to provide African-American art and literature with a political and national cohesiveness but was employed more problematically by Hurston and Hughes to establish an authentic racial identity.

These early debates are important for a consideration of Morrison's aesthetic as her project for the recovery and transformation of language extends the efforts of the Harlem writers to use language in ways that counteract its power to limit and define. Building upon the Harlem writers' concern with minstrelsy and primitivist preconceptions, Morrison extends the critique of dominant modes of language to include ideologies of education, beauty and twentieth-century cultural hegemony. As a leading intellectual, academic and literary figure, Morrison, like Du Bois before her, bears a pedagogical responsibility. In effect, the political intent of Morrison's project extends Du Bois's privileging of an African-American epistemology and her work dramatizes group and individual consciousnesses struggling for self-determination and psychological freedom from within a violent history and in dialogue with a romantically conceived folk discourse.

W.E.B. Du Bois and Harlem Renaissance modernism

In 1985, Toni Morrison remarked that black women writers were beginning to enjoy a 'renaissance' (Morrison intv. with Naylor, 1994, p. 213) and her choice of word is significant as it echoes the cultural, aesthetic and communal confidence articulated by Alain Locke in his introduction to *The New Negro* (1925). This collection of essays, African-American visual art, poetry, drama and fiction, first published in 1925, was a cultural and artistic signpost for the creative energy of the Harlem Renaissance and a positive attempt to synthesize and direct a sense of identity for an emerging generation of African Americans. Critics have identified the main period of Harlem Renaissance creativity as occurring between 1917 and 1935 and yet, as Henry Louis Gates has shown, the publication of *The New Negro* signalled a second African-American renaissance, the first being marked by the activities of critics, essayists and creative writers such as W.E.B. Du Bois, William Stanley Braithwaite, Paul Dunbar and Pauline Hopkins (Gates, 1997, pp. 162–7). Contrary to criticism that concentrates on the Harlem Renaissance as a brief period of creativity that reached its apotheosis with the publication of *The New Negro*, Gates outlines several different, but interrelated, African-American renaissance movements extending from the 1890s to the resurgence in black art, music and literature during the late 1990s (Gates, 1997, pp. 162–7). Morrison and others have sustained and developed the themes and aesthetic techniques formulated by such literary and intellectual precursors. Du Bois's writing, from his undergraduate work in the 1880s to his mature output in the 1960s, encompassed politics, fiction, philosophy, sociology and meditations on colonialism. Moreover, his political activism and international position as a racial leader places Du Bois at the centre of African-American political and literary traditions. Of particular relevance here are Du Bois's efforts to put black art and literature to political use, his role in initiating the particular modernisms of the Harlem Renaissance and the tensions within the movement's endeavours to establish an aesthetic language. Whereas Du Bois, in *The Souls of Black Folk* (1903), is preoccupied with the 'problem' (Du Bois, 1903, p. 1) of black identity, Locke's philosophical manifesto is constructed around cultural self-determination, an aesthetic to combine the folk and the modern with a positive sense of identity. Often regarded as a failure, the Harlem Renaissance in fact helped establish the modern African-American voice and allowed artists to develop a distinct language that held political and aesthetic meaning and spoke beyond both Harlem itself and the 1930s.[1]

The Souls of Black Folk is regarded as an African-American classic text and yet, as Shamoon Zamir points out, it is 'among the most widely quoted works of African-American literature, but also one of the most neglected' (Zamir, 1995, p. 2). In order to understand the full range and complexity of this text it is important, as Zamir suggests, to examine Du Bois's relationship with both European and American social science. Du Bois's experience of studying in the 1880s in the racially affirmative atmosphere of Fisk, Tennessee intensified his burgeoning racial consciousness and allowed him to reconstruct his identity from that of a New Englander American into a 'Negro'. In his autobiography he writes:

> So I came to a region where the world was split into white and black halves, and where the darker half was held back by race prejudice and legal bonds, as well as by deep ignorance and dire poverty. But facing this was not a lost group, but at Fisk a microcosm of a world and a civilization in potentiality. Into this world I leapt with enthusiasm. A new loyalty and allegiance replaced my Americanism: hence-forward I was a Negro. (Du Bois, 1968, p. 122)

Although Du Bois makes references to 'Negro blood' in *The Souls of Black Folk*, they are largely strategic attempts to appease the expectations of a white readership and the volume, in general, reveals a subtle, anti-essentialist approach to race and an understanding of racial identity as socially constructed. Du Bois writes with great care about this issue and qualifies any lapses into nineteenth-century racial discourse.[2] In an earlier essay, 'The Conservation of the Races' (1897), he

---

[1] See, for example, Nathan Huggins, *Harlem Renaissance* (1971) and David Levering Lewis, *When Harlem Was in Vogue* (1981). Houston Baker in *Modernism and the Harlem Renaissance* points out, 'While Huggins adduces provinciality and narrowness as causes for a failed Harlem Renaissance, . . . Lewis ascribes Harlem's failings to a tragically wide, ambitious and delusional striving on the part of renaissance intellectuals' (Baker, 1987, p. 10).

[2] The extent to which Du Bois regards race as socially rather than biologically constructed has been the subject of considerable debate. In his reading of Du Bois's 1897 speech to the American Negro Academy, 'The Conservation of the Races', Anthony Appiah argues that Du Bois's definition of race does not transcend nineteenth-century scientific concepts and that Du Bois relies on biological definitions even as he offers a 'revaluation of the Negro race in the face of the sciences of racial inferiority' (Appiah, 1986, p. 25). In contrast to Appiah, Lucius Outlaw reads Du Bois's definition of race as a political project for the 'social reconstruction of identity' and for 'self appropriation by a particular people suffering racialized subordination' (Outlaw, 1996, p. 28). Robert Gooding-Williams is in broad agreement with Outlaw (Gooding-Williams, 1996, pp. 39–56). See also Bernard R. Boxhill's argument that, rather than the claim of a common history committing Du Bois to a biological concept of race, 'What is essential is that the group inherit a common way of life that has developed over generations' (Boxhill, 1996, p. 62).

disingenuously claims how 'we must all acknowledge that physical differences play a great part, and that, with wide exceptions and qualifications, these eight great races of today follow the cleavage of physical race distinctions', but goes on to stress:

> The deeper differences are spiritual, psychical, differences – undoubtedly based on the physical, but infinitely transcending them. The forces that bind the Teuton nations are, then, first, their race identity and common blood; secondly, and more important, a common history, common laws and religion, similar habits of thought and conscious striving together for certain ideals of life. (Du Bois, 1897, p. 41)

If Fisk provided Du Bois with a new-found racial awareness, then Harvard ensured his exposure to the work on pluralism and relativism initiated by the psychologist and philosopher William James. This distinctly American form of philosophical pragmatism questioned existing thought on the nature of reality and challenged any form of absolutism by stressing the relativity of ideas in time and in place. James believed in the notion of a pluralistic society that would contribute to the formation of a philosophical, social humanism and the extent to which Du Bois was influenced by James is the subject of debate. Cornel West, for example, situates Du Bois firmly in a genealogy of pragmatism that includes Emerson, Dewey, James and Rorty, claiming that Du Bois succeeded in offering an African-American perspective that provided 'American pragmatism with what it lacks' (West, 1989, p. 147). Zamir, however, in an analysis of Jamesian pragmatics and Hegelian theory and their relation to Du Bois's early work, makes clear the limitation of notions of free will and relativism that rely on an assumption of the inherent integrity of the collective will in allowing for individual or group self-expression in a pluralistic society. James ultimately fails to understand the nature and ramifications of the role of terror in the construction of black identity and culture. As Zamir writes:

> It is not that James offers Du Bois nothing that can today be recuperated as positive value. James's emphasis on contingency and striving in the real world does play a significant part in turning Du Bois toward politically committed social science work . . . But what is most radical in Du Bois's early work is his ability to confront, through complex descriptions of the outer contours and inner torments of black life in America [the process and inheritance of slavery]. In this endeavour James is of little help to him. (Zamir, 1995, p. 46)

Du Bois's encounter with the rigours of German methodology, as a student at Berlin University, enabled a more objective understanding of the highly racialized nature of American society and also helped refine his study of Hegel's writing, from which he drew selectively. He rejected Hegelian historical idealism – freedom through the logic and destiny of history – but instead filtered Hegelian notions of civilization through what he calls in *The Souls of Black Folk* 'the gift of second sight'.

> After the Egyptian and Indian, the Greek and Roman, the Teuton and Mongolian, the Negro is a sort of seventh son, born with a veil, and gifted with second-sight in this American world, – a world which yields him no true self-consciousness, but only lets him see himself through the revelation of the other world. It is a peculiar sensation, this double-consciousness, this sense of always looking at one's self through the eyes of others, of measuring one's soul by the tape of a world that looks on in amused contempt and pity. One ever feels his two-ness, – an American, a Negro; two souls, two thoughts, two unreconciled strivings; two warring ideals in one dark body, whose dogged strength alone keeps it from being torn asunder. (Du Bois, 1903, p. 2)

We see here the first intimation of the idea of double consciousness and its importance as a unifying theme connecting the disparate essays collected in *The Souls of Black Folk*. As a member of the African-American elite, Du Bois's double consciousness is an intensely personal and theoretical device. By this I mean that part of the struggle in *The Souls of Black Folk* is the conflict between western academic and literary traditions and African-American particularisms.[3] Each chapter is headed with a quotation from the western literary canon, juxtaposed against the musical notation of an appropriate Negro spiritual. Without their accompanying lyric these notations become esoteric subversions of the ornamental quotation as employed in the western canon[4] and it is this synthesis of folk art and western literature that underlies Du Bois's project

---

[3] See also Bernard Bell's argument that for Du Bois, 'double consciousness was a mythic blessing and a social burden: an ancestral gift for making sense of the mystery of life in the cosmic scheme of things, a product of institutionalized racism, and a dialectic and a dialogic process in American society between the bearers, on the one hand, of residually oral sub-Saharan African cultures and, on the other, of industrialized print cultures' (Bell, 1996, p. 95).

[4] See Eric Sundquist's detailed analysis of Du Bois's treatment of the Sorrow Songs in *To Wake the Nations*. Sundquist's purpose is 'to estimate the centrality of song to African-American culture, both its extension of the folk traditions of slavery into a later era and its incorporation of the tonal semantics of vernacular culture into modern literary form; to trace Du Bois's own remarkably comprehensive theorizing about African-American economic labour, political rights, and aesthetic endeavour in its continual reference to the grounding principles of survival and salvation articulated in the communal art of the spirituals' (Sundquist, 1993, p. 459).

for the advancement of African Americans. He wishes to exploit the double consciousness of African-American existence by placing the Sorrow Songs, or spirituals, as the classical music of America, their poetry the equal of any from the western tradition. Toni Morrison has appropriated this aspect of double consciousness in her own work and, as I argue in Chapters 2 and 4, exploits its potential as a 'strategy' for participation in American society without the loss of a politicized, marginal consciousness.

It is in Du Bois's strategic use of fiction, history, sociology and autobiography, combined with his privileging of folk expression, that *The Souls of Black Folk* is a distinctly modernist text. More than this, and in common with much modernist art, Du Bois's exposure of the hollowness of rationality's promise, for the enslaved at least, stands as a critique of modernity. As Paul Gilroy notes in *The Black Atlantic*, Du Bois's critical appraisal of Booker T. Washington's 'attitude of adjustment and submission' contains an implicit critique of American economic rationality, the 'gospel of Work and Money' readily adopted by Washington (Gilroy, 1993b, p. 128). Also, in his journey across Georgia, Du Bois describes the ravished landscape and poverty of African Americans in the aftermath of Reconstruction and reveals a profound sense of modernity's ultimate destiny to fail, declaring: 'With such foundations a kingdom must in time sway and fall' (Du Bois, 1903, p. 77). This finds echo in Zygmunt Bauman's discussion of modernism's place within modernity in which he describes how 'In modernism, modernity turned its gaze upon itself and attempted to attain the clear-sightedness and self-awareness which would eventually disclose its impossibility' (Bauman, 1991, p. 4, f.n.1). This distinguishes Du Bois's modernism from later white modernists such as Gertrude Stein, William Carlos Williams, Sherwood Anderson and Waldo Frank, who I will refer to in more detail later in this chapter. These writers tended to romanticize and homogenize black experience and their perceptions contrast sharply with Du Bois's vision of the South and the struggle for individual existence in the face of economic and racial discrimination in Georgia. For Du Bois, racial cohesion is only to be found in the articulation of the Sorrow Songs in the hallowed halls of the black institution, Atlanta University, where he taught economics and history at the time of writing *The Souls of Black Folk*.

The influence of *The Souls of Black Folk* on subsequent black writing has been profound. James Weldon Johnson wrote in 1968 that the work 'had a greater effect upon and within the Negro race in America than any other single book published in this country since *Uncle Tom's Cabin*' (Johnson, 1968, p. 203). This effect, especially in terms of the importance of double consciousness, can be seen in works as diverse as Johnson's own novel of 1912, *The Autobiography of*

An Ex-Colored Man, Ralph Ellison's *Invisible Man* (1952) and in Toni Morrison's fiction. *The Souls of Black Folk* is also an early example of the political use of folk culture, echoed in later Harlem Renaissance literature and art and, indeed, in Morrison's novels; as I argue in Chapter 2, Morrison, in *Sula* (1973) follows Zora Neale Hurston in exploring the anxieties of a migratory female identity in relation to a folk consciousness. Much criticism of the Harlem Renaissance has focused on the division between Du Bois's views on literature, as revealed in his editorship of the African-American journal *Crisis* from 1910 and which were generally regarded as conservative, and the vitalist modernism of later writers such as Langston Hughes and Zora Neale Hurston.[5] There were, of course, important differences between them, but would argue that Du Bois's work helped set the tone for the radicalism of late Harlem Renaissance artists in ways that he himself could not have foreseen.

Hurston was to use African-American dialect and folk stories in much less of an elitist fashion than that envisaged by Du Bois's elevation of folk art and his ordination of spirituals as the classical music of America. In an essay on the subject, Hurston rebuffs Du Bois's description of the Sorrow Songs as predominantly 'the music of an unhappy people' that 'tell of death and suffering and unvoiced longing toward a truer world, of misty wanderings and hidden ways' (Du Bois, 1903, p. 157). Instead, Hurston argues, 'The idea that the whole body of spirituals are "sorrow songs" is ridiculous. They cover a wide range of subjects from a peeve at gossipers to Death and Judgement.' She goes on to point out, 'What is being sung by the concert artists and glee clubs are the works of Negro composers or adaptors *based* on the spirituals. . . . All good work and beautiful, but *not* the spirituals' (Hurston's italics, 1934a, pp. 359–60). For Hurston, the importance of the spirituals lies in their existence as living, vibrant art, rather than as conserved classical music that loses spontaneity in the concert hall

---

[5] In *The Art and Imagination of W.E.B. Du Bois* Arnold Rampersad provides a detailed account of Du Bois's involvement with *Crisis*. In 1910, Du Bois left his teaching post at Atlanta University and helped found the National Association for the Advancement of Colored People (NAACP) and its monthly magazine, *Crisis*. Rampersad summarizes the main aims of *Crisis*: 'to defend, praise, and instruct black people; more simply put its goal was black power. A secondary but ultimately indispensable end was to extol certain principles that were only indirectly related to race but were irresistible in Du Bois's grand vision of man: morality, interracial harmony, socialism and world peace' (Rampersad, 1976, p. 143). In 1912, *Crisis* launched as a literary journal and it was the most important forum for black literature until Charles Spurgeon Johnson founded *Opportunity: A Journal of Negro Life*, in 1923, for the National Urban League, and established the journal as a platform for the younger Harlem Renaissance artists who reacted against Du Bois's view of their literature as decadent and his opinion that art should have a propagandistic purpose. Rampersad points out that Du Bois, in his *Crisis* editorial comments, became increasingly concerned that Harlem writers were not representing 'Negroes of Education and Accomplishment' (W.E.B. Du Bois, 'A Questionnaire', *Crisis* 31 February 1926, quoted in Rampersad, 1976, p. 195). For a general analysis of Du Bois and *Crisis* see pp. 184–201.

setting and she thought it unnecessary to sanitize African-American creativity in order to demonstrate its aesthetic worth. Toni Morrison takes her place much later within these debates as an advocate of folk art and sensibility not, like Du Bois, to prove African-African folk expression to be worthy of consideration by a white readership, but instead to privilege it, in the novel form, as a valuable source of knowledge for black Americans. Morrison invests the folk stories of the South with new meanings, for example in her reworking of the tar baby story for a 1980s readership in *Tar Baby* (1981), and her approach to folk culture, like Hurston's, stresses the spontaneous and dialogical functions of folk art as stories and songs that are never concluded, but constantly open to new and multiple interpretations.

The Souls of Black Folk is a carefully orchestrated work that addresses both black and white readers in an effort to show how, through the powerful expression of the Sorrow Songs, African Americans could transcend the Veil of racial segregation by demonstrating they possessed cultural qualities to enrich America's 'dusty desert of dollars and smartness' (Du Bois, 1903, p. 7). Du Bois argued that through the regenerative experience of higher education black people could articulate 'the rich and bitter depth of their experience, the unknown treasures of their inner life, the strange rendings of nature they have seen' and that these 'may give the world new points of view and make their loving, living and doing precious to all human hearts' (Du Bois, 1903, p. 66). This calculated attempt to illustrate the redemptive potential of African-American spirituality for all Americans is analogous to Alain Locke's showcase for black art and literature, *The New Negro*. However, in the 20 years between *The Souls of Black Folk* and *The New Negro*, a new confidence had emerged among African-American artists. In *The Souls of Black Folk* Du Bois remains concerned with the 'problem' of being African American and, although he saw possibilities in the spirituals for the 'uplift' of the race, the book ends with a refrain from 'Let Us Cheer the Weary Traveller' as he resists optimistic closure in its intimation of a journey to self-fulfilment which in many ways had only just begun (Du Bois, 1903, p. 164). *The New Negro* constitutes another stage in the journey, another renaissance. In *The Souls of Black Folk* Du Bois traversed the broken South in his sociological and psychological investigation of post-reconstruction America. In *The New Negro* Harlem has become the positive location, or as Locke put it, the 'Mecca', for African-American creative energy.

Alain Locke and *The New Negro*

Locke's project, like Du Bois's, was informed by the complex theories of race and culture he had developed during his formal study of philosophy at the universities of Howard, Oxford, Berlin and Harvard between 1904 and 1918. He taught at Howard, chairing the Department of Philosophy from 1917 to 1954, beginning a tradition of African-American philosophy that influenced departments and students across the country (Harris, 1989, p. 22). Founded in 1867 in Washington DC, Howard University was originally established and funded by the Freedmen's Bureau to provide education for recently emancipated African Americans. Locke's period of tenure saw the University grow in national and international stature and Morrison herself, reading English and Classics at Howard from 1949, would have been aware of Locke's ideas.

During his early career Locke was also influenced by William James's work on pluralism and relativism that he adapted to make a specific link between pluralism and dispossessed peoples. Locke focused his analysis of pluralism on African-American particularisms and their relationship to democracy and culture. He saw an ideal democracy as one allowing those group and individual freedoms that repression would deny (Rutledge, 1982), but he also wished to expose the reality of an America in which minorities were voiceless (Belles, 1982, p. 56). In his introductory essay to *The New Negro* he comments that 'an intelligent realization of the great discrepancy between the American social creed and the American social practice forces upon the Negro the taking of the moral advantage that is his' (Locke, 1925a, p. 13). Here, Locke transfers the emphasis from 'the Negro' as a 'problem', as characterized by Du Bois, to democracy itself and the book is as much a challenge to white America to open the 'channels' of its political system as it is a showcase for black art and literature (Locke, 1925a, p. 12). We can see this in Locke's cautionary tone: 'Only the steadying and sobering effect of a truly characteristic gentleness of spirit prevents the rapid rise of a definite cynicism and counter-hate and a defiant superiority of feeling' (Locke, 1925a, p. 13). What appears at first to be a stereotype of the gentle, spiritual Negro is in fact constructed as a 'counter stereotype' that Locke later admitted was necessary for the destruction of the old images of submission and minstrelsy (Locke, 1942, p. 210).

As Houston Baker writes, Locke, like Du Bois before him, developed strategies to explicate his radical call for a national cultural expression which necessarily meant he 'had not only to filter the absurd noises of minstrelsy but also, and at the same instant, to recall sounds of African origin in an age characterized by divided aims, betrayed hopes, and open brutalities. What was required was a shrewd combination of formal mastery and deformative creativity'. (Baker, 1987, pp. 71–2)

Baker makes a distinction here between the knowing, pragmatic use of African-American minstrelsy stereotypes by Booker T. Washington and Charles Chesnutt – what Baker terms *formal mastery*, and perhaps best exemplified by the perpetuation of those innocuous stereotypes calculated to elicit a sympathetic response from the white readership – and the more open *deformation of mastery* (Baker's italics, 1987, p. 50) involving the deliberate exaggeration of African-American *sounds*, as seen in the poet Paul Laurence Dunbar's use of dialect and Du Bois's evocation of the folk. Locke employs both these strategies but combines them in an act of *radical marronage*, an idea Houston Baker derives from the Maroons' deliberately exaggerated and fearful use of sound and language that does not make any sense to the outsider. The result is a rebellious, sophisticated variant of nationalism that finds expression in Locke's philosophy and the editorial decisions he makes in *The New Negro*.

Despite his affirmations of the racial particularisms of African-American artists and the merits of a culturally pluralistic society, Locke denied that he was advocating a form of separatism, arguing that 'The racialism of the Negro is no limitation or reservation with respect to American life; it is only the constructive effort to build the obstructions in the stream of his progress into an efficient dam of social energy and power' (Locke, 1925a, p. 12). Locke's desire for a racialized aesthetic was rendered more complex by his apparently contradictory argument that African-American art should aim at objectivity and universality. 'The newer motive, then, in being racial is to be so purely for the sake of art' (Locke, 1925b, p. 51). This tendency towards universality accounts, to some extent, for the inclusion in Locke's anthology of poetry that attempted to emulate western form and technique in its depiction of African-American experiences. The poetry of Countee Cullen, for example, was influenced by the English Romantics and Claude McKay employed the sonnet form in 'White Houses'. The desire for universality and the impulse to reveal to a white readership how African-American art could attain the standards set by a dominant aesthetic has been interpreted as a form of mimicry that both denied the tradition of dialect, music and rhythm available to the African-American poet and served to undermine the quality of their art. Bruce Kellner, for example, has claimed that 'the genteel tradition to which Cullen clung only weakened his poems eventually'

(Kellner, 1984, p. 88) and Gates, while accepting the rejection of dialect by the Harlem Renaissance poets because of its association with slavery and minstrelsy, feels that in doing so the African-American lost 'a peculiar sensitivity to black speech as music, poetry, and a distinct means of artistic discourse on the printed page' (Gates, 1989, p. 181).

Minstrelsy

The relationship between minstrelsy, American and African-American culture is a complex one that highlights some of the most conflicted and psychological aspects of race in America and has implications, as we shall see, for the language of contemporary, as well as Harlem Renaissance, African-American literature. As the most popular form of nineteenth- and early twentieth-century entertainment, blackface minstrelsy appropriated black dialect, music and dance in order to play out and exorcize the sexual, economic and racial anxieties of white America and served to deny the African American his humanity. Ralph Ellison offers insight into the ways in which the minstrel tradition worked psychologically to consolidate white America as a nation. He sees a contradiction between the white American's 'Judeo-Christian morality, his democratic political ideals' and 'his daily conduct' that forces a dualism of consciousness. From this he concludes that

> it was our Negro 'misfortune' to be caught up associatively in the negative side of this basic dualism of the white folk mind, and to be shackled to almost everything it would repress from conscience and consciousness. The physical hardships and indignities of slavery were benign compared with this continuing debasement of our image. Because these things are bound up with their notion of chaos it is almost impossible for many whites to consider questions of sex, women, economic opportunity, the national identity, historic change, social justice – even the 'Criminality' implicit in the broadening of freedom itself – without summoning malignant images of black men into consciousness. (Ellison, 1964, pp. 47–8)

Ellison remarks that central to the ideology of minstrelsy was the adoption of the blackface 'mask' of burnt cork or greasepaint which facilitated an exploration of the 'fascination of blackness'. Rather than seeing the application of the blackface mask as a crude act of racial domination, Ellison hints at the importance of unconscious desire in the construction of an African-American persona. This has parallels in the work of the postcolonial critic Homi Bhabha, who uses the psychoanalytic concept of ambivalence to analyse 'otherness' in terms of existing simultaneously as the 'object of desire and derision' (Bhabha, 1994, pp. 66–84). The introduction of desire thus complicates the power of minstrelsy, infusing it with ambiguity, fluidity and multiplicity in its historical and cultural manifestations.

In a genealogy of ante-bellum minstrelsy, Eric Lott extends Ellison's ideas and anticipates Bhabha, in his study *Love and Theft*. He shows how, as the Civil War approached, blackface portrayals became increasingly sympathetic to the anti-slavery movement and yet remained inherently racist, 'Underwritten by envy as well as repulsion, sympathetic identification as well as fear the minstrel show continually transgressed the color line even as it made possible the formation of a self-consciously white working class' (Lott, 1993, p. 8). Through his concept of 'transgression' Lott reveals the full intricacies of minstrelsy and its ambivalent relationship with African-American art and culture. The success of the first major sound movie *The Jazz Singer* (1927), starring the blackface minstrel Al Jolson, underscores not only the extent to which minstrelsy was inextricably linked to popular culture but how it could also blur the colour line by flouting white American cultural authority. The film's protagonist Jakie Rabinowitz, the son of a Jewish cantor, rejects traditionalism in his search for an authentic personal identity by becoming the black-faced jazz singer, Jack Robin. As in the modernist literary texts discussed later, we see here how race, or the adoption of race, becomes an experiment in forging a new American identity. With its images of Jolson continually applying and removing the grease paint, this famous film reminds us that, for the white rebel, convention and normality can be easily regained. As Michael North argues,

> the very mask that makes this rebellion possible also guarantees that it will not go beyond mime. The blackface masquerader can give himself up to the insurrectionary rhythms of jazz and at the same time identify these with another race which he resembles so little in his clumsy makeup as almost to emphasize his distance from it. (North, 1994, pp. 81–2)

The Harlem Renaissance, modernism and modernity

It is not surprising that the emerging African-American artists of the Harlem Renaissance were wary of employing a dialect already appropriated by the dominant culture throughout the minstrel tradition and in the written works of white Americans such as Joel Chandler Harris. Even if Booker T. Washington and Charles Chesnutt successfully moved 'behind – within, and through – the mask of minstrelsy to ensure survival, to operate changes, to acquire necessary resources for continuance, and to cure a sick world' (Baker, 1987, p. 47), the self-confidence of the Harlem poets was characterized by the desire to transcend what they perceived to be the trap of minstrelsy and to achieve new expressions of race through the objectivity of art. That the standard for this art was set by a dominant western aesthetic seemed less important to the Harlem poets than the need to disentangle themselves from 'the minstrel tradition and the fowling nets of dialect' in the way that Locke believed they had (Locke, 1925b, p. 48). However, in this declaration lay another potential problem. African-American writers wanting to escape the strictures of minstrelsy were enabled, ironically, by those writers and artists who were establishing a new standard of art in an emerging modernism that exalted a form of primitive spontaneity identified in Africans and African Americans. The earliest moment of this awareness, according to Locke, was the discovery of Benin art by Felix von Lushaun, a curator at the Berlin Museum. The pieces, looted from Benin city by the British in 1896, were bought by Lushaun and by the early 1900s had begun to influence young painters living in Paris, most notably Matisse and Picasso (Locke, 1969, pp. 34–7). Picasso appropriated African masks in *Les Demoiselles d'Avignon* in 1907 and in his portrait of Gertrude Stein in 1906. Stein herself utilized a literary form of the black mask in the 'Melanctha' section of *Three Lives* (1909), a reconfiguration of an earlier fictionalization of her own unhappy love affair, this time transposed onto black characters. Using the dialect of black Baltimore, Stein forged what she regarded as a new language that marked 'the first definite step away from the nineteenth century and into the twentieth century in literature' (Stein, 1933, p. 58). Stein's creative strategies meant the rejection of conventional literary techniques that could not adequately express the new concern with individual subjective consciousness that William James did so much to initiate. The most radical aspect of her work was the way in which she articulated African-American dialect in a representational, rather than a realist, form.[6] For McKay, this was nothing more than a fad to be resisted, in his case, by writing intensely political poetry in a traditional style (cited in North, 1994, p. 115).

---

[6] Ann Chartres, in her introduction to Stein's *Three Lives*, acknowledges Stein's use of racial and ethnic stereotypes but argues, 'Stein's portraits have authenticity because she used her own language for the descriptions of her fictional characters' life and speech rather than relying on the degrading stereotypical speech patterns of the "stage German" or the blackface "minstrel show" Negro' (Chartres, 1990, pp. xvii–xviii).

Locke saw the importance of these developments for the dislocation of artistic conventions and realized how the early modernist application of African art provided possibilities for a new generation of African-American artists and writers. He identified an answer to the problem of expressing a folk sensibility while at the same time negotiating the pernicious nature of the minstrel tradition. As Du Bois, 20 years earlier, had tried to resolve this problem by elevating the Sorrow Songs to the status of classical art, Locke now saw, in European and American modernism, opportunities for the affirmation of African-American racial expression. Writing on Negro art, he discusses the European interest in African art and music. 'There is a vital connection between this new respect for African idiom and the natural ambition of Negro artists for a racial idiom in their art expression. To a certain extent contemporary art has pronounced in advance upon this objective of the younger Negro artists, musicians and writers' (Locke, 1925c, p. 262). Locke called for the Harlem Renaissance writers to seek inspiration in the work of European artists and contemporary Americans interested in black America, thus establishing a temporary and uneasy alliance between the primitivist modernists and the new Harlem writers.

Central to this was Jean Toomer's relationship with Waldo Frank, the white cultural critic and novelist who believed the answer to America's moribund conservatism, materialism and individualism lay in the artist's ability to articulate what he felt to be the Southern, rural African-American's sense of group wholeness. The prose pieces, poetry and experimental drama of Toomer's *Cane* (1923), some of which are included in *The New Negro*, provided the synthesis that Locke sought. Toomer added a 'musical folk-lift' to the style of the American prose modernists and an ability to 'transpose the dialect motive and carry it through in the idioms of imagery rather than in the broken phonetics of speech' (Locke, 1925b, p. 51) and hence, like Claude McKay, avoided the taint of minstrelsy. A 'bright morning star' of the Harlem Renaissance, Toomer was linked more generally with those avant-garde writers, Gertrude Stein, William Carlos Williams and Sherwood Anderson, interested in primitivism as a form of artistic rebellion against an aesthetic standard. In a review of *Cane* Du Bois revealed how these most modern of modernist literary trends had begun to move beyond his aesthetic sensibilities. He admired the 'strange flashes of power' but found *Cane* difficult or even impossible to understand (Du Bois and Locke, 1924, pp. 161–2). The book certainly could not offend his moral sensibilities; Du Bois was not a conservative in this sense, as shown by his own novel, *The Dark Princess* (1928) that deals sympathetically with adultery and illegitimacy. Du Bois's objection, by 1926, when Harlem was perceived to be at the height of its decadence, was to those portrayals of African-American life which he viewed as debased and ultimately debasing, 'the continual portrayal of the sordid, foolish and criminal among Negroes' (Du Bois, 1926b, p. 165).[7] Like nineteenth-century minstrelsy, this kind of art, he argued, took crude and degenerate forms merely in order to fulfil the voyeuristic demands of a white audience.

In terms of technique, Toomer was undeniably influenced by the economical, impressionistic phrasings of the Imagists and his themes do foreshadow the concerns of other modernist writers. Indeed, George Hutchinson claims that the major importance of Harlem Renaissance modernism lies in its wholly interracial character and argues that an interpretation focusing only on white modernism's preoccupation with exoticism or primitivism overlooks the complexity of this relationship. Hutchinson refigures conventional definitions of a monolithic American modernism that mainly includes expatriates Eliot, Pound, Stein and Fitzgerald, to embrace the lesser known forms with which black writers and artists were associated. Most notable among these was the journal, *The Seven Arts*, concerned with developing a new polyglot, self-determining American culture by fostering the 'native' modernism of white writers Van Vechten, Marianne Moore and Sherwood Anderson and black writers like Toomer and Claude McKay. Hutchinson concedes that the radicalism associated with *The Seven Arts* was not entirely free of racism, but concludes: 'If Greenwich Village cultural nationalists shared certain stereotypical images of Africa with Eliot, they evaluated them in a radically opposed manner, one that affiliated them with the African-American writers of Harlem more than with their white compatriots in London' (Hutchinson, 1995, p. 97). Hutchinson also associates both black and white non-canonical modernism with the wider philosophical and anthropological work of key figures such as William James and Franz Boas. The pragmatism and cultural pluralism of James and others is related by Hutchinson to a 'low' modernism, or a form of 'critical realism', that characterizes much of the Harlem Renaissance literature and helps to explain why it has come to be seen as modernist.

> Even the formal experiments of Harlem Renaissance authors are most often attempts to incorporate folk forms into poetry or fiction, or to bend generic conventions from Western literary tradition to their own uses, while the so-called bourgeois writers such as Larsen and Fauset were unabashedly 'realistic', in an

---

[7] Examples of the novels that Du Bois particularly objected to are: Carl Van Vechten's *Nigger Heaven* (1926); Julia Peterkin's *Black April* (1927) and Claude McKay's *Home to Harlem* (1928).

almost old-fashioned sense, except for the nature of their subject matter and the people to whom they gave voice. (Hutchinson, 1995, p. 119)

By redefining the academy's delineation of modernism as always being anti-realist, Hutchinson recovers neglected black writers previously overlooked because they were concerned to portray middle-class black life rather than express a more fashionable, gritty modernism. Hutchinson's delineation of an interracial modernism, however, overlooks some of the serious problems encountered by black writers in their relationships with white patrons and New York publishing houses. Toomer, for example, bridled at his publisher Liveright's request that he exploit his blackness when publicizing *Cane* and Langston Hughes had a famous disagreement with the wealthy patron Mrs. Osgood Mason when his work became too critical of white high society (Wintz, 1988, pp. 180–3). Hutchinson also ignores those forms of black art, such as the burgeoning black film industry, that were intended only for a black audience (Stewart, 1997, p. 93). More importantly he fails to consider the full implications of aesthetic modernism's relationship with modernity that involved an early dependence on primitivism as the means to redefine American culture and critique the ongoing degenerate rationality of the Enlightenment project.[8] It is remarkable that the regenerative properties of primitivism began the process by which modernism was to establish itself as high art. Early American modernists, weary of rationality, were enabled by the most extreme example of Enlightenment excess, racial slavery, to draw upon the African-American's existence as the antidote. As Robert Young notes in his discussion of culture and modernism in *Colonial Desire*, 'the notion of culture developed so that it was both synonymous with the mainstream of estern civilization and antithetical to it. It was both civilization and the critique of civilization, and this characteristic form of self-alienation has marked culture from the start' (Young, 1995, p. 53). What differentiated black modernism from all other forms was the African-American's particular experience of modernity. As Paul Gilroy writes in *The Black Atlantic*, 'the literary and philosophical modernisms of the black Atlantic have their origins in a well-developed sense of the complicity of racialized reason and white supremacist terror' (Gilroy, 1993b, p. x). Gilroy traces the development of black 'double consciousness' as a counter culture of modernity, a transnational and intercultural black Atlantic

---

[8] I am using Zygmunt Bauman's definition of modernity in *Modernity and Ambivalence*, as 'a historical period that began in Western Europe with a series of profound social-structural and intellectual transformations of the seventeenth century and achieved its maturity: (1) as a cultural project with the growth of Enlightenment; (2) as a socially accomplished form of life – with the growth of industrial (capitalist, and later also communist) society' (Bauman, 1991, p. 4, f.n.1).

with a philosophical and literary tradition expressed in two different, but closely related forms, the *politics of fulfilment* and the *politics of transfiguration*. The former embraces the promise and language of the Enlightenment's demand for justice and equality. The politics of transfiguration has more creative and utopian ambitions and has its origins in the need for plantation slaves to express the unsayable through song and is verbal, textual and semiotic. Gilroy stresses that black performative expression is distinctly political and rooted in 'commentary on the systematic and pervasive relations of domination that supply its conditions of existence' (Gilroy, 1993b, p. 38). Together, the politics of fulfilment and transfiguration comprise a critique of racial capitalism that is unique in its denial of modernity's insistence on separating art and life. Thus, for Gilroy the black Atlantic exists within modernity and yet transcends it. The expressive culture of black people has its foundations in a slave system itself integral to the development of western civilization and yet provides the impetus for a new and liberating poetics that reflects the politics and history of black culture.

Gilroy seeks this new poetics through an analysis of black music, literature and orality and is concerned to map its changing shape and hybridity as a 'non-traditional tradition', a 'changing same' (Gilroy, 1993b, p. 101). Writers and artists working within this volatile aesthetic take on board the ambivalence of black consciousness and its historical and contemporary struggle with the project of the modern nation state. The techniques employed include a manipulative use of the spoken word, social memory, historiography and the disruption of linearity and together constitute a powerful critique of representation and subjectivity that confronts the terror of racial slavery.

Toni Morrison takes her place in Gilroy's vision of black poetics as a writer whose narratives of African-American experience stand outside conventional literary and historical discourse. It is their shared concern with racial memory and a Southern past of slavery, the tradition of the changing same, that brings Morrison together with many of her Harlem precursors. Toomer's *Cane*, for example, is concerned with twentieth-century black existence and yet the presence of slavery pervades. Through his complex use of language Toomer sought to express African-American experience in ways that the aesthetic strictures of modernism, as the racially tempered critique of modernity, would otherwise have obstructed. In a sense, he engaged in the process of 'signifying' on both the primitivist preconceptions of modernist discourse – which, despite its radical beginnings, quickly became the dominant discourse – and on the limitations of the Imagists in terms of form and style.

The term 'signifying' has its origin in the experience of slaves for whom a secretive, coded language became essential and is used generally to denote word games of playful insult or serious critique. As a semantic art form, signifying constitutes a creative, performative oral act used for the negotiation and critique of the white world and as a form of individual and communal expression. An exclusive and exclusionary form of communication, it is characterized by the indirect statement, always implying more than what is said, a private, encoded language born of the necessity for slaves to communicate in English while disguising meaning in the presence of the white master. It can involve the repetition, with embellishments, of well-known folk tales as well as verbal insults and more supportive word play.[9] As Rap Brown puts it:

> Signifying allowed you a choice – you could either make a cat feel good or bad. If you had destroyed someone or if they were down already, signifying could help them over, Signifying was also a way of expressing your own feelings . . . Signifying at its best can be heard when the brothers are exchanging tales. (Brown qtd. in Gates, 1988, p. 73)[10]

In *The Signifying Monkey* Henry Louis Gates attempts to construct a theory of the vernacular as a critical framework for the examination of the African-American literary tradition. Signifying provides, for Gates, a metaphor for the evolution of African-American literature as writers have drawn on the creative wordplay and language of signifying, and related oral traditions to create a 'double voiced' aesthetic, unique to African Americans. Moreover, artists within this aesthetic signify on, that is comment on and revise, texts in the western tradition as well as the texts of their precursors in African-American literature.

> Signifyin(g) is black double-voicedness; because it always entails formal revision and an intertextual relation . . . [It is] an ideal metaphor for black literary criticism, for the formal manner in which texts seem concerned to address their

---

[9] Geneva Smitherman provides an example of signifying. 'The blunt, coded language of enslavement *sigged* [signified] on Christian slaveholders with the expression, *Everybody talkin' 'bout Heaven ain' goin' there*. . . . In this instance, enslaved Africans were commenting on the hypocrisy of European Americans who professed Christianity but practiced slavery' (Smitherman, 1998, p. 216). See also Thomas Kochman, 1977, pp. 145–62. Lawrence Levine provides an invaluable account of early African-American cultural forms. He points out that across America signifying is known variously as the Dozens, Sounding or Woofing – a list which does not exhaust the different names given to the art of African-American wordplay. Levine refers to African-American verbal contests collectively as the Dozens. He points to the importance of humour in the Dozens (signifying) as a means for African Americans to understand, negotiate and survive the oppressive realities of their existence in America (Levine, 1977, pp. 344–58).

[10] Rap Brown from *Die Nigger Die!* (Brown, 1969, pp. 25–6).

antecedents. Repetition, with a signal difference, is fundamental to the nature of Signifyin(g). (Gates, 1988, p. 51)

In his discussion of the 'double-voicedness' of signifying Gates also makes use of Mikhail Bakhtin's theories of narration to which I will return in the next chapter.

Interpretations of Toomer's work focus on *Cane* as a lyrical 'swan-song' for the dying folk spirit of the rural South, as black Americans now faced the modern wasteland.[11] Yet, 'Seventh Street' also stands as a celebration of the new urban life and aesthetic possibilities that Toomer recognized would not match idealized visions of African-American existence.[12] Toomer spoke about the pain of creating *Cane*. 'It was born in an agony of internal tightness, conflict and chaos . . . the creations of the forms were very difficult' (Toomer, 1923, p. 156). It became the swan-song to his life as both artist and African American – he said he gave the book his 'last blood' and never really returned to literature. Instead, Toomer remade himself as 'The First American' in what he believed to be a new race of Americans of mixed of nationality and *Cane* was not recovered again until the Black Aesthetic movement of the 1960s (Turner, 1975, p. 122). In a review of a newly published collection of Toomer's writing in 1980, Toni Morrison commented that he had conveniently declared the end of Southern rural life in order to free himself of his race (Morrison, 1980). Morrison has revived Toomer's project, extending his themes and building upon his aesthetic through the use of call and response, mythic character representation, black dialect and music. Both writers dismantle white America's constructions of blackness and explore the negative effects of the adoption of white values by African Americans on their sense of self, community and culture. Morrison's *Jazz* (1992), for example, balances the spiritual cost of migration against a truly modernist vision of the city, 'when everything's ahead at last' (*J*, p. 7), in indeterminate combinations of good and evil. In articulating the experience of African-American communal life, Toomer and Morrison politicize black existence by drawing on the tools of western aesthetics while simultaneously privileging the African-American tradition of orality. Toomer does this by invoking the songs of the South; Morrison by emphasizing the vital, active and

---

[11] See for example 'The Aesthetic Structure of Jean Toomer's *Cane*', in *Negro American Literature Forum* (Krasny, 1975, pp. 42–3).

[12] Jean Toomer felt that in the urban segments of *Cane* he was depicting '[a] life, I am afraid, that Sherwood Anderson would not get his beauty [of the Negro] from. For it is jogged, strident, modern' (Toomer, 1923, p. 151). Nellie Y. McKay recognizes Toomer's ambivalence towards both the South and the North (McKay, 1984).

collective nature of black orality. The educated protagonist in Toomer's drama piece 'Kabnis', in *Cane*, goes south to elevate his people but searches in vain for a constructive and nourishing language; 'Th form thats burned int my soul is some twisted awful thing that crept in from a dream, a godam nightmare, an wont stay still unless I feed it. An it lives on words. Not beautiful words. God Almighty no. Misshapen, split-gut, tortured, twisted words' (Toomer, 1923, p. 111). In a wider sense, Toomer's search for the right words is symptomatic of the problems faced by the Harlem Renaissance writers in establishing and developing a language with which to articulate their changing sense of identity.

Zora Neale Hurston

Toomer's struggle with language and his ambiguous depiction of individual and group consciousness contrasts with the confident evocation of a folk voice found in Zora Neale Hurston's contribution to *The New Negro*. Her short story 'Spunk' explores the folklore of her Southern hometown of Eatonville and marks Hurston's emergence as a writer concerned with the authentic portrayal of African Americans rather than with racial or political rhetoric. Hurston took her place among an emerging group of artists who were to become increasingly critical toward what they regarded as a 'nordicized Negro intelligentsia', exemplified by Du Bois and, to some extent, Alain Locke. This shift was initiated by Langston Hughes in 'The Negro Artist and the Racial Mountain' (1926), published just one year after *The New Negro* and in which he articulated the views of a new generation of writers who were already beginning to distance themselves from the genteel morality expressed by many of their precursors. Hughes declared: 'We younger Negro artists who create now intend to express our individual dark-skinned selves without fear or shame' (Hughes, 1926, p. 694). For her part, Hurston created positive, complex characters in ways that built upon Toomer's realistic rendering of dialect and his delineation of Southern experience, yet without his bleak sensibility. Crucially, the static and tragic portraits of women in *Cane* are replaced by a complexity and sense of identity that establish the beginnings of an African-American female aesthetic, a poetics that is at once both theory and autobiography. Ironically, Hurston's art is more autobiographical than her famously, and perhaps deliberately, obscure autobiography, *Dust Tracks on a Road* (1942). Her first novel *Jonah's Gourd Vine* (1934) provides, for example, a detailed picture of the lives of her own mother and father, and Janie, in *Their Eyes Were Watching God* (1937), is a figure reflecting not only Hurston's life, but also the unwritten lives of all African-American women; Hurston's fiction is simultaneously autobiography and biography.

Hurston's break with the rhetorical endeavours of her literary contemporaries has a parallel with her radical work as an academic anthropologist and folklorist. Her presentations of black American folklore, published in 1935 as *Mules and Men* (1935), is a collection of stories, 'lies' and songs that signalled a turning point in the efforts of anthropologists to record black American experience and constituted an early attempt to combine the discipline of social science with literary technique. Hurston's ethnographic fieldwork led her away somewhat from the scientific credentials that anthropology had sanctioned for itself by the 1930s (Clifford, 1988, p. 25). Her multiple identities as a black artist, a rural Southerner and academically trained social scientist meant that Hurston's work, as Deborah Gordon has pointed out, 'violated one of the most important ideologies of Western history and culture, namely that authorship be neutral, unique and transcendent' (Gordon, 1990, p. 162).

It is not surprising that *Mules and Men* was, at the time of publication, regarded with suspicion by academics doubting the scholarly rigour of Hurston's methods. Anthropological discourse, however, now concedes that 'no sovereign scientific method or ethical stance can guarantee the truth' (Clifford, 1988, p. 23), and we can recover Hurston's anthropology of black folklore and re-inscribe her work with a significance not always recognized. *Mules and Men*, and Hurston's literary works, have been re-examined in attempts to uncover and consecrate a black literary canon. Gates, for example, cites Hurston as the first black writer concerned with privileging an oral literary tradition (Gates, 1988, p. 181), and Alice Walker, who is largely responsible for rebuilding Hurston's reputation, has described *Mules and Men* as 'perfect' because of its delineation of the wholly black community of Eatonville. For Walker, the strength of Hurston's collection lies in its 'racial health; a sense of black people as complete, complex, undiminished human beings, a sense that is lacking in so much black writing and literature' (Walker, 1983, p. 85). In Chapter 2, I discuss how Hurston in fact exposes the tensions within Eatonville's black community, but would concur that in all areas of her creativity Hurston certainly strived to represent African Americans 'as they are' without projecting ideological or political notions about what they should become. Her overriding focus on the personal life of her characters has left Hurston open to the charge that she lacked any real political conviction. Alain Locke, for example, praised her use of folklore in *Their Eyes Were Watching God*, but would have preferred the novel to have been 'motive fiction and social document fiction' (Locke qtd. in Hemenway, 1986, p. 241). This was in spite of Locke's claim that Harlem Renaissance art should be racial 'purely for the sake of art', a contradiction recognized by Du Bois who saw *The New Negro*, positively, as an exercise in racial 'uplift' and propaganda and not one of 'pure' literature (Du Bois, 1926a, p. 141). In a devastating review of *Their Eyes Were Watching God*, Richard Wright argued that Hurston perpetuated a minstrel image of folk life that did nothing to further the political struggle in which African Americans were engaged. He noted that 'Her characters eat and laugh and cry and work and kill; they swing like a pendulum eternally in that safe and narrow orbit in which America likes to see the Negro live: between laughter and tears' (Wright, 1937a). Wright's review is surprising when viewed in the light of another essay in the same year, 'Blueprint for Negro Writing' (1937b), in which he reveals an attitude towards African-American folklore that is remarkably close to Hurston's own views. It was in

> a folklore moulded out of rigorous and inhuman conditions of life that the Negro achieved his most indigenous and complete expression. Blues, spirituals, and folk tales recounted from mouth to mouth; the whispered words of a black mother to her black daughter on the ways of men, to confidential wisdom of a black father to his black son; the swapping of sex experiences on street corners from boy to boy in the deepest vernacular; work songs sung under blazing suns – all these formed the channels through which the racial wisdom flowed. (Wright, 1937b, p. 104)

In his call for an African-American fiction that utilizes folklore hitherto 'unwritten and unrecognised', Wright denies its burgeoning existence in Hurston's fiction and anthropology. Hurston did not write the overtly political protest fiction that came, under Wright's powerful influence, to dominate black literature during the 1940s, but she did pre-empt those ideas as expressed in his 'Blueprint for Negro Writing'. Wright felt that if the writer's 'conception of the life of his people is broad and deep enough, if the sense of the *whole* life he is seeking is vivid and strong in him, then his writing will embrace all those social, political, and economic forms under which the life of his people is manifest' (Wright's italics, 1937b, p. 104). Wright could, in fact, be describing those very elements that do characterize Hurston's work. Hurston achieves a political, even perhaps a theoretical, project by means of a deceptively simple presentation of 'her people' that belies complex representations of identity, community and female/male relationships. It is a crystallized and pure form of literature in which, although no one is lynched or hounded, her characters' lives are nonetheless informed by a history of racial violence and Janie's quest for identity serves to render the personal as political and as history: 'Janie saw her life like a great tree in leaf with the things suffered, things enjoyed, things done and undone. Dawn and doom was in the branches' (Hurston, 1937, p. 20). It is understandable that Wright overlooks Hurston's originality and importance when we remember that her work was out of print for most of his career. It is, however, a tragic interruption in the tradition that, again, finds reflection in Hurston's personal life, and meant that women like Janie could not be figured again until Morrison created Sula during the 1970s.

Nancy Cunard and *Negro*

Ironically, it was the English heiress and Communist sympathizer Nancy Cunard who considered Hurston's work radical enough for inclusion in her anthology *Negro* (1934). This eclectic collection marked a break with Locke's carefully orchestrated anthology and revealed a new development in African-American radicalism that was much less concerned to protect the readership from the more contentious realities of black existence and culture. Furthermore, the tentative beginnings of an African-American modernist sensibility found, for example, in Toomer's contribution to *The New Negro* had, by the 1930s, evolved into a high modernism aligned with the radical politics of the left. Almost 1000 pages of quarto size, *Negro* was internationalist in scope and ambition, including works from the West Indies, South America, Europe and Africa. Again, like Hurston's work from the same period, Cunard's anthology quickly disappeared, a fact that may be attributed to its open affiliation with Communism and to the infamous unorthodox behaviour of Cunard herself. Certainly, there is a naivety about many of Cunard's editorial intrusions, particularly those in which she espoused the international Communist Party line.

Jane Marcus discusses Cunard's racial performance in terms of a modernist appropriation of slavery and primitivism that allowed freedom from both racial and sexual limitation.

> Her body is here very much part of the history of the period, draped in tiger skins, wrapped in leopard, or backed by metal as in a Metropolis landscape of Thirties Berlin. Breastless, white and phallic, stretched in pleasure or perhaps it's pain, caught in soft cloth manacles, bound by silken scarves, held by ivory chains, she becomes a boy or an androgynous creature (a different kind of woman, the

imaginary lesbian of Sapphic modernism?) from the African fertility figures with their pointed breasts which stand at the centre of modernist primitivism. (Marcus, 1995, p. 38)

This is not a negative assessment of Cunard's racial performance, but is in fact Marcus's acknowledgement of Cunard's ability to create herself in advance of a late twentieth-century femininity in which the creative construction of the body is considered acceptable, if not desirable. Cunard's performance of bondage is an attempt to identify with black suffering and her metaphorical use of race went beyond fashionable primitivism as her intense efforts to further African-American civil rights testify. As Toni Morrison, however, makes clear in her collection of essays *Playing in the Dark* (1992) race, as a social construction, has consistently played a far more iniquitous role when operating to establish a white American cultural and social identity (Morrison, 1992c, p. 63). This has involved the invention and employment of a black persona, a form of Africanism that allows white America to know itself as free. 'The metaphorical and metaphysical uses of race occupy definitive places in American literature, in the "national" character' (Morrison, 1992c, p. 63). Thus, in literature as well as in the forms of minstrelsy discussed earlier, we can see how the creation of an African persona functioned to define white America and to establish difference. Henry Louis Gates, like Morrison, situates his own discussion of the trope of race clearly at the site of language. 'The biological criteria used to determine "difference" in sex simply do not hold when applied to "race". Yet we carelessly use language in such a way as to *will* this sense of *natural* difference into our formulations' (Gates's italics, 1986a, p. 2). Hurston herself regarded race as a cultural, rather than a biological, product and was able to reverse and subvert the invented representations of Africans that served the dominant cultural hegemony.

Barbara Johnson reads Zora Neale Hurston in order to reveal the strategies that she employs when representing racial identity and difference and argues that 'questions of difference and identity are always a function of a specific interlocutionary situation – and the answers matters of strategy rather than truth' (Johnson, 1986, p. 324). Hurston then, inscribes a racial identity into the text according to the audience that is being addressed. In 'How It Feels to Be Colored Me' she creates a stereotype for the white readership of *World Tomorrow* which functions as a mask. In a comparison of her reaction to a jazz performance with that of a white male companion Hurston invokes the stereotypical savage that lies beneath a civilized exterior.

I am in the jungle and living in the jungle way. My face is painted red and yellow and my body is painted blue. My pulse is throbbing like a war drum. I want to slaughter something – give pain, give death to what, I do not know. But the piece ends. The men of the orchestra wiped their lips and rest their fingers. I creep back slowly to the veneer we call civilisation with the last tone and find the white friend sitting motionless in his seat, smoking calmly.

'Good music they have here', he remarks, drumming the table with his fingertips.

Music. The great blobs of purple and red emotion have not touched him. He has only heard what I felt. He is far away and I see him but dimly across the ocean and the continent that have fallen between us. He is so pale with his whiteness then and I am *so* colored. (Hurston's italics, 1928, p. 154)

Here, Hurston is masking and unmasking, shifting between her blackness and the civilization she mockingly undermines. Apparently accentuating racial difference Hurston in fact, through the ironic use of the collective pronoun 'we', denies its significance. The significant difference between Hurston and her white companion is that she has an artistic sensibility that enables her to *feel*, literally, 'colored'; an empowering sensibility which, like the blue paint, she is able to apply and remove at will.

The Harlem Renaissance and folk discourse

'How it Feels to Be Colored Me' reflects a major preoccupation in Harlem Renaissance writing, that of how to construct the self in ways that negotiate preconceived notions of blackness without relinquishing racial identity. Hurston's response to this paradox was to claim an identity for herself beyond the 'pigeonholes' of racial demarcation; a pre-figuration of the postmodern preoccupation with fluidity and ambivalence.[13] In this sense, Hurston is not so far removed from Du Bois as she believed herself to be.[14] As we have seen, Du Bois emphasized the cultural construction of race rather than its biological determinations and his recognition of the inherent ambiguity of black identity as

---

[13] In *Dust Tracks on a Road*, Hurston objects to 'the pigeonhole way of life' and claims 'I do not wish to deny myself the expansion of seeking into individual capabilities and depths by living in a space whose boundaries are race and nation' (Hurston, 1942, p. 237).

[14] See also Ross Posnock's discussion of Du Bois, Hurston, Patricia Williams, Darryl Pinckney and Toni Morrison. Posnock traces incongruities in Du Bois's political allegiances to both segregation and integration during the course of his career and concludes that Du Bois adhered to a pragmatist 'politics of non-identity', (Posnock, 1995, p. 251), a politics which Posnock aligns with Hurston's rejection of 'conventional political coherence' (Posnock, 1995, p. 253).

expressed in his explication of double consciousness had profound ramifications for the subsequent development of an African-American literary aesthetic. Determined to counteract negative constructions of race in the minstrel tradition and segregationist Jim Crow legislation, Du Bois and others sought to construct the 'New Negro' as a racially transformed figure, modern and adaptable to a new urban existence, and yet, paradoxically, aware of and determined to preserve, the cultural particularisms of a folk past.[15] This inevitably involved the writers of the Harlem Renaissance in complex and, at times, fraught relationships with a discourse of the folk.[16] Du Bois, Locke, Hughes, Toomer and Hurston all sought to negotiate the psychological, political and aesthetic problems they encountered in establishing a new 'black' literary movement through the deployment of folk discourse. By the 1920s, migration to the urban North had begun to disrupt African-American rural culture in the South and necessitated the creation of new forms of expression and conceptualization that could still be designated as folk culture. Reformulations of the folk aesthetic in the cities of North America are expressions of the desire for cultural continuity among dislocated rural migrants and were encouraged by the concomitant development of new markets for the folk as commodity.[17] Alain Locke seized upon the 'transformed and transforming psychology' of the 'migrating peasant' as the source of authentic racial expression that should lead and inform both artist and critic in a project towards cultural self-determination (Locke, 1925a, p. 7).

---

[15] Posnock points to another paradox in Du Bois's position. 'Du Bois's characteristic movement of mind is to revise and complicate all his assertions in accordance with his famous belief that black identity is inherently a problem, a "double consciousness". . . . Thus Du Bois's proclamation of his own exemplary significance and his general demand that the talented tenth serve the race inspire a project of racial unity founded on stable identity and at the same time make it problematic' (Posnock, 1995, p. 250).

[16] Favor in *Authentic Blackness: The Folk in the New Negro Renaissance* criticizes vernacular theories of literary criticism. For him, they privilege 'certain African-American identities and voices over others' (Favor, 1999, p. 3). In his study of James Weldon Johnson, Jean Toomer, Nella Larsen and George Schuyler, Favor argues that black writers often have a problematic relationship with folk culture and while 'many writers feel the necessity of writing themselves into a privileged discourse of black identity, . . . some authors, as they engage in a specific discourse of black identity, [folk discourse] also undermine a "natural" or, more precisely, "naturalized" – sense of African-American literary identity by asking pointed questions about the underlying ideologies of "race" and engaging in a sometimes playful, sometimes disturbing destabilization of the black subject' (Favor, 1999, pp. 3–4).

[17] See Evelyn Brooks Higginbotham, 'Rethinking Vernacular Culture: Black Religion and Race Records in the 1920s and 1930s'. Through an analysis of African-American religion and a growing record industry, Higginbotham traces the development of folk culture in the Northern states of America during the period of migration. 'Building on patterns from the folk tradition and thus rejecting a rational, dispassionate style, the recorded sermons and religious songs were especially appealing to the waves of rural migrants who poured into northern cities, uprooted and in search of cultural continuity. Record companies catered to the migrants' preference for a "down-home", that is, more rural, southern style by adopting such phrases as "old-fashioned", "real Southern style" and "old-time" in their record titles and advertisements' (Higginbotham, 1997, p. 166).

Locke's focus on the centrality of folk expression for black literary and artistic creation led him to compare Harlem's efforts as a cultural capital with nationalist struggles for political self-determination in Europe after the First World War: 'Harlem has the same rôle to play for the New Negro as Dublin has had for the New Ireland or Prague for the New Czechoslovakia' (Locke, 1925a, p. 7). Locke's introductory essay to *The New Negro* reveals a Herderian understanding of the *Volk* as nationhood, formed from the creative expressions of a cultural community, rather than as a political and geographical unit. Johann Gottfried von Herder's emphasis on folk culture and its representations of national characteristics in music and poetry, folk music being an important display of 'the internal character of the peoples' (Herder qtd. in Bluestein, 1972, p. 8), and as a focus for cohesive national consciousness, is apparent in both Locke's and Du Bois's reflections on the importance of transforming a folk past into a regenerative form of racial identity. Their admiration for the German intellectual tradition led them to equate the German struggle for national unity with African-American efforts towards a self-determined racial integrity. In fact, as Arnold Rampersad points out, Du Bois's 'definition of "folk" is primarily a political one and should be understood as interchangeable with the more daring term "nation"' (Rampersad, 1976, p. 74). Du Bois went so far as to claim that in the Sorrow Songs 'The same voice sings here that sings in the German folk-song' (Du Bois, 1903, p. 161). Du Bois's formulations of the folk were also informed by Herderian frameworks that extended as far back as Emerson, Whitman and earlier, and which had been adopted by the Communalist scholars that he encountered at Harvard. Francis James Child, Francis Barton Gunmere and George Lyman Kittredge's work on folklore held that folk poetry was the expression of a collective consciousness generated by an essentially classless society before the formation of the modern state. Within his own Herderian framework Du Bois was able to privilege the Sorrow Songs as the classical art form of America, not peripheral or exclusively for African Americans, but essential for the moral regeneration of an American culture driven by materialism and economic rationality. Concerned to emphasize the redemptive potential of African-American folk culture for America as well as affirm its quality as art, Du Bois provides a deeper and more politicized understanding of the folk as presented by late nineteenth-century American folklorists.[18] Despite this break, Du Bois's conception of the folk did not go beyond the Sorrow Songs to include other vernacular or musical expressions, and

---

[18] See Shamoon Zamir's discussion of the final chapter of *The Souls of Black Folk* in relation to the Communalists and nineteenth-century folklorists (Zamir, 1995, pp. 173–4).

his commitment to a 'talented tenth' vanguard of black intellectuals to lead the African-American masses served to obscure his own ideas on the transcendent potential of the folk.

As we have seen, Hurston and Hughes refused to be constrained by Du Bois's narrow and elitist conception that merely took one aspect of the folk, namely the Sorrow Songs, as the basis for a mature aesthetic far removed from the expressions of lower-class African Americans. For Du Bois the primitive folk song had to be filtered through the concert hall setting to attain its status as high art. This is partly attributable to his awareness of the debasement of the spirituals in the minstrel tradition but, for Hurston and Hughes, an authentic identity was to be found precisely in the sensibilities of black lower-class vernacular forms, not in a bourgeois intelligentsia. These very different interpretations and appropriations of folk culture illustrate the indeterminacy of the 'folk' as a concept and show how blackness, for the Harlem writers, was not a monolithic essence but instead offered many different subject positions.

Despite their differences, many of the Harlem writers drew heavily on the folk in their anxiety and ambivalence about becoming part of the newly emerging black urban bourgeoisie. The development of an authentic literary identity became, then, bound up with issues of class as membership of a black bourgeoisie meant succumbing to white American materialism and the loss of racial consciousness. In their efforts to define an identity the Harlem writers wrote themselves into a discourse of the folk. *The Souls of Black Folk* had set the tone for the Harlem Renaissance movement as Du Bois, the brilliant middle-class intellectual, travelled south in geographical and literary identification with the folk spirit of the masses. Toomer, Hughes, Hurston and later Morrison herself, were to make the same journey in their efforts to recover a folk aesthetic, memory and sensibility. Toomer, like Du Bois, turned to the spirituals and also positioned himself as the interpreter of a lost tradition. In 'Song of the Son' Toomer's poet narrator is the 'seed' from the 'dark purple ripened plums' of the folk spirit as expressed in the spirituals, and he filters these primitive, dying Southern forms through a northern intellectual sensibility (Toomer, 1923, p. 14). Hughes's privileging of blues and jazz forms reveals a closer identification with the art of the urban lower-class but his entry into folk discourse is problematic as his own middle-class background conflicts with his desire to identify a mass, African-American experience. At the heart of Hughes' appropriation there exists a crisis of identity, expressed very clearly in 'The Weary Blues' (1925), in *The New Negro*, in which the narrator distances himself from the subject of the poem, the Blues Man, saying 'I heard a Negro play' and thereby casting doubt on his own racial identity (Hughes, 1994, p. 50). The oral vernacular art of the blues singer, the expression of 'a black man's soul' is framed within, and contrasts with, the narrator's conventional poetic form and Hughes is at once both immersed in, and detached from, the blues experience.[19] This double consciousness is also evident in his novel, *Not without Laughter* (1930) as the Episcopal aspirations of the protagonist's aunt are juxtaposed with the sensibility of his jazz singing younger aunt, Harriett. The tension remains unresolved as Harriett's itinerant lifestyle is likely to lead to her premature death while his older aunt is confined to a deadening life of constraining respectability. Hughes' ambivalence becomes heightened anxiety in Nella Larsen's *Quicksand* (1928), in which her central character, the elegant, accomplished and light-skinned Helga Crane, seeks a meaningful identity for herself as distinct from the Harlem elite. In a highly improbable move, that itself reveals Larsen's own problematic relationship with folk culture, Helga marries a Southern preacher and the novel ends with her suffocation in the 'quicksand' of a Southern folk existence of child bearing and drudgery. Larsen's novel, like Morrison's *Sula* and *Tar Baby*, complicates the relationship between the artist and folk culture through the interjection of gender. Even Zora Neale Hurston, who set out to record, preserve and contribute to folk experience and expression, does not represent the community as a holistic entity in romantic abstraction, but in fact explores the woman's quest for a female identity within and against the folk culture.

In the next chapter I argue that Morrison's *Sula* exposes the complex relationship between female identity, migration and the folk community. As we shall see, Morrison's entry into the discourse of the folk extends the concerns and dilemmas faced by the Harlem writers as she negotiates ideologies of materialism and assimilation. In *The Bluest Eye* (1970), the love of whiteness is pathological and leads ultimately to the fracturing of Pecola's identity and the loss of the racial self in a passionless existence of misplaced desire. In their migration to the Midwest and their assumption of white bourgeois values, the light-skinned

---

[19] Arnold Rampersad claims that Hughes's 'initiative in the blues remains the only genuinely original achievement in form by any black American poet' (Rampersad, 1993, p. 67), but also argues: 'In his willingness to stand back and record, with minimal intervention, aspects of the drama of black religion (and, later, of music and dance), Hughes clearly showed that he had begun to see his own learned poetic art, even with his individual talent, as inferior to that of "ordinary" blacks.... At the heart of his sense of inferiority – which empowered rather than debilitated Hughes – was the knowledge that he (and other would be poets) stood to a great extent *outside* the culture he worshipped. Perhaps Hughes stood at a greater distance from the masses than did most other black poets' (Rampersad, 1993, p. 56).

Mobile girls have lost the 'dreadful funkiness of passion, the funkiness of nature, the funkiness of the wide range of human emotions' (*BE*, p. 64). By the time Morrison came to write *The Bluest Eye* the burgeoning folk consciousness of the Harlem Renaissance had become the cultural nationalism of the Black Aesthetic movement and its extreme proclamations of racial pride rooted firmly in black lower-class expression.

2

Ideology, Identity and the Community: *The Bluest Eye* (1970) and *Sula* (1973)

It is as an intervention into the affirmative aesthetic of Black Power politics that I now consider Morrison's first two novels *The Bluest Eye* (1970) and *Sula* (1973). I first examine how the Black Aesthetic movement of the 1960s drew upon the work of Harlem writers in their recovery of an appropriate vernacular and communal sensibility that could speak to all African Americans. This chapter focuses on *The Bluest Eye* and *Sula* as texts emerging from the Black Aesthetic as Morrison engages with the political and intellectual debates of the 1960s. A Bakhtinian critical framework is used here to highlight *The Bluest Eye* as an oppositional text in which Morrison contests both nineteenth-century scientific racism and the cultural hegemony of 1940s America. In discussing *Sula* I examine how Morrison's imaginative reconstruction of African-American female identity in the 1920s is informed by feminist debates of the late 1960s and early 1970s. I end by returning to the Harlem Renaissance and Morrison's engagement with folk discourse in *Sula* in the context of an intertextual relationship with Zora Neale Hurston within a female, non-linear, African-American literary tradition.

The Bluest Eye (1970)

Toni Morrison and the Black Aesthetic

In the mid-1960s, when African Americans had begun to express a newfound political awareness in the Black Power movement and a corresponding cultural energy in the Black Aesthetic, Toni Morrison chose to set her first novel, *The Bluest Eye*, in 1940s Ohio rather than in the positively charged atmosphere of her contemporary world. The work is, all the same, very much influenced by the political agenda of the Black Power era, but Morrison's decision reveals her concern that a particular period in African-American history might be forgotten in the impulse to celebrate black consciousness and 'the age of Black is Beautiful', a celebration which 'was going too fast in 1965' (Morrison intv. with Houston, 2008, p. 256). Moreover, her focus on a female protagonist in *The Bluest Eye*, from the perspective of a female narrator, signals a concern with the intersection of gender and race, absent in the literature and criticism of more vocal proponents of the Black Aesthetic. Morrison also wanted to render the complexities of personal and class relationships within the African-American community for that community itself, rather than for a white readership. In the work of her literary precursors from the 1940s and 1950s, Morrison has said that she

> always missed some intimacy, some direction, some voice. Ralph Ellison and Richard Wright – all of whose books I admire enormously – I didn't feel were telling *me* something. I thought they were saying something about *it* or *us* that revealed something about *us* to *you*, to others, to white people, to men. Just in terms of the style, I missed something in the fiction that I felt in a real sense in the music and poetry of black artists. (Morrison's italics, intv. with Ruas, 1994, p. 96)

The innovative form with which Morrison experiments in her first novel, and which characterizes her subsequent work, involves a return to the vernacular that was initiated by the poets Jean Toomer and Langston Hughes. Toomer and Hughes were recovered by the Black Arts movement during the late 1960s and it is significant that Toomer's *Cane*, last printed in 1927, was republished in 1967. The late 1960s appeared to provide, after the achievements and disappointments of the Civil Rights movement, a fitting mood for Toomer's poetic evocation of the spiritual and for Hughes's urban blues and jazz expression. For the Black Aestheticians, Hughes's poetry became important because his work fulfilled the criteria they had set, namely that art should have at least the potential for mass appeal for African Americans. In fact, the defining features of the Black Aesthetic can be identified in Hughes's 1926 manifesto for artistic expression that originated in the experiences of the majority rather than aspiring to meet the standards of the dominant literary establishment:

> These common people are not afraid of spirituals, as for a long time their more intellectual brethren were, and jazz is their child. They furnish a wealth

of colorful, distinctive material for any artist because they still hold their own individuality in the face of American standardizations. And perhaps these common people will give to the world its truly great Negro artist, the one who is not afraid to be himself.... And they accept what beauty is their own without question. (Hughes, 1926, p. 693)

These sentiments are echoed repeatedly by those Black Aestheticians concerned with promoting a literature that has at its centre a profound belief in the artistic validity of African-American folk, vernacular and musical traditions. In the 1960s LeRoi Jones, for example, followed Hughes when arguing that

Negro music alone, because it drew its strengths and beauties out of the depth of the black man's soul, and because to a large extent its traditions could be carried on by the lowest classes of Negroes, has been able to survive the constant and wilful dilutions of the black middle class. (Jones, 1962, p. 106)

For Jones and others, an authentic African-American literature must construct its own criteria and language from the achievements and experiences of its people and, importantly, build upon the foundations of cultural nationalism established during the Harlem Renaissance. Larry Neal, claimed in a seminal essay of the period, 'The Black Arts Movement', that the movement

represents the flowering of a cultural nationalism that has been suppressed since the 1920s. I mean the 'Harlem Renaissance' – which was essentially a failure. It did not address itself to the mythology and the life-styles of the Black community. It failed to take roots [sic], to link itself concretely to the struggles of that community, to become its voice and spirit. Implicit in the Black Arts Movement is the idea that Black people, however dispersed, constitute a *nation* within the belly of white America. This is not a new idea. Garvey said it and the Honorable Elijah Muhammed says it now. And it is on this idea that the concept of Black Power is predicated. (Neal's italics, 1968, p. 39)

Here, Neal makes a direct connection between African-American literature and Black Power, significantly conflating art with politics. He also reveals the desire, typical of Black Aestheticians, to identify a tradition of African-American art and politics even while being dismissive of the endeavours of the Harlem Renaissance writers. His remarks may now seem misjudged given that the 'voice and spirit' of the 'community' had already been articulated during the 1930s by Zora Neale Hurston. The concern to celebrate neglected African-American texts from the past did not extend to the full recovery of Hurston's novels until the late 1970s when African-American feminism began to gain momentum. The

Black Aestheticians were also discriminating in their praise of those writers who did not entirely meet their criteria. If Morrison felt that black novelists were 'saying something' primarily to a white readership, Black Aestheticians were as likely to be critical of those writers using mainstream conventions in their delineation of African-American experiences and not concerned to articulate a collective consciousness. Addison Gayle in *The Way of the New World* (1976), for example, admires Ralph Ellison's *Invisible Man* (1952) because it 'is rich in imagery, myth, and legend, adorned with suggestive, figurative language, and infused with the wealthy language and life-style of a people'. Yet he criticizes Ellison's characterization of the nameless protagonist claiming that Ellison chose 'individualism as opposed to racial unity' by accepting a European existentialist 'image of the faceless, universal man, trapped in the narrow world of his own ego' (Gayle, 1976, pp. 255, 258). Ellison, in *Shadow and Act*, made clear how he felt morally obligated to write about the African-American experience, but stressed he wanted to communicate the full range of this experience while simultaneously articulating a universal, 'larger concern with the tragic struggle of humanity' (Ellison, 1964, p. 169). To reveal the 'diversity of American life with its extreme fluidity' went beyond narrow, even essentialist representations of African Americans for purely political ends (Ellison, 1964, p. 103). In direct opposition to the Black Aesthetic, and to Richard Wright's earlier protest fiction, Ellison was not 'primarily concerned with injustice, but with art' being committed to the original, frontier ideals of American democracy and a belief that the dual identities of African Americans were not irreconcilable. He declared that he was more influenced by writers within the western canon, most notably Eliot, Hemingway and Faulkner, than by Langston Hughes or Ellison's former mentor, Richard Wright (Ellison, 1964, p. 140). Ellison knew how many of the writers he admired perpetuated negative representations of African Americans and he stressed that his relationship to them was one of appropriation rather than imitation. 'Negro Americans have a highly developed ability to abstract desirable qualities from those around them, even from their enemies, and my sense of reality could reject bias while appreciating the truth revealed by such art' (Ellison, 1964, p. xx). Ellison's views are further complicated by his attitude towards folklore, which for him was of literary, rather than political, importance, was closely related to his ideas about the 'universality' of the African-American experience and to his commitment to modernist experimental forms. 'I use folklore in my work not because I am Negro, but because writers like Eliot and Joyce made me conscious of the literary value of my folk inheritance' (Ellison, 1964, p. 58).

Ellison's privileging of art over social protest, and his focus on the individual rather than on the life of the race, left him open to attack from the new movement. Gayle, and many others, demanded that the focus for black writing must be one in which 'substance is more important than form', sociology more important than any kind of literary experimentation and each 'act' and 'gesture' a political one (Gayle, 1976, p. xii). In *The Bluest Eye* Morrison shows how the objectives of the new movement and those of Ellison were never in fact mutually exclusive as her literary techniques are able to embrace both sensibilities and create powerful and often surreal tensions between them. For Morrison, in her essay 'Rootedness', art as for the Black Aestheticians, should be 'unquestionably political' but, equally important, 'irrevocably beautiful at the same time' (Morrison, 1984, p. 64). Morrison also brings elements to the black tradition that had been largely neglected since Hurston, namely the experience of black women and a complex treatment of community that goes beyond Black Power's use of the term as a euphemism for a fictitiously cohesive and monolithic black urban proletariat. 'If anything I do, in the way of writing novels (or whatever I write) isn't about the village or the community or about you, then it is not about anything' (Morrison, 1984, p. 64). The concern of this chapter is to examine Morrison's politicization, through language, of the spirit of the community.

In 'Rootedness', on her role as a novelist, Morrison has written:

> There are things that I try to incorporate into my fiction that are directly and deliberately related to what I regard as the major characteristics of Black art, wherever it is. One of which is the ability to be both print and oral literature: to combine those two aspects so that the stories can be read in silence, of course, but one should be able to hear them as well. It should try deliberately to make you stand up and make you feel something profoundly in the same way that a Black preacher requires his congregation to speak, to join him in the sermon, to behave in a certain way, to stand up and to weep and to cry and to accede or to change and to modify – to expand on the sermon that is being delivered. In the same way that a musician's music is enhanced when there is a response from the audience. (Morrison, 1984, p. 59)

Morrison outlines here the characteristics of call and response as an important structural device that both privileges African-American vernacular forms and displays her concern to engage the reader in the construction of her texts. Morrison's novels convey the communal characteristics of African-American religious practices and musical expression in secular narratives that retain the interplay between the individual and the community expressed in call and response patterns, originating in pre-slavery Africa.

Lawrence Levine in *Black Culture and Black Consciousness* (1977) provides an account of early African–American cultural forms in which he traces the development of call and response, also known as 'antiphony', and shows how in gospel music call and response is characterized by solo and choir singing in which the congregation, as audience, participate and respond to the preacher with shouts, comments and assents. In slave work songs workers would respond to a lead singer's lines, or call, with their own words, vocal punctuations or the sounds of their tools at the appropriate interval. The blues form that emerged after Emancipation was the first personalized African-American music. Call and response forms remained, but in blues it was the singer who responded to him or herself either vocally or instrumentally.[1]

The Black Aesthetic poet Don L. Lee said that in the effort to find a new and political voice with which to delineate the concerns of the African-American community and develop a separatist black aesthetic 'we must destroy Faulkner, dick, jane, and other perpetuators of evil' (Lee qtd. in Neal, 1968, p. 185). Ironically, it is by keeping these characters alive, if only in order to subvert them, that Morrison is able to construct her first novel. *The Bluest Eye* is a deceptively simple story about a lonely black girl, Pecola Breedlove, whose desire for the blue eyes she regards as the ultimate symbol of beauty and the key to gaining acceptance and love from those around her, drives her into madness. Pecola's insanity is charted through her relationships with other members of the community who have, in varying ways and degrees, also been affected by the imposition of white cultural values. Morrison complicates Pecola's story through the innovative use of an extract from the white middle-class Dick and Jane school primer as a preface to the novel. Morrison then frames the subsections of *The Bluest Eye* with lines taken from this extract of the primer, a text she contrasts ironically with the experiences and voices of the children, Pecola, the narrator Claudia MacTeer and her sister Frieda. The primer extracts are the ideological 'call' of white, beautiful middle-class America,

---

[1] Lawrence W. Levine, in *Black Culture and Black Consciousness: Afro-American Folk Thought from Slavery to Freedom* describes the development of call and response, which he refers to as antiphony, in his chapter, 'The Rise of Secular Song', (Levine, 1977, pp. 190–297). In an earlier reference, Levine points out that the Protestant practice of lining-out of hymns and the first African-American slaves' antiphonal call and response patterns were analogous. '[T]hese conditions were conducive to a situation which allowed the slaves to retain a good deal of the integrity of their own musical heritage while fusing to it compatible elements of Euro-American music. The result was a hybrid with a strong African base' (Levine, 1977, p. 24).

Morrison's text and the voices within it, the 'response'. To undermine further its hegemonic status, Morrison renders the text of the primer meaningless through the omission of punctuation and, as in Don L. Lee's reference to 'dick and jane', capital letters. This subversive technique is maintained as elements of the primer – house, garden, father, mother, cat, dog – reverberate in Pecola's life. This technique allows Morrison to interrogate a dominant value system without resorting to direct authorial intervention and create a dialogical relationship with her readers who must contribute meaning to the text and its construction.

Like Ellison before her, Morrison wants to exploit the existing qualities of African-American vernacular art for the novel form, but for more overt political ends. Her use of the Primer extracts signifies on the call and response practice that marks African-American religion, a form of signifying in itself. Moreover, she signifies on strategies adopted by writers of slave narratives, such as Frederick Douglass and Harriet Jacobs, of authenticating their work by including a formal testimony or preface by a respected white personage (see the discussion of signifying in Chapter 1). In rendering the Primer extracts as meaningless, *The Bluest Eye* is testimony to how the African-American writer, by 1970, can articulate a confident aesthetic that is not dependent on white authentication. Morrison privileges the vernacular over the western tradition while at the same time revealing a deep understanding of that tradition, a facility with its form and technique and the ability to 'change' and 'modify' it.

Bakhtin

It is appropriate at this point to examine further the use of language in *The Bluest Eye* by returning to Mikhail Bakhtin's *The Dialogical Imagination* (1981). Until the 1940s, criticism had been largely concerned to analyse literature in terms of categories of style, or 'schools', and creative writing was regarded essentially as the expression of an individual artistic personality. Bakhtin, however, considered this stylistic analysis inadequate for the novel, which for him was a hybrid 'dialogized system' that could not be seen to contain a single unitary language. The term 'dialogic' refers to the writer's representations of the different languages used in the novel.

> The author represents this language, carries on a conversation with it, and the conversation penetrates into the interior of this language-image and dialogizes it from within. And all essentially novelistic images share this quality: they

are internally dialogized images – of the languages, styles, world views of another (all of which are inseparable from their concrete linguistic and stylistic embodiment). (Bakhtin, 1981, p. 46)

Importantly, this system has its roots in the pre-literary stages of verbal culture, an ancient oral tradition that could 'transmit, mimic and represent from various vantage points another's word, another's speech and language' (Bakhtin, 1981, p. 50). In early literature, one of the most common forms for representing the direct word of another is that of 'Parodic-travestying'. This provided a means to satirize and critique the 'serious word' and created the conditions for the emergence of the novel and its unique ability to transcend, by drawing upon the vernacular, outdated literary styles and language. Morrison renders the mode of the Primer as outdated and inadequate, or in Bakhtin's terms, 'monological', through her complex use of the vernacular as its response.

Bakhtin's theories relating to the novel have been invoked in discussions of African-American literature, notably in Henry Louis Gates's *The Signifying Monkey* (1988). In his discussion of the 'double-voicedness' of signifying, referred to in Chapter 1, Gates utilizes Bakhtin's theory of narration. Bakhtin discusses how a single utterance is 'double-voiced' in the way it 'serves two speakers at the same time and expresses simultaneously two different intentions' (Bakhtin, 1981, p. 324) its meaning split between a first speaker's intention and a second speaker's reception and response according to his own understanding and perspective. We shall see later how Bakhtin emphasizes the political and ideological conflict within the double-voiced utterance. Gates, however, is concerned to yoke Bakhtin's linguistic theory to his own ideas on signifying as Bakhtin's notion of 'double voiced' discourse theorizes the hidden polemic and parodic narration embedded in the utterance. This adds to Gates's understanding of literary signifying as an adaptation of the parody and rhetoric characteristic of the original form of signifying as verbal wordplay (Gates, 1988, pp. 110–11). Gates also appropriates and extends the notion of 'double-voiced' discourse to explain the African-American writer's relationship to language and the western tradition; in an earlier essay, 'Criticism in the Jungle' (1984), which does not refer directly to Bakhtin, the text is necessarily 'double voiced' as the writer expresses an African-American oral sensibility in the English language and furthermore comments on, or signifies upon, the language and form of western texts. The African-American text, then, is also 'double voiced' because it has a place in both the western literary tradition and the African-American tradition. African-American texts occupy spaces in at least two traditions: a European or American literary tradition, and one of the several related but distinct black traditions. The 'heritage' of each black text written in a Western language is, then, a double heritage, two-toned, as it were. (Gates, 1984, p. 4)

In his appropriation of signifying and Bakhtin's theories of narrative, Gates is concerned to reveal the formal properties of African-American texts within the context of literary traditions, rather than to examine the political impulse behind any linguistic and narrative choices made by writers. Gates's argument that African-American texts such as Morrison's, which she claims are both 'print' and 'oral' literature, are 'double-voiced' and 'occupy spaces in at least two traditions', an African-American oral tradition and a European or American literary tradition, is useful. I would, however, argue that the applicability of Bakhtin's ideas to Morrison's fiction becomes even clearer if we consider her as a writer who is actively engaged in developing a dialogical relationship with her readers as well as being aware of the ideological nature of different languages, and who knowingly dialogizes these languages from within the text – most obviously in *The Bluest Eye*.[2]

Bakhtin's ideas provide a plausible theoretical perspective from which to examine the duality of African-American literature and the way in which language is used to disrupt authority and liberate alternative voices. However, the appropriation of Bakhtinian philosophy as a tool of literary analysis is, for various reasons, problematic. Bakhtin's thinking moved through conceptual changes and his writing was characterized by ambiguities that have produced very different interpretations of his work, and indeed his ideas can be applied to serve a variety of political purposes and intentions. Robert Young, in *Torn Halves*, attributes the popularity of Bakhtinian critical perspectives to the crisis in Marxist theory in the late 1970s resulting from the conflict between scientific structuralism, Marxist humanism and Derridean poststructuralism. 'Bakhtin was heralded as offering a "way out" of the impasse that had threatened to cut Marxist knowledge off from the social. Bakhtin's attraction was that he seemed to offer

---

[2] Apart from the general discussions of African-American literature in relation to Bakhtin in Gates's, *The Signifying Monkey*, see also Linden Peach's *Toni Morrison*. At times, (Peach, 2000, pp. 16, 85), Peach employs a loosely Bakhtinian model for his analysis of Morrison's novels. He is in broad agreement with black literary criticism that has been 'resistant to the various trends in Euro-American critical practice, from New Criticism to structuralism, that posit the separation of the literary text from its author, because reclaiming an identity and (narrative) voice has been important to the black writer in countering centuries of dispossession and misrepresentation' (Peach, 2000, p. 1). Marilyn Sanders Mobley also invokes Bakhtin in her discussion of *Beloved*'s intertextual relationship with the slave narratives (Mobley, 1993, pp. 356–65).

the possibility for Marxism to return to the old certainties of the everyday world outside' (Young, 1996, p. 34). Others, not necessarily Marxists, were also drawn to him because Bakhtin appeared to 'offer a reconciliation between poetics and hermeneutics, between questions of form and questions of interpretation in the context of their relation to society and history' (Young, 1996, p. 35). It is true that Bakhtin emphasized the 'concrete' nature of discourse and offered the possibility of philosophical enquiry grounded in materialism that could, paradoxically, resolve the tensions in Marxism while simultaneously satisfying the exactions of liberal academicians. As Ken Hirschkop suggests, debates surrounding the concepts of the Bakhtin School 'are to a great extent arguments about democracy, and the kind of linguistic and cultural life it implies' (Hirschkop, 1989, p. 3). It is perhaps futile to attempt to ascertain the real Bakhtin, but fruitful to recognize his abstruseness as a condition of 'the way in which he himself represents rather than resolves the conflictual struggles in society' (Young, 1996, p. 40). If we can accept the ambiguities inherent in Bakhtin's conceptualizations and agree, as Graham Pechey suggests, that Bakhtin's 'concepts are always in internal exile, paradoxically situated both within and beyond the borders of disciplines as traditionally defined and institutionally policed', then we can freely apply his philosophy of language and 'push his concepts still further on in their journey, putting them to still more demanding tests' (Pechey, 1989, pp. 40, 57). This for Pechey includes the 'migration' of Bakhtinian concepts from the realm of the European novel and culture, with which Bakhtin himself was primarily concerned, to postcolonial contexts in which they may be helpful in resolving the very real 'life-or-death ferocity' of Third World cultural struggle (Pechey, 1989, p. 62). 'The problems encountered in this struggle need for their solution a theory which neither submits politics to a cultural sublimation nor reduces culture to a mere expression of the political or economic.' For Pechey, a Bakhtinian understanding offers the opportunity for 'the notion of a multilingual field where the languages of colonizer and colonized are indelibly inscribed within each other and which oppositional initiatives should seek to exploit rather than escape' (Pechey, 1989, pp. 62–3).

In *The Location of Culture* Homi Bhabha has adapted Bakhtin's concept of hybridity to rethink questions of identity and social agency and to comprehend the history of colonialism and current postcolonial situations. For Bhabha, there is a 'disturbance' or 'undecidability' in the 'authoritative representations' of colonial discourse, a consequence of 'the uncanny forces of race, sexuality, violence, cultural and even climactic differences which emerge in the colonial discourse as the mixed and split texts of hybridity' (Bhabha, 1994, p. 113). This hybridity helps disrupt the authority of colonial discourse and affords agency on the part of the colonized in that it 'enables a form of subversion, founded on the undecidability that turns the discursive conditions of dominance into the grounds of intervention' (Bhabha, 1994, p. 112). This emphasis on the transactional or negotiated nature of colonialism, rather than on its conflictual aspects, has left Bhabha open to the accusation that because knowledge, for him, can only be found within linguistic representation that is textual rather than social, human agency, conflict and struggle become obscured (Parry, 1994, p. 18). Moreover, simplistic appropriation of the concept of hybridity is not adequate for understanding the very different relations of domination and struggle in the history of American slavery and liberation. As Anne McClintock argues, what is needed is 'a proliferation of historically nuanced theories and strategies' to understand the various workings of colonialism across the world (McClintock, 1995, p. 396). Morrison herself, in *Playing in the Dark*, contributes to an awareness of the specific operations of white America's dominance through literary discourse. Her project continues the work of those who have carried out 'sustained critiques' of European 'racialized discourse' and demands similar examinations of the ambivalence of American literature. 'Yes, I wanted to identify those moments when American literature was complicit in the fabrication of racism, but equally important, I wanted to see when literature exploded and undermined it' (Morrison, 1992c, pp. 7, 16).

As Robert Young points out, appropriations of Bakhtin's work such as Pechey's and Bhabha's hold obvious attraction for minority politics, but perhaps overemphasize their claims for agency and evade the intent of Bakhtin's project. Young's understanding of Bakhtin's notion of hybridity allows for an understanding of the ways in which texts subvert authority. In *The Dialogical Imagination*, Bakhtin defines hybridity as the way in which language is double-voiced. 'It is a mixture of two social languages within the limits of a single utterance, an encounter, within the arena of an utterance, between two different linguistic consciousnesses, separated from one or another by an epoch, by social differentiation or by some other factor' (Bakhtin, 1981, p. 358). While identifying the phenomenon of unintentional or organic hybridity, which Bhabha adapts, Bakhtin emphasizes the conflictual, contestatory and always socially concrete ways in which languages operate within texts. The will to interpret Bakhtin for a variety of purposes poses particular problems for the literary critic seeking to understand Toni Morrison's work. Appropriations of Bakhtinian criticism can yield a false sense of optimism, focusing as they do upon the destabilization of the language of a standard authority or by celebrating the contestatory possibilities of minority discourse. What remains is a form of enclosure or entrapment in which texts produce endless hybrid constructions that may indeed be conflictual, but ultimately rendered as being benign. An effective use of Bakhtin's ideas must recognize the internal dynamic of dialogism that is itself, as Robert Young notes, dialectical:

> Dialogism works as an internally riven economy, whereby in one domain it consists of the benign openness of intersubjective exchange between multiple voices, while in another it also enables a critical, subversive, contestatory challenge to monological, hegemonic forms of authority which it shows can be transgressed and contested. Dialogism thus itself involves a dialogic hybridity: of a dissonant heterogeneity which retains a critical, dialectical cutting edge. (Young, 1996, pp. 61–2)

This recognition of the ambivalence and contradiction in Bakhtin's notion of dialogism and hybridity enables an understanding of Morrison's complex language that, on one level, does not work towards a final resolution in the presentation of diverse voices and, on another, constitutes a radical challenge to authority. Later in this chapter I return to the ways in which *The Bluest Eye* is, in Bakhtin's terms, 'authentic', comprised as it is of varied and competing voices with no single indisputable 'finished off' language. I consider how this lack of resolution is achieved through Morrison's innovative narrative structure and her employment of characteristic forms of black art and expression. Before doing so, the particular contestatory function of language in *The Bluest Eye* is to be considered in more detail.

Language and ideology

In *Playing in the Dark*, Morrison, as critic, academic and public intellectual, wants to investigate the nature and literary operandi of a 400-year African presence in American literature. She explains, 'The scholarship that looks into the mind, imagination, and behavior of slaves is valuable. But equally valuable is a serious intellectual effort to see what racial ideology does to the mind, imagination, and behavior of masters' (Morrison, 1992c, pp. 11–12). However, Morrison wants to foreground the African-American presence in history to privilege the African-American community, its myths, folklore and language. In her first novel a vital part of this project, and analogous to that of her later work as a critic, is an exploration of the ideological and cultural operations of hegemony in order then to dismantle America's construction of blackness through an investigation of the adoption of white values by African Americans. In *The Bluest Eye* Morrison is 'interested in racism as a cause, consequence, and manifestation of individual and social psychosis' (Morrison, 1997, p. 9). Morrison is concerned with a particularly impalpable form of racist ideology that, because of its indefinable nature, is paradoxically more pervasive, psychologically damaging and difficult to contest than extreme, overt forms of racism. When Cholly Breedlove reduces his family to a state of homelessness, puts them all 'outdoors', the older Claudia reflects upon her new awareness of the social, psychological and economic constraints on the black community:

> Outdoors was the end of something, an irrevocable, physical fact, defining our metaphysical condition. Being a minority in both caste and class, we moved about anyway on the hem of life, struggling to consolidate our weaknesses and hang on, or to creep singly up into the major folds of the garment. Our peripheral existence, however, was something we had learned to live with – probably because it was abstract. (*BE*, p. 11)

The finality of homelessness is easily understood by the community in terms of their material, economic marginality. More difficult is the 'abstract' mechanism supporting this marginality and which the young Claudia, and other characters, cannot comprehend, a lack of understanding that has tragic consequences for Pecola. Claudia, Frieda and Pecola are racially insulted by their prosperous, light-skinned fellow pupil, Maureen Peal, and again the mature Claudia reflects with retrospective knowledge, 'And all the time we knew that Maureen Peal was not the Enemy and not worthy of such intense hatred. The *Thing* to fear was the *Thing* that made her beautiful, and not us' (Morrison's italics *BE*, p. 58). It is this indefinable *Thing*, the ideology of racial hierarchy and its devastating impact on the community and the individual, that Morrison explores and contests. Claudia's childhood struggle with the *Thing* becomes manifest in misdirected anger and violence. Her narration begins with the prediction of a violent encounter between Frieda, herself and the Greek girl next door. 'When she comes out of the car we will beat her up, make red marks on her white skin, and she will cry' (*BE*, p. 5). The white plastic doll given to her at Christmas is loathed and dismembered by Claudia in order to ascertain 'what it was that all the world said was loveable' (*BE*, p. 13). Morrison's deconstruction of notions of beauty and desire finds reflection as Claudia destroys the doll in her effort to unlock the mystery within. Even Claudia, however, succumbs to the beauty myth and is converted 'from pristine sadism to fabricated hatred, to fraudulent love' (*BE*, p. 16), not because she believes but because she recognizes the futility of contesting its power with blind, unmediated aggression. It is not until Claudia reaches adulthood and a conscious, radicalized understanding of her childhood that she turns to language in order to bear witness, record and contest.

Language is crucially important for Morrison as the medium of ideology:

> Oppressive language does more than represent violence; it is violence; does more than represent the limits of knowledge; it limits knowledge. Whether it is obscuring state language or the faux-language of mindless media; whether it is the proud but calcified language of the academy or the commodity-driven language of science; whether it is the malign language of law-without-ethics, or language designed for the estrangement of minorities, hiding its racist plunder in its literary cheek – it must be rejected, altered, and exposed. (Morrison, 1993, p. 16)

This resonates with Bakhtinian, dialogical language, as the vehicle of ideology, enacting and representing the struggle for meaning among groups competing for political and social recognition. Language has a material function, 'it is violence', as Morrison says, as well as a representational role. Morrison, like Bakhtin, recognizes the possibilities in language for contesting representations, 'as agency – as an act with consequences' (Morrison, 1993, p. 13), and wishes to expose the ideological deployment of language through a critique of education, culture and religion.

Robert Young notes that, in Bakhtin's theoretical formulations, ideologies may die or be generated within the conflict of dialogism and how this means that there can be no utopian end to the struggle over the sign (Young, 1996, pp. 44–5). Bakhtin's concept of ideology therefore departs from classical accounts, whereby conflict inherently retains possibilities for resolution through class consciousness. Again, his approach to ideology as an open and contested site appeals to cultural theorists, now that the narratives of resolution have dissipated. Literary critics have, in a different way, taken a moribund, fatalistic model of ideology from which to construct forms of criticism that revel in radical possibilities for contestation and change. An aesthetic and literary tradition has been created whereby 'minor literatures'[3] operate with a twofold dimension:

---

[3] I am using the term 'minor literatures' here in the sense that Gilles Deleuze and Félix Guattari employ it in *Kafka: Towards A Minor Literature* (1975). They theorize a 'minor literature' as the collective enunciation of the margin; a dominant language is subsumed and reconstructed in the creation of a 'minor' language appropriate for the expression of a communal sensibility. Writers in a 'minor' tradition are not 'minor' in the sense that they are not great writers, rather they create a 'minor' literature from within the heart of the canon. I discuss Deleuze and Guattari's conception of a 'minor literature' in more detail in Chapter 3.

first, the critique of dominant modes of thought remains constant and, secondly, those producing minor literature comment on, critique and extend the work of earlier writers within their own tradition (see in particular, Gates's *The Signifying Monkey*).

We have seen how, in *The Bluest Eye*, Morrison uses the Primer extracts to signify on the slave narratives and interrogate codified and institutional language and ideology. Morrison presents the language of the primer in order to highlight its contrast with her own voice, fulfilling Bakhtin's principle that 'it is impossible to represent an alien ideological world adequately without first permitting it to sound, without having first revealed the special discourse peculiar to it' (Bakhtin, 1981, p. 355).

Nineteenth-century racial discourses

Standards of beauty, order and cleanliness are central to this 'special discourse' and Morrison attacks the core of racist ideology by turning her attention to the French philosopher and diplomat Count Joseph de Gobineau. She quotes directly in *The Bluest Eye* from his *Essay on the Inequality of the Human Races* (1853–5) to show how Elihue Micah Whitcomb's family have internalized the racist doctrine of Gobineau's assertion that 'All civilizations derive from the white race, that none can exist without its help and that a society is great and brilliant only so far as it preserves the blood of the noble group that created it' (*BE*, p. 133, and de Gobineau, 1853–5, p. 348). Gobineau outlined the decline of civilizations, with race the driving force of history, progressing only through the civilizing instinct of the white race and its 'marriage' with other races, the absorption of the weak by the strong; black people, untouched by the white race, remain 'immersed in profound inertia' (qtd. in Young, 1995, pp. 99–118). Paradoxically, inter-racial union leads to the degeneration of civilizations through the adulteration of pure, white blood.

Gobineau's theories are partly dependent on western cultural notions of what constitutes 'civilisation' and in this sense his model of race is founded on cultural, as well as physical, difference. The conflation of cultural and physical differences proved persuasive in racial discourse, gaining credence in America with the publication of Josiah Nott's and George Gliddon's *Types of Mankind* (1854). Nott, an anatomist, was concerned to demonstrate that physical differences between races were innate and presented, as evidence, the infertility of hybrid offspring from the union of black and white races. The Egyptologist Gliddon, on the other hand, asserted there had never been a black civilization and that the race was therefore inferior. Nott's and Gliddon's intellectual alliance allowed them to draw the 'scientific and the cultural together in order to promulgate an indistinguishably scientific and cultural theory of race. Biology and Egyptology thus constituted *together* the basis of the new "scientific" racial theory' (Young's italics, 1995, p. 124). Nott also helped revise the tone of Henry Hotze's American edition of Gobineau's book, re-titled as *The Moral and Intellectual Diversity of Races* (1856), in which Gobineau's idea of degeneration was withdrawn and his recognition of the fertility of hybrids discredited (Young, 1995, p. 125). That Nott was prepared to amend the work of others betrays the importance, for a relatively young country, of constructing racialized theory as the ideological bolster for America's racial policy.

Reginald Horsman, in *Race and Manifest Destiny* (1981), offers a historically specific account of the origins and role of racial ideology in America. For Horsman, its development is inextricably linked to the desire of Americans during the nineteenth century to claim descent from Anglo-Saxons, a notional racial group considered to be a superior branch of the Caucasian race. This invented heritage became important for consolidating American identity through a common language and culture and ensuring that new white immigrants conformed to this identity. Crucially, Anglo-Saxonism again served to promote the expansionist ethos of America in the nineteenth century and from an early stage it seemed clear to Americans that theirs was a civilizing mission and their elevated heritage fitting for the task. This originally took form as an Enlightenment belief in the ability of advanced government to instruct the indigenous population of the Continent. In the period between the American Revolution and 1850 there was a predominant monogenesist belief that all races were descended from Adam and Eve and therefore potentially equal. The recalcitrance of Native Americans and Mexicans and the need for justifications of slavery meant polygenesist theories such as Nott and Gliddon's gained much support. What was originally a genuine belief in the tenets of democratic republicanism became, by 1850, a conviction that the American Anglo-Saxon branch of the Caucasian race was innately superior to other races. The rhetoric of Nott and Gliddon's *Types of Mankind* illustrates the will to disseminate this ideology as an explanation for 'the enslavement of blacks, the disappearance of Indians, and the defeat of the Mexicans in a manner that reflected no discredit on the people of the United States' (Horsman, 1981, p. 301).

> Nations and races, like individuals, have each an especial destiny: some are born to rule, and others to be ruled ... No two distinctly-marked races can dwell together

> on equal terms. Some races, moreover, appear destined to live and prosper for a time, until the destroying race comes, which is to exterminate and supplant them. (Nott and Gliddon, 1854, p. 77 and qtd. in Horsman, 1981, p. 137)

The polemical tone makes clear that this is no objective 'scientific' account of racial difference, but rather one in which the desire to plunder the American continent is refigured as the 'especial destiny' of American Anglo-Saxons. Nott and Gliddon's book was in its eighth edition by 1860 and their thesis acceptable to the American reading public, despite being rejected by anthropologists and many Americans, particularly in the South, surrounded by evidence that hybrids were not in fact infertile.

Racialized theory in America was not, then, solely based on spurious science but also culturally and intellectually constructed. Excessive forms of racial doctrine are often regarded as a phenomenon of the late nineteenth century, but Horsman argues that racialized ideas were extant in America's literature and culture by the early 1800s. 'When Gobineau published his work on the inequality of the human races in 1854, he was summarizing and amplifying more than half a century of ideas on race rather than inaugurating a new era' (Horsman, 1981, p. 2). The beginning of these ideas are to be found in particular forms of American Romanticism which

> clearly represented a rejection of eighteenth-century reason and universalism in favor of intuition and particularism. The American Romantics were less interested in the features uniting mankind and nations than in the features separating them. Like the scientists, who shared many of their preconceptions, they looked for what was special and different, not what was general and alike.... In one sense, with all their emphasis on scientific measurement and physical comparison, the new scientific racial theorists were themselves responding to the changes in thought embodied in the general concept of Romanticism. Many of their scientific measurements in effect reinforced intuitive beliefs about racial peculiarities and uniqueness. (Horsman, 1981, p. 159)

Gobineau's thesis consolidated the foundations of what Morrison, in her essay 'Home' has called 'the race house', a compelling metaphor for linguistic, cultural and scientific constructions of race. By the 1940s the powerful fusion of scientific, intellectual and economic rationality established in the nineteenth century had fractured into the uncountable symbols of an America embarking upon new waves of expansionist consumer capitalism and its attendant ideologies, including, of course, persuasive cinematic images of white beauty. Pauline Breedlove acquires an 'education in the movies', in repressive notions of 'romantic love' and 'physical beauty', constructions described by Morrison's narrator as 'Probably the most destructive ideas in the history of human thought' (*BE*, p. 95).

Morrison focuses on Hollywood and popular culture as conduits for ideologies of racial superiority and reveals how Gobineau's doctrines crystallized in the images of the 1940s as representations of physical beauty; references to the movies, billboards, magazines, window signs, dolls, Mary Jane candy and Shirley Temple films pervade *The Bluest Eye*.[4] By the 1940s, Gobineau's thesis is submerged, taken as given. Hollywood reinforced, without needing to justify, the scaffolding of eighteenth- and nineteenth-century racism and implicitly articulated Gobineau's doctrine that the 'white race' is 'superior to all others in beauty', that 'human groups are unequal in beauty; and this inequality is rational, logical, permanent and indestructible' (Gobineau, 1853–5, p. 151).[5]

Popular culture and the beauty myth

Pauline Breedlove's internalization of this doctrine is passed down in pathological repetitions that have devastating consequences for her family. Pecola suffers the same obsessions as her mother, but by now the pathological damage is intensified and Pecola literally consumes whiteness, devouring Mary Jane candy wrapped in the image of the blonde, blue-eyed beauty. 'To eat the candy is somehow to eat the eyes, eat Mary Jane. Love Mary Jane. Be Mary Jane' (*BE*, p. 38). She also imbibes whiteness by drinking milk from a Shirley Temple cup in a grotesque re-enactment of transubstantiation. Pecola's cannibalization of whiteness reverberates with Shirley Temple's appearance in *Kid 'n Africa* (1931) as a civilizing infant missionary rescued from the cauldron by a small white boy with whom she gathers, civilizes and leads a colony of black infants. Morrison reverses the cannibal myth in Pecola's literal consumption of whiteness to reveal the effect of cinematic racist ideology on Pecola's sense of self. As we saw in the discussion of minstrelsy in Chapter 1, the racism of Shirley Temple films is complicated by the use of racial difference and childhood as a means of transgressing social

---

[4] Donald Gibson argues that *The Bluest Eye*, 'for all its eloquence and beauty of expression, engages in sustained argument with modes of thought and belief explicitly stated in Gobineaus's assertion . . ., but likewise, and perhaps more vividly presented in cultural icons portraying physical beauty' (Gibson, 1993, p. 160).

[5] In an intriguing footnote on page 151, Gibineau makes a comment that contradicts this statement and shows he realized that hybrids were not infertile: 'It may be remarked that the happiest blend, from the point of view of beauty, is that made by the marriage of white and black. We need only put the striking charm of any mulatto, creole and quadroon women by the side of such mixtures of yellow and white as the Russians and Hungarians.'

boundaries. In a 1935 film, *The Littlest Rebel*, Temple's character manipulates the adults around her and she 'blacks up' to evade detection by the Yankees, violating boundaries that limit her power as a child and as 'black'. As with Jolson in *The Jazz Singer* (1927), her blackness, like childhood itself, is merely a temporary state of playful transgression. Set in an ante-bellum Southern State, *The Littlest Rebel* has the earliest example of an on-screen inter-racial relationship (Bogle, 1992, p. 49). Bill 'Bojangles' Robinson is Temple's surrogate parent and playmate, as well as her servant, and his warmth and ability to provide solutions to her problems contrasts with the detached pomposity of her real family and other white characters. Any suggestion of the transgression of racial boundaries is, however, undermined by the film's evocations of nineteenth-century racial doctrine. As late as the mid-1930s, Hollywood found it necessary to reinforce the familiar stereotypes of the plantation; Bojangles is merely the childlike foil for Temple and, like the other slaves in the film, regards his liberation by the approaching Yankees as both unnecessary and undesirable. On one level, then, we have a straightforward debasement to the Uncle Tom figure, the happy minstrel; and on the other, we have what James Snead calls the 'mythification by contrast' of the blonde, blue-eyed Anglo-Saxon ideal: mythification is 'a process of glorification or magnification by contrast, and the comparatively grand stature that Shirley Temple attains in these movies is quite revealing about the nature of cinematic mythification in general, especially given her actual diminutiveness' (Snead, 1994, p. 47).

In *The Bluest Eye* the cinematic image, as part of this mythification process, leaves Pecola overwhelmed, her self-worth shattered. She will 'never know her beauty' (*BE*, p. 35), while Claudia, by contrast, has an alternative to celluloid images in the form of her mother's blues. Claudia's reactions to the world depicted in such films centre not on Shirley Temple but on Bojangles himself, with whom she claims a kinship beyond Hollywood's reification of blackness: 'Frieda and she had a loving conversation about how cu-ute Shirley Temple was. I couldn't join them in their adoration because I hated Shirley. Not because she was cute, but because she danced with Bojangles, who was *my* friend, *my* uncle, *my* daddy, and who ought to have been soft-shoeing it and chuckling with me' (Morrison's italics *BE*, p. 13). Unlike Pecola and her sister, Frieda, Claudia senses the absurdity of Bojangles's relationship with the infant character. Racist ideology, even when communicated by the medium of popular cinema, is rendered impotent by Claudia's resistance as her own history and culture are capable of withstanding white ideology and the ideal represented by Temple becomes instead the focus for hatred. As a child, Claudia possesses an instinctive awareness of the exploitative nature of the relationship between the film's white characters and the Bojangles figure; and as the mature narrator of later years, she refines this understanding and takes her place in the tradition as artist/storyteller. Her anger as a black girl in the 1940s is directed not simply at whiteness, or even white ideology, but rather at the economic and material restrictions it endorses. The childlike, petty violence she inflicts on her white neighbours emanates from a dim awareness of their relative economic advantage, her shame fostered artificially by a system of exclusion and marginalization.

Morrison plays out some of the key concerns occupying social scientists and the proponents of Black Power during the 1960s. In this sense, *The Bluest Eye* is more than a consideration of African-American existence in 1940s Ohio; it is also a confrontation of 1960s political and intellectual thought and its relationship to African Americans. Morrison's treatment of Pecola as a victim of white cultural values reflects those interpretations of race, prevalent among the predominantly white social theorists of the period, in which emphasis was placed upon the self-perpetuating pathologies considered endemic in African-American families and widely regarded as the legacy of slavery, racism and a concomitant self-hatred and desire for whiteness.[6] Morrison, however, like the black aestheticians and social theorists, stresses how this interpretation of race ignores the characteristics and strengths of the African-American community, taking for granted white middle-class culture as the norm against which African Americans were measured and usually found wanting (Blauner, 1970, p. 364).

Frantz Fanon in 1960s America

To counter these views black intellectuals, social theorists and psychologists turned to Frantz Fanon, the black psychiatrist who combined a career as a physician and scholar with his role as a revolutionary in the Algerian war of

---

[6] In *Dark Ghetto: Dilemmas of Social Power*, Kenneth Clark's study of African-American urban life, Clark sees the black experience in wholly negative terms, as 'chronic, self-perpetuating pathology' (Clark, 1965, p. 81). In relation to Morrison's treatment of Pecola it is also interesting to note that Clark argues: 'Many Negroes live sporadically in a world of fantasy.... In childhood the delusion is a simple one – the child may pretend that he is really white' (Clark, 1965, p. 64).Nathan Glazer and Daniel Patrick Moynihan in *Beyond the Melting Pot: The Negroes, Puerto Ricans, Jews, Italians, and Irish of New York City* are sympathetic towards those African Americans aspiring to meet Glazer and Moynihan's own middle-class norms. They also argue that 'the Negro is only an American, and nothing else. He has no values and culture to guard and protect' (Glazer and Moynihan, 1963, p. 53).Elliot Liebow in *Tally's Corner: A Study of Negro Streetcorner Men* concludes that African Americans have no distinctive culture of their own. Their form of social organization 'is rather the cultural model of the larger society as seen through the prism of repeated failure' (Liebow, 1967, p. 221).

independence. The two key works appropriated by the Black Power Movement, *Black Skin, White Masks* (1952) and *The Wretched of the Earth* (1961) were not specifically concerned with the condition of African Americans:

> The Negroes of Chicago only resemble the Nigerians or the Tanganyikans in so far as they were all defined in relation to the whites. But once the first comparisons had been made and subjective feelings were assuaged, the American Negroes realized that the objective problems were fundamentally heterogeneous. . . . and that the problems which kept Richard Wright or Langston Hughes on the alert were fundamentally different from those which might confront Leopold Senghor or Jomo Kenyatta. (Fanon, 1961, pp. 173–4)

For Fanon, celebrations of a pan-African culture risked overlooking important historical, economic and geographical differences. In spite of this, proponents of Black Power adopted and adapted core concepts of Fanon's writing as part of their strategy for self-empowerment and liberation from the internal colonization of African Americans and constructions of pathology. By 1970, almost one million copies of *The Wretched of the Earth* had been sold and Eldridge Cleaver called the book 'the bible of the black liberation movement', and fellow Black Panther Bobby Seale claimed to have read it six times (Van de Burg, 1992, p. 60). Its appeal lay in Fanon's revolutionary anti-colonialism that stressed the necessity and inevitability of violence from the very start: 'Decolonization is always a violent phenomenon' and colonialism is itself 'violence in its natural state and it will only yield when confronted with greater violence' (Fanon, 1961, pp. 27, 48). The application of Marxist principles to the colonial encounter needed, according to Fanon, to be 'slightly stretched' in order to take account of extreme forms of domination in colonized countries that dispense with the necessity for a powerful ideological superstructure as a veil for capitalist exploitation (Fanon, 1961, p. 31). Fanon did not underestimate the power of ideology as an adjunct to the colonial process; it was rather a question of emphasizing his belief that negotiated political liberation would only lead to premature and distorted versions of bourgeois democracy.

> [I]t so happens sometimes that decolonisation occurs in areas which have not been sufficiently shaken by the struggle for liberation, and there may be found those same know-all, smart, wily intellectuals. We find intact in them the manners and forms of thought picked up during their association with the colonialist bourgeoisie. Spoilt children of yesterday's colonialism and of today's national governments, they organise the loot of whatever national resources exist. (Fanon, 1961, p. 37)

Fanon's formulation has complex ramifications for any discussion of the United States as a colonizing country – oppressor of indigenous Native Americans and enslaved Africans as well as perpetrator of global economic exploitation. His edict for decolonization attracted African-American militants clearly aware of the violent oppression of black people in America. However, America is also a postcolonial country that, after all, conducted its own violent war of independence against British oppression, despite failing to live up to the ideals in the name of which that war was waged (Hayes, 1996, pp. 11–34). As Helen Carr points out, 'Being postcolonial may mean a wrongful oppression has been overthrown, but it is no guarantee of moral rectitude. Postcoloniality is a historical stage, not a virtue' (Carr, 1996, p. 7). What is at stake here is an understanding of the form of government adopted by the United States after the war of independence. Despite its constitution, America proceeded to imitate Europe to such a degree that it 'became a monster, in which the taints, the sickness and the inhumanity of Europe have grown to appalling dimensions' (Fanon, 1961, p. 252). Fanon urged emergent nation states to avoid duplication and aim instead towards the development of alternative governing concepts and practices, and 'not pay tribute to Europe by creating states, institutions and societies which draw their inspiration from her' (Fanon, 1961, p. 254).

It is from within this milieu that Toni Morrison emerged as a writer. She was in fact involved in the early Civil Rights movement as a member of the Howard University Players and in 1962 taught Stokeley Carmichael as an undergraduate at Howard (Goulimari, 2011, p. 18). During the early to the mid-1960s Morrison was herself ambivalent about integration as a panacea for the 'race problem'. The 'terror' and 'abuses' of segregation were clear, but she was aware that integration would mean 'no fine black college' or 'fine black education' (Morrison intv. with Lester, 1988, p. 51) and by the time Carmichael had become a national figure in Black Power, the movement, Morrison felt, had become 'embezzled by the media which made it into fashion' (Morrison intv. with Lester, 1988, p. 52). The momentum was in fact diffused not only by its commodification through television and print media, but also by emergent, parallel protests from feminists and white middle-class students.

Instead, Morrison's activism was to take form in imaginative fiction and, as we have seen, many of the psychological, ideological and cultural preoccupations of American and European intellectuals permeate *The Bluest Eye*. In spite of her ambivalence about segregation and African-American nationalism, Morrison's novel resonates with the new militancy of the period and Fanon's conception of the role of the intellectual and the rejection of bourgeois standards of culture.

His focus on the importance of culture for the nation state is reformulated by Morrison, and culture now becomes, for her, the expression of the community. The writer, for Fanon, must produce an effective 'literature of combat', 'inert episodes' from the past, including folklore, myths and song, alive again but with modification and attuned to developing social consciousness (Fanon, 1961, p. 193). Fanon's reference to 'inert' art forms from the past reveals his problematic relationship with folklore, which for him constituted a debilitating form of superstition based upon sterile customs that merely played into the hands of the colonizer. Any real art, art of national consciousness, would instead represent the past 'with the intention of opening the future, an invitation to action and a basis for hope' (Fanon, 1961, p. 187).

Morrison, in fact, makes extensive, subversive use of folk language and music in her representations of the past to create possibilities for the future of African Americans, 'to identify those things in the past that are useful and those things that are not', and for the future of the novel as a delineation of African-American experience (Morrison intv. with LeClair, 1994, p. 121). As I pointed out in the Introduction, Morrison believes that as music is no longer the exclusive preserve of African Americans its healing function has to be replaced by the novel (Morrison, 1984, p. 58). She has said, 'The music kept us alive, but it's not enough anymore. My people are being devoured' (Morrison intv. with LeClair, 1994, p. 121). Through the novel form Morrison wants 'to do what the music did for blacks, what we used to be able to do with each other in private and in that civilization that existed underneath the white civilization' (Morrison intv. with LeClair, 1994, p. 121). Morrison here reveals her desire to renew existing forms of African-American expression, while maintaining its collective, oral function.

Vernacular responses to ideology

In *The Bluest Eye*, Claudia's narration is presented in standard English punctuated by the occasional slippage into the vernacular idiom. Her opening phrase, 'Quiet as it's kept' is, as Morrison has said,

> a piece of information which means exactly what it says, but to black people it means a big lie is about to be told. Or someone is going to tell some graveyard information, who's sleeping with whom. Black readers will chuckle. There is a level of appreciation that might be available only to people who understand the context of the language. (Morrison intv. with LeClair, 1994, p. 124)

That Claudia occasionally mixes black idiom with standard English shows that she, like Morrison, whose authorial voice at times blends with Claudia's, knows 'standard English' and wants 'to use it to help restore the other language, the lingua franca' (Morrison intv. with LeClair, 1994, p. 124).

Morrison has said:

> There are certain things I cannot say without recourse to my language. It's terrible to think that a child with five different present tenses comes to school to be faced with those books that are less than his own language. And then to be told things about his language, which is him, that are sometimes permanently damaging. (Morrison intv. with LeClair, 1994, p. 124)

This critique of the educational system is executed in her exposure of the school primer as inadequate for the expression of real experience and in her satirical representation of Elihue Soaphead Church, the 'Reader, Adviser, and Interpreter of Dreams' (*BE*, p. 131), 'reared in a family proud of its academic accomplishments and its mixed blood – in fact, they believed the former was based on the latter' (*BE*, p. 132).

> Little Elihue learned everything he needed to know well, particularly the fine art of self-deception. He read greedily but understood selectively, choosing the bits and pieces of other men's ideas that supported whatever predilection he had at the moment. Thus he chose to remember Hamlet's abuse of Ophelia, but not Christ's love of Mary Magdalene; Hamlet's frivolous politics, but not Christ's serious anarchy'. (*BE*, p. 134)

He is the one character who could grant Pecola blue eyes, his internalization of imperialist ideology leaving him without any sense of his own blackness. As Morrison has said, Soaphead, like Pecola herself, 'would be convinced that if black people were more like white people they would be better off' (Morrison intv. with Stepto, 1994, p. 22). His voice finds expression in writing rather than in the spoken word, a reversal of the oral preaching tradition whereby Soaphead can relate to God only on paper, his business card enclosed. When he does speak it is in the affected tones of the English clergyman; 'What can I do for you, my child?' (*BE*, p. 137) and 'Courage. Courage, my child. These things are not granted to faint hearts' (*BE*, p. 138).

Voices, and the languages used to express them, cannot of course be divorced from the specific historical situation that has helped to create them. Morrison's representation of Soaphead is not, as Bakhtin would say, 'accomplished at the level of linguistic abstraction: images of language are inseparable from images of various world views and from the living beings who are their agents – people who think, talk, and act in a setting that is social and historically concrete' (Bakhtin, 1981, p. 131). Morrison creates Soaphead from the hegemonic discourse of nineteenth-century English colonialism, the 'soundless cave' (*BE*, p. 135) of his mind in need of the nourishing orality that sustains the MacTeer family. The MacTeers, even Claudia, have to some extent internalized white standards of beauty and yet they resist this ideology through the spoken word that functions to keep them sane. Without creative orality, Pecola has no sense of self, a lack that sends her into madness.

Using dance as a metaphor, Morrison emphasizes the collective vitality of black orality that contrasts so vividly with the tone of the Dick and Jane primer:

> Their conversation is like a gently wicked dance: sound meets sound, curtsies, shimmies and retires. Another sound enters but is upstaged by still another: the two circle each other and stop. Sometimes their words move in lofty spirals; other times they take strident leaps, and all of it is punctuated with warm-pulsed laughter – like the throb of a heart made of jelly. (*BE*, p. 9)

Claudia, as mature narrator, recalls the nurturing orality of her childhood and is moved by the memory of her mother's singing.

> But her voice was so sweet and her singing-eyes so melty I found myself longing for those hard times, yearning to be grown without 'a thin di-i-ime to my name'. I looked forward to the delicious time when 'my man' would leave me, when I would 'hate to see that evening sun go down . . .' 'cause then I would know 'my man has left this town'. Misery colored by the greens and blues in my mother's voice took all of the grief out of the words and left me with a conviction that pain was not only endurable, it was sweet. (*BE*, p. 18)

Claudia learns from her mother the idiom, function and structure of the blues and knows the value of this expressive inheritance that will be hers to pass on. It is this and the kitchen gossip, not the gift of an unyielding plastic white doll, that Claudia affectionately remembers and which helped the MacTeers and families like them to 'deal' with their 'peripheral existence' (*BE*, p. 11). Claudia is fully aware of her family's economic and social position but she is given the voice that enables her to transcend it.

The Breedloves, and especially Pecola, have a more problematic relationship with language. Pauline tells her story, albeit with the omniscient intervention of the author, but her daughter Pecola barely speaks at all. When buying the Mary Jane candy she loves so much, Pecola is struck dumb by the store-owner's disavowal of her existence and only at the end of the novel does she find an authoritative voice but sadly only to converse with her imaginary friend. The victim of family neglect and racism, Pecola descends into hysteria and delusion.

Sula (1973)

Pecola's individual delusion is the result of racism in both its ideological and more overt manifestations, but Morrison also considers descrimination in relation to the community of Lorain, Ohio. As we have seen, the community is sustained by African-American oral tradition and yet it is not idealized as the environment for a positive and racially healthy existence.[7] Instead, the community remains as the background to the lives of Claudia and Frieda MacTeer and the Breedlove family, affirming itself mainly through Lorain's moralistic condemnation of the Breedlove's tragic history. When Cholly Breedlove puts his family 'outdoors' they are also outside of the community and, as Claudia says, 'to be slack enough to put oneself outdoors, or heartless enough to put one's own kin outdoors – that was criminal' (*BE*, p. 11). Pecola becomes the community pariah, raped by her father and, by the end of the novel, the wild child living on the edge of town. The people of Lorain, however, retain Pecola as the repository for their anxieties and guilt about their marginal status and the novel closes with Claudia's admission of her own complicity in Pecola's descent into madness:

> All of us – all who knew her – felt so wholesome after we cleaned ourselves on her. We were so beautiful when we stood astride her ugliness. Her simplicity decorated us, her guilt sanctified us, her pain made us glow with health, her awkwardness made us think we had a sense of humor. (*BE*, p. 163)

Retrospective self-understanding and acknowledgement of the community's guilt reflects Claudia's awareness of the punitive effects of a collective, choral sensibility that, by the very end of the novel, exists as a disembodied voice. The choral voice of the community is also evident when Morrison introduces Mrs. MacTeer and her nameless women friends. The reader is unaware exactly who is speaking, but taken together the voices form a commentary on the

---

[7] Morrison uses the term 'community' with certain reservations 'because it came to mean something much different in the sixties and seventies, as though we had to forge one – but it seemed to me that it was always there, only we called it the "neighbourhood"' (Morrison intv. with Stepto, 1994, p. 11).

neighbourhood, more significant than mere gossip as it constitutes their attempt for autonomy.

The Caribbean-American novelist, Paule Marshall, in 'The Making of a Writer: From the Poets in the Kitchen' (1983), describes the importance of her mother's kitchen talks with female friends as forms of therapy, refuge and, importantly for Marshall's own development as a writer, creativity. They were women in whom the need for self-expression was strong and, language being the only vehicle readily available, they made of it an art form that was, in keeping with the African conflation of art and life, an integral part of their lives (Marshall, 1983, p. 6).

Orality alleviates feelings of 'powerlessness' and 'invisibility' engendered by the women's peripheral existence in American society (Marshall, 1983, p. 7). 'They were in control, if only verbally and if only for the two hours or so that they remained in our house' (Marshall, 1983, p. 7). Morrison has herself spoken of the value of her own oral heritage for her work. 'It's always seemed to me that black people's grace has been with what they do with language. . . . when I think of things my mother or father or aunts used to say, it seems the most striking thing in the world. That's what I try to get into my fiction' (Morrison intv. with Watkins, 1994, p. 45). She also relates the creativity of black speech and storytelling to the community and its choral role in her novels. A Classics minor from Howard, Morrison was to incorporate the Greek chorus into her work and see similarities between its function and the function of black art forms for the community:

> [T]here was something about the Greek chorus, for example, that reminds me of what goes on in Black churches and in jazz where there are two things. You have a response obviously. The chorus being the community who participates in this behaviour and is shocked by it or horrified by it or they like or support it. Everybody is in it. And it has something also to do with the way in which those stories are told because the reader becomes a participant in the books, and I have to make it possible for the reader to respond the way I would like the chorus to in addition to the choral effects in the book itself. (Morrison intv. with Jones and Vinson, 1994, p. 176)

Here Morrison reiterates a Bakhtinian understanding of her novels as dialogical, a participatory event for reader and writer, and as 'double-voiced' in her utilization of specifically African-American forms of expression and classic Greek drama. There is a double purpose to her aesthetic in that Morrison makes her own contribution to African-American art and the community through the act of novel writing and she represents the community itself; its choral characteristics, myths, folklore, history and language. In *The Bluest Eye*, the community is important for Morrison's articulation of the effects of racism on group cohesion and their treatment of Pecola, but serves as background rather than as a central presence. It is in *Sula* that Morrison is interested in 'making the town, the community, the neighbourhood, as strong as a character I could' (Morrison intv. with Stepto, 1994, p. 11). Place in *Sula* is conflated with the voice and actions of the community to create a unifying force for the novel in which the prominence given to Bottom, the black section of Medallion, allows Morrison to probe a complex range of connected themes and issues. These include the tension between the concerns of the community and individual self-expression, the intersection of gender and race, and the nature of good and evil.

Place, community and history

Sula is in certain respects a continuation of Morrison's first novel; the delineation of the childhood friendship of Nel and Sula has parallels with the childhood relationships between Pecola, Claudia and Frieda in *The Bluest Eye*. In *Sula*, however, Morrison explores Nel's and Sula's adult lives and Sula, unlike Pecola, does not capitulate to the condition of being female and black in a society that devalues both. Rather, Sula has the strength and ability to articulate the self, ultimately at the cost of her own life. Crucially, in *Sula* Morrison privileges the black community and its cultural forms in ways that go beyond her concern in *The Bluest Eye* to delineate the manifestations of white ideology and culture and considers issues within the black community itself. This constitutes an important political shift as Morrison is aware that a wholly 'black-topic text' has possibilities for challenging western ideological boundaries in its very denial of whiteness.[8] As the Black Aesthetic poet Etheridge Knight noted, the contestatory or 'protest' black novel implicitly appealed to a white audience in the author's 'belief that a change will be forthcoming once the masters are aware of the protestor's "grievance" (the very word connotes begging, supplications to the gods). Only when that belief has faded and protestings end, will Black Art begin' (qtd. in Neal, 1968, p. 30). In an interview with Salman Rushdie, originally

---

[8] Robert Grant argues that 'Morrison deliberately avoids the rhetorical/polemical features generally associated with socio-political Afro-American novels, or the "protest" fiction exemplified in Richard Wright's *Uncle Tom's Children* and *Native Son*. Morrison's acknowledgements of white American racism's circumscription of black life are neither trumpeted nor elaborated' (Grant, 1988, p. 90).

broadcast in 1992, Morrison discussed her feelings of marginality as an African American, saying that she

> began to value more the marginality, the sort of peripheral existence, because it seemed to offer so much more. It was deeper, more complex, it had a tension, it related to the centre but it wasn't the centre. So of that sense of feeling American, I was deprived. I was deprived of that, and I felt bereft. Now, of course, I take it as a position of far more interesting possibilities. (Morrison intv. with Rushdie, 2008, p. 55)

Morrison admits, however, that on beginning *Sula* in 1969 she did not have the courage of these convictions. In 'Unspeakable Things Unspoken' (1989) she outlines ways in which the language of her novels is informed by an African-American cultural specificity. She knew that *Sula* 'would be about people in a black community not just foregrounded but totally dominant; and that it was also about black women – also foregrounded and dominant.' In spite of this, and in fact partly because of it, and because the late 1960s was a period of intense political activity on the part of black Americans, Morrison felt it necessary 'to cater to the diminished expectations of the reader, or his or her alarm heightened by the emotional luggage one carries into the black-topic text.' Morrison makes clear from the beginning of *Sula* that she is concerned with community and place, the first line establishing the novel's premise. 'In that place, where they tore the nightshade and blackberry patches from their roots to make room for the Medallion City Golf Course, there was once a neighbourhood' (*S*, p. 3). Morrison came to regret introducing the community from the 'point of view of the stranger – the "valley man" who might happen to be there on some errand, but who obviously does not live there and to and for whom all this is mightily strange, even exotic' (Morrison, 1989, pp. 221–2). The need to create a 'welcoming lobby' for the reader may seem surprising, given that proponents of the Black Aesthetic had been proposing literature that 'speaks directly to the needs of Black America' (Neal, 1968, p. 29). The decision to welcome the white reader to the text perhaps reflects a desire for distance from the controversies of Black Power, but more importantly Morrison knew that with *Sula* she was radically questioning essentialized notions of black women dominant at this time. As Deborah McDowell says of *Sula*

> Coming significantly on the heels of the Black Power Movement that rendered black women prone or the 'queens' of the male warrior – an updated version of a familiar script – the narrative invites the reader to imagine a different script

for women that transcends the boundaries of social and linguistic convention. (McDowell, 1989, p. 60)

For McDowell, Morrison transcends boundaries through an interrogation of the 'positive black self', articulated in the characterization of Sula. In a subsequent section of this chapter, I will consider how *Sula* constitutes a move forward in the representation of black women as ambiguous and defying codification through a fluidity, symbolized by the use of water imagery and Sula's split identity. Similarly, as in *The Bluest Eye*, Morrison renders the community itself as ambiguous, a far from monolithic and racially positive entity, presented in ways which question notions of good and evil and invite the reader into a dialogical relationship with the text.

Sula begins with a reflection on the life of a community that no longer exists. Yet despite the sense of loss, Morrison does not idealize Bottom in her evocation of it as a place,

> where on quiet days people in valley houses could hear singing sometimes, banjos sometimes, and, if a valley man happened to have business up in those hills – collecting rent or insurance payments – he might see a dark woman in a flowered dress doing a bit of cakewalk, a bit of 'messing around' to the lively notes of a mouth organ. Her bare feet would raise the saffron dust that floated down on the coveralls and bunion-split shoes of the man breathing music in and out of his harmonica. The black people watching her would laugh and rub their knees, and it would be easy for the valley man to hear the laughter and not notice the adult pain that rested somewhere under the eyelids, somewhere in the palm of the hand, somewhere behind the frayed lapels, somewhere in the sinew's curve. (S, p. 4)

Morrison here draws on the blues aesthetic to establish the importance of the economic and ritualistic culture of Bottom. Despite the beauty of this description, and the nostalgia for a vanishing folk past, Morrison makes clear that the expressive art form of the cakewalk and accompanying music derive from the community's attempt to negotiate powerlessness and marginality rather than as a positive form of self-expression. The community's art and expression may be seen as a reaction to, and resistance against, oppression. The placement of the black community at the centre of *Sula* is framed by an understanding of this oppression.[9] In the prologue we learn how Bottom owes its very existence to the

---

[9] I would agree with Houston Baker's remark that the 'apparently tranquil intimacy and autonomy' of Bottom 'remain romantic mystifications if they are not read as reaction formations of certain Western confinements' (Baker, 1993, p. 244).

deception of a slave by a white farmer who allotted the infertile hill land to the black population, assuring him that it was fertile land – 'the bottom of heaven' – rather than supply him with the genuine bottom land of the fertile valley. The community transpose this story into a 'nigger joke' that becomes part of its folk past and a strategy for gaining 'a little comfort somehow' (S, p. 5).

The aesthetic of Bottom is a blues expression of pleasure and pain, the artists – the girl performing the cakewalk and her musician – expressing and living in the moment. Their performance constitutes a space for release from the pressing economic and ideological realities surrounding them. The prologue, which we have seen was problematic for Morrison, contrasts with representations of the community in the rest of the novel. We see this form of pure expression only in the prologue, a spontaneous living of the blues in which the easy grace of music and movement belie an underlying history, and future, of pain. The white trick is repeated at the end of the novel when the inhabitants are persuaded to move to the once prized, but now urbanized valley land, leaving the Bottom to leafy suburban development and a new golf course.

The centrality of the community in *Sula* is framed by wider historical events, peripheral to the lives of the people of Bottom but nevertheless affecting their existence in important ways. The first chapter, '1919', indicates the impact that the First World War could have on such a remote 'little river town in Ohio'. Shadrack's horrific wartime experience in France leaves him permanently traumatized and, back home in Bottom, he holds a yearly remembrance of the war and calls it National Suicide Day.[10] 'It was not death or dying that frightened him, but the unexpectedness of both. In sorting it all out, he hit on the notion that if one day a year were devoted to it, everybody could get it out of the way and the rest of the year would be safe and free' (S, p. 14). Originally a way for Shadrack to create order out of the chaos of war, National Suicide Day becomes an important ritual in the life of Bottom, an alternative and communal commemoration that helps define and shape the community. As America enters the Second World War, Shadrack loses faith in the redemptive value of Suicide Day after his realization that Sula has died and his efforts to prevent death 'were never going to do any good' (S, p. 158). The function of Suicide Day as a safety valve for the community is revealed as its dissolution provokes an eruption of chaos and death as people parade to the tunnel from which, because they are black, they have been excluded from building. The community suddenly needs definite 'respite' from the 'very adult pain that had undergirded them all those

---

[10] For a detailed analysis of trauma in *Sula* see Jill Matus, *Contemporary World Writers: Toni Morrison* (Matus, 1998, pp. 55–71).

years before' (S, p. 160). This pain, previously assuaged by music, folk mythology and ritual becomes too much to bear. Enraged and disillusioned, the people of Bottom attempt to destroy the tunnel, the material representation of their exclusion, and many die as the entrance collapses. The public parade through the white part of town and the ensuing disaster assumes significance in the context of Black Power politics during the early 1970s. America was committed to winning the war in Vietnam and there was a renewed recognition among African Americans that they had the freedom to die for their country yet denied equal political, social and economic opportunities at home despite the legislative gains made in the 1960s. In her historicization of the work of African-American women novelists, Melissa Walker argues:

> In 1973, it would have been virtually impossible for readers of a novel like *Sula* to be oblivious to the public history of years that saw the passing of the Voting Rights Act; the escalation of the Vietnam War, with its disproportionate number of African-American casualties; Lyndon Johnson's announcement that he would not seek re-election; the assassination of Martin Luther King, Jr; increasing outbreaks of urban riots; the election and re-election of Richard Nixon; and the systematic attack on the advocates of black power. With all this came the rapid retrenchment from public policies intended to combat racism. (Walker, 1991, p. 128)

In a passage as relevant in 1973 as it was in 1941, Morrison characterizes the hope that by the end of the novel, as in the 1970s, has finally dissipated.

> The same hope that kept them picking beans for other farmers; kept them from finally leaving as they talked of doing; kept them knee-deep in other people's dirt; kept them excited about other people's wars; kept them solicitous of white people's children; kept them convinced that some magic 'government' was going to lift them up, out and away from that dirt, those beans, those wars. (S, p. 160)

War and the trick of Bottom's very existence are, then, incorporated into ritual, mythology and folklore of the through National Suicide Day and the retelling of the 'nigger joke'. These events begin and end the novel, literally marginalized in its structure to give the community its central position. *The Bluest Eye* is set in the real town of Lorain, Ohio; in *Sula*, however, we see place mythologized in the invented setting of Bottom. The imaginative creation of Bottom inflects *Sula* with surreal and mythical qualities, but the encroachment of actual historical and political events are crucial for its creation.

That the community's spontaneous uprising brings death and failure suggests that disorganized rebellion is not a viable solution to oppression. Significantly, those who refuse to take part in the parade and who consequently survive are those

> who understood the Spirit's touch which made them dance, who understood whole families bending their backs in a field while singing as from one throat, who understood the ecstasy of river baptisms under suns just like this one, did not understand this curious disorder, this headless display and so refused also to go. (S, p. 160)

Those who understand the sustaining qualities of culturally specific forms of dance, music and religion are more likely to endure. Ultimately, though folk expression can sustain the inhabitants of Bottom, it cannot materially alter their condition and any openly contestatory challenge to intolerable poverty and exclusion will fail. Morrison's evocation of slavery in the reference to 'families bending their backs in a field' is a celebration of a group cohesion that is disappearing by the end of the novel. *Sula* is, in part, a testimony to a semi-rural community that by 1965 has been relocated to the town of Medallion and absorbed by faceless urbanization. In the epilogue Nel bears witness to the demise of Bottom, noting how its former inhabitants are more prosperous than ever: 'You could go downtown and see colored people working in the dime store behind the counters, even handling money with cash-register keys around their necks. And a colored man taught mathematics at the junior high school' (S, p. 163). However, Nel recognizes that in gaining certain social and economic advantages the community has been sacrificed along with the defining art forms that their collective history and geography compelled them to articulate.

> These young ones kept talking about the community, but they left the hills to the poor, the old, the stubborn – and the rich white folks. Maybe it hadn't been a community, but it had been a place. Now there weren't any places left, just separate houses with separate televisions and separate telephones and less and less dropping by. (S, p. 166)

Morrison's delineation of a community's adoption of bourgeois aspiration in *The Bluest Eye* is extended in *Sula* as she implies that marginality, and not life as a dime store clerk, holds potential as a liberating space.

Autonomy and folk discourse

As we have seen, Morrison regards the 'peripheral existence' of African Americans as offering 'far more interesting possibilities' than life in the dominant social, economic and cultural mainstream (Morrison intv. with Rushdie, 2008, p. 55).

Central to a political analysis of *Sula* is the question of whether marginality can provide agency beyond the expression of individual or group identity. Philip Richards, on folk discourse in *Sula*, summarizes the problem of interpretation here, emphasizing individual or group cultural identity rather than issues of agency. 'The question of whether to identify with the ghetto [Bottom] as the fantasized fulfilment of self that cannot be had in the integrated world, or as a disruptive world of lower class disorganization, is the central ambiguity played out in the shifting point of views of Morrison's *Sula*' (Richards, 1995, p. 295).

Morrison regards writing and language 'as agency – as an act with consequences' (Morrison, 1994, p. 13), evident in Claudia's retrospective narration of an untold history in *The Bluest Eye* to contest western literary and ideological constructions. Central to Claudia's narration are her memories of the orality of family life and, similarly, when Morrison takes over the narration of Cholly's and Pauline's young lives, the qualities of oral culture are affirmed. It is in the process of migration that Cholly and Pauline neglect to pass on remembered stories, experiences and feelings to their children. In *Sula*, too, urbanization and integration promise only alienation and the dissolution of community. As often noted in discussions of *Sula*, Morrison writes in confrontation with white bourgeois ideology, privileging a folk spirit as its liberatory antithesis,[11] but it is evident that this conceptualization of folk culture is filtered through her experiences as a public intellectual and established novelist. The space in the margins, the literal space of Bottom and the expression of its people, are aesthetically and intellectually mediated in order for Morrison to accomplish what is in effect a political project to give voice to the community, recover history and achieve agency.

In this respect Morrison belongs to a tradition of intellectuals and writers who have appropriated African-American cultural forms for political purpose. In *Narrative of the Life of Frederick Douglass* (1845), Douglass remembers the collective singing of his fellow slaves as unconscious expressions of resistance and outlines how songs were composed for his uninitiated white reader: 'They would compose and sing as they went along, consulting neither time nor tune. The thought that came up, came out – if not in the word, in the sound – and as frequently in the one as in the other. They would sometimes sing the most pathetic sentiment in the most rapturous tone, and the most rapturous sentiment in the most pathetic tone.' Like the white 'valley man' in *Sula*, hearing the laughter

---

[11] See for example, McDowell, 'Boundaries: Or Distant Relations and Close Kin'; Baker, 'When Lindbergh Sleeps with Bessie Smith'; Cynthia Davis, 'Self, Society and Myth in Toni Morrison's Fiction'; Byerman, 'Beyond Realism: The Fictions of Toni Morrison', in *Toni Morrison: Modern Critical Views* (Bloom, ed., 1990).

but not seeing the pain, white listeners hearing slave songs mistakenly 'speak of the singing, among slaves, as evidence of their contentment and happiness'. In fact, the songs 'breathed the prayer and complaint of souls boiling over with the bitterest anguish. Every tone was a testimony against slavery, and a prayer to God for deliverance from chains.' Douglass admits that it is only with hindsight that he recognizes the significance of the songs as a form of resistance. 'I did not when a slave, understand the deep meaning of those rude and apparently incoherent songs. I was myself within the circle; so that I neither saw nor heard as those without might see and hear.' As a free man Douglass appropriates and reinterprets the slave songs in an effort to convince the nineteenth-century reader of the inhumanities of slavery. Being 'within the circle' is a precondition for instinctive understanding of the expressions of pain and resistance inherent in the songs, but there is a contradiction in Douglass' analysis in that being 'within the circle' means that the true significance of the songs cannot be appreciated. He also distances himself from the slaves with whom he expresses solidarity, inferring that he did not participate in the singing himself and draws attention to the act of narration as his own form of resistance. The songs were nevertheless vitally important to Douglass, supplying him with the 'first glimmering conception of the dehumanizing character of slavery', but it is only through the retrospective act of 'writing these lines' that he feels their full affect. Douglass's strategic appropriation of the slave songs involves a transformation of the 'incoherent' and the 'rude' into lucid expressions of resistance (Douglass, 1845, pp. 497–8).

Fifty years later in *The Souls of Black Folk* (1903), Du Bois infuses the slave songs with political significance and like Douglass finds it necessary to distance himself from the group he represents. Assuming the role of a cultured observer, Du Bois offers a sociological analysis of the 'disorganised' African-American rural experience and makes clear that real agency can be achieved only if this experience is refined through higher education. For Du Bois the songs of the South assume power as forms of resistance and propaganda when relocated from the Georgia cotton field to the university concert hall for the edification of a cultured audience. Zora Neale Hurston, too, who objected to the *embourgeoisement* of the spirituals, paradoxically distances herself from the folk experience in order to recover it. In *Mules and Men* (1935) she says of her folk heritage, 'I couldn't see it for wearing it. It was only when I was off in college, away from my native surroundings, that I could see myself like somebody else and stand off and look at my garment. Then I had to have the spy-glass of Anthropology to look through at that' (Hurston, 1935, p. 1). For Philip Richards, the paradox of an educated, literary middle class finding solidarity with folk culture characterizes the African-American literary tradition to which Douglass, Du Bois, Hurston and Morrison belong. Richards attributes the origin of this tradition to the black writer's 'quest to achieve autonomy in a world of patrons, to escape inferior caste status in an egalitarian democracy, or to overcome psychological distance from the unlettered black masses with whom one claimed solidarity.' He concludes that the resulting tension 'constituted serious contradictions that often over-determined black expression, and shaped its representations of African-American folk culture.' This perspective offers possibilities for enriched readings of African-American texts that take into account the intersection of race and class and conflicts in literary representations of folk culture in the African-American tradition, 'a tradition which features the provocative confrontation between psychologically complex cultivated blacks and the seeming simplicities of folk life' (Richards, 1995, p. 271).

In Richards' discussion *Sula* takes its place within the tradition as an 'ironic' text. Morrison knowingly articulates this tension between the folk as offering an autonomous space for self or group expression and a deeply entrenched, middle-class ideology derived historically from the forms of black Protestantism displayed in the slave narratives. The treatment of community and self in *Sula* is characterized by a conscious ambiguity that this tension fosters and which means Morrison does not idealize the community as a homogeneous environment for racial cohesion. Richards notes how Sula's and Nel's quest for self-hood is influenced by their different social environments: Sula's background offers self-hood through the experience and expression of moments to be lived, Nel Wright's through the appropriation of the values and aspirations of bourgeois accumulation. The order of the Wright family home offers clearly defined possibilities for the self in that it provides the economic and psychological space for the consideration of identity. Although each family represents different African-American value systems they are both, as Richards points out, ultimately shaped by the same economic and social restrictions. Ironically, the scope for self-expression Nel is afforded by her stable environment is also restricted by her mother's middle-class values and, as Richards says, 'Morrison's narration brilliantly captures the central truth of the folk discourse, that the middle-class impedes the selfhood which it cultivates' (Richards, 1995, p. 281).

Sula's relationship with the community is one of confrontation and recrimination as she aspires to move beyond the conventional values of Bottom and, as she says, 'make myself' (S, p. 92). To construct her identity necessarily involves the transgression of the value system that many of Bottom's inhabitants have established for themselves in their desire for racial 'uplift'. Eschewing the conventions of marriage and domestic existence, Sula explores her identity through an untrammelled sexuality unacceptable to the community, not only sleeping with Nel's husband, Jude, but also with white men, transgressions of sexual and social boundaries that finally confirm her as 'evil'. 'There was nothing lower she could do, nothing filthier' (S, p. 113). As in *The Bluest Eye*, however, in which the community accommodates Pecola's madness, Sula's 'evil' functions to define the protective essence of the neighbourhood and she becomes the repository for fear, the source of bad things and the community seek new forms of cohesion in the face of such evil. Morrison interrogates 'good' and 'evil', blurring the boundaries between them in ways that reflect her understanding of religious and moral codes. Within this discourse of the folk, evil is accommodated, allowed to run its course and, as borne out in Hurston's collections of folklore, God and the Devil are stoically regarded as equals in a world that can produce plagues of robins, severe climate change and an individual such as Sula herself.

Sula's complex, disruptive individualism is accentuated by the years she spends away from Bottom, allowing her to develop a sense of self and to view the neighbourhood objectively. Nel, on the other hand, remains in Bottom and her individuality erodes until she is, in effect, subsumed by the community. For Sula, an artist seeking an art form, the community is not enough and neither the autonomy of the folk world of Bottom nor its opposite, the adoption of bourgeois values, can offer self-fulfilment. Sula lacks any formal means of expression and 'like any artist with no art form, she became dangerous' (S, p. 121). Morrison here reiterates similar reflections made in *The Bluest Eye* in which the narrator says of the young Pauline Breedlove, 'She missed – without knowing what she missed – paints and crayons' (BE, p. 87) and of Cholly, 'The pieces of Cholly's life could become coherent only in the head of a musician' (BE, p. 125) and, like Sula, without means of expression Cholly becomes 'dangerously free'. The restrictive economic environment does not foster any form of creative imagination and instead a nihilistic, self-destructive impulse overrides sensory and aesthetic feeling. Sula has a 'gift for metaphor' (S, p. 121) that remains un-channelled, turning in upon itself until she becomes the only art form her material conditions will allow. Morrison uses a trope here that is central to her later novel *Beloved* (1987), namely that her 'lawless' characters are profoundly aware of their status, or history, as commodities. When confronted by racism or, as in Sethe's case in *Beloved*, the loss of newly found freedom from slavery, the only resort is self-destruction or infanticide. In a typically nihilistic and metaphorical gesture

Sula cuts off the tip of her finger when threatened by racism as a girl, an act that both disarms her attackers and constitutes a defining moment in her journey towards self-invention.

Migration

Through her characterization of Sula, Morrison articulates the complexities of identity and empowering forms of self-expression in the face of social, geographical and economic restrictions. As the community is shaped, being compelled to negotiate displacement and the lack of economic power, whether by maintaining autonomous folk traditions or adopting assimilationist practices, so the development of individual identity is indelibly marked by these same constraints. Sula is inescapably a product of the community, but the conditions that create such an individual are also restrictive and her attempts at self-creation embody the wider struggle of the community to define itself in times of social upheaval for populations encouraged to migrate to the North. The semi-rural community of Bottom constitutes an intermediary space between the rural South and the Northern city and as such allows Morrison to consider the anxieties of African-American migration. In an interview with Claudia Tate, Morrison explains her choice of Ohio as a setting for *Sula*.

> The northern part of the state had underground railroad stations and a history of black people escaping into Canada, but the southern part of the state is as much Kentucky as there is, complete with cross burnings. Ohio is a curious juxtaposition of what was ideal in this country and what was base. It was also a Mecca for black people; they came to the mills and plants because Ohio offered the possibility of a good life, the possibility of freedom, even though there were some terrible obstacles. Ohio also offers an escape from stereotyped black settings. It is neither plantation nor ghetto. (Morrison intv. with Tate, 1983, p. 119)

The possibilities that movement northwards offered for economic advancement also created new dilemmas of identity as African Americans faced the potential erasure of the black self in their attempts to participate economically in a white world. At the heart of Morrison's appropriation of folk discourse is the recognition of the psychological anxiety and fear permeating a fragile migratory identity. Sula's life is the literary representation of this tension as she gains a college education, made possible by her uncle's war pension and which until the 1920s would have been denied to women of her race and class. She is also representative of a transitory moment in the history of black women in that Sula, at least psychologically, has rejected existence as circumscribed by her community and yet she is denied any alternative aesthetic or economic empowerment. This psychological tension means Sula occupies an intermediary and marginal space that reflects the social and geographical placing of Bottom and its community. She becomes a 'pariah figure' in a 'pariah community' and, although her individualism conflicts with the community, it is clear that the relationship between the two is, paradoxically, one of mutual dependence.[12]

Narrative strategies

Sula is, as Robert Grant maintains, a text rich in such 'calculated indeterminacies' (Grant, 1988, p. 94), and to attempt a definitive reading is fraught with complications as Morrison confounds the reader's expectations through a variety of narrative strategies. Although written in the third person, there is no guiding central voice; instead, events or emotions are described from a range of positions. Bottom is introduced from the perspective of both the white 'valley man' and of the future, a perspective infused with loss and absence; Jude and Sula's relationship is told from Nel's point of view, suggesting that we should identify with her and condemn Sula's behaviour. The changes, however, from Nel's point of view to Sula's complicate our identification with Nel as Morrison invites us to engage with Sula's construction of herself. Furthermore, at times the community's choral voice becomes central as Morrison denies herself any direct moral commentary of her own, describing grotesque and reprehensible acts such as maiming, infanticide and adultery without drama or interjection.

Morrison's innovative use of point of view has been noted, as have discontinuities in the novel's 'spiral' structure.[13] The use of dates as chapter titles suggests linearity and yet the content belies any implication that significant events are continuous, but rather are contingent and important only in the context of other past or future events. Morrison also disrupts conventional linear narrative form through the evocation of absence, the novel's structure broken in the middle by Sula's time away from Bottom allowing Morrison to create presence out of absence; there are many examples of significant missing 'things', including the tip of Sula's finger, Eva's leg, Chicken Little, Jude and

---

[12] Morrison has said of the relationship between the community and Sula: 'Medallion is a sustaining environment even for a woman who is very different. Nobody's going to lynch her or call the police. They call her bad names and try to protect themselves from her evil; that's all. But they put her to good use, which is a way of manipulating her' (Morrison intv. with Tate, 1983, p. 130).

[13] See, for example, 'Absence into Presence' (Grant, 1988). Morrison has described the structure of *Sula* as 'spiral' (Morrison intv. with Tate, p. 124).

Ajax (Grant, 1988). *Sula* is a technical *tour de force*, but its formal excellence should not overshadow the political impulse behind such literary innovation. More than a narrative device, the significance of absence in the novel indicates Morrison's purpose to record a history that is missing in conventional literary forms. In 'Unspeakable Things Unspoken' Morrison focuses on the 'great, ornamental, prescribed absence' of African Americans from early American literature and points out

> that invisible things are not necessarily 'not there'; that a void may be empty, but is not a vacuum. In addition, certain absences are so stressed, so ornate, so planned, they call attention to themselves; arrest us with intentionality and purpose, like neighbourhoods that are defined by the population held away from them. (Morrison, 1989, pp. 210, 212)

In *Sula*, Morrison signifies on the absence of African Americans from American literature in order to restore them as a central presence. The reference to white America's ghettoization of black communities in an attempt to render them invisible and exposed to codification reverberates with her ironic introduction of Bottom, the black ghetto of Medallion, as an absence. It is by evoking Bottom's absence that Morrison establishes its presence and indicates how the experiences of African Americans are in fact central to the 'body politic' of America (Morrison, 1992c, p. 5).

Female identity and social mobility

Morrison's determination to record what has been absent in American history is focused, in *Sula*, specifically upon women and she emphasizes how the experiences of African-American women living in the 1920s should not be prescribed as either 'tragic mulatto' or the black 'mammy figure'.[14] Historically, black women have been shadows, fixed within a taxonomy that is at once exotic

---

[14] Barbara Christian in *Black Feminist Criticism: Perspectives on Black Women Writers* identifies the stereotypical use of these figures in both Anglo- and African-American literature. 'Throughout the novels of the slavery and reconstruction periods, Anglo-American literature, particularly southern white literature, fashioned an image of the black woman intended to further create submission, conflict between the black man and woman, and importantly, a dumping ground for those female functions a basically Puritan society could not control' (Christian, 1985, p. 2). 'Whilst I acknowledge this assessment of Anglo-American representations of black women, I agree with Hazel Carby that the apparent use of these stereotypes in African-American fiction is more complex than Christian suggests. In *Reconstructing Womanhood: The Emergence of the Afro-American Woman Novelist* Carby claims that Christian has 'concentrated on the explication of stereotypes at the expense of engaging in the theoretical and historical questions raised by the construction of a tradition of black women writing' (Carby, 1987, p. 14).

but knowable, readily appropriated and controlled. *Sula* instead constitutes a radical theoretical moment for feminism by revealing the unspoken, unrecorded complexities of female experience. It is literature, as Barbara Johnson has reiterated, that remains central for feminism as 'the place where impasses can be kept and opened for examination, where questions can be guarded and not forced into a premature validation of the available paradigms.' In fact, literature is a 'mode of cultural work' for Johnson, articulating contradiction and ambivalence (Johnson, 1998, p. 13). In *Sula*, individual or communal agency is attenuated into tragedy and sacrifice; everything has a price when choices are so stark and Sula indeed kills herself in the very act of self-creation. Any gains are to be found only in the mediation of Morrison's alternative epistemology in the act of writing itself, through the translation of the life experiences of her characters into theory.

Despite her literary and professional standing, Morrison maintains that her position is one of marginality and in fact her position as an African American within the academy exemplifies a particular aspect of Du Boisian double consciousness. More than outlining the psychological dilemma of being African-American and American, Du Bois also articulated the potential that being both black and American could offer in terms of 'second sight'. In her opening address, 'Home', to the Race Matters Conference at Princeton in the 1990s Morrison referred directly to Du Bois's concept in relation to those academics working to contest western hegemony from a position of difference. Morrison remarked how double consciousness should be viewed as a 'strategy, not a prophecy or a cure' and envisaged the role of the academic as a contestatory one to create a space where 'political action, legal and social thought, and cultural production can be generated sans racist cant, explicit or in disguise' (Morrison, 1997, p. 11).

Morrison's comments can be related to developments in feminism where a position, both within and without the academy, has increasingly radical possibilities. At the time Morrison began *Sula* feminists were moving towards theorizations of experience as being constituted by gender and viewed the experiences of certain groups of marginalized women as more revealing of inequality and oppression than others. In 1969, Mary Ann Weather in 'An Argument for Black Women's Liberation as a Revolutionary Force' argued that black women constituted the most oppressed minority, not only in the United States but also across the world (Weathers, 1970, pp. 303–7).

The late 1960s saw black women beginning to take positions in American academic institutions; Morrison herself had taught at Howard and New

York Universities and had embarked upon a publishing career as an editor at Random House by the time *Sula* was published in 1973. In certain respects *Sula* plays out the tension that this kind of social mobility, post Civil Rights, engendered for a small minority of African Americans. As well as exploring the more obvious effects of migration in the 1920s, *Sula*, as Philip Richards points out, also reflects the anxieties of an emerging black middle class in the 1970s. 'Written in the early seventies, *Sula* represents a bourgeois point of view reacting to the stresses of the movement of black middle-class Americans from the isolation of black ghetto life to the tensions of integrated existence in the corporations, publishing houses, universities and suburbs' (Richards, 1995, p. 289). By 1997, when Morrison opened the Race Matters Conference at Princeton, these 'stresses' were being openly discussed in the academy and strategies for moving forward in an integrated middle-class world without sacrificing the 'second sight' of marginalization were being established.[15] *Sula* constitutes an early intervention in the theoretical, even therapeutic, effort to open the terrain surrounding issues of black, and more specifically black female, identity.

The tentative explorations of female identity, mobility and race of the late 1960s and early 1970s had, by the end of the 1990s, found new confidence as academics and writers established for themselves a safer place, not 'paradise' but at least a 'home', once the expectations and disappointments of the black power movement had stabilized. Morrison is in fact central to this epistemological shift which in itself, and for a period of 30 years, has really meant the move, in bell hooks' terms, from margin to centre (hooks, 1984). This site is marked by the mediation of marginal knowledge or 'wisdom' into an effective and contestatory epistemology that can, as Patricia Hill Collins maintains, challenge established 'truth' and hegemonic knowledge claims (Collins, 1991).[16] Much of the work necessary for the this resistance has been carried out by black women who,

---

[15] See, for example, bell hooks, 'Choosing the Margin as a Space of Radical Openness', in *Yearning: Race, Gender, and Cultural Politics*. hooks makes it clear that in becoming an academic she did not want to lose her position of marginality, rather she regards it as 'a site one stays in, clings to even, because it nourishes one's capacity to resist. It offers to one the possibility of radical perspective from which to see and create, to imagine alternatives, new worlds' (hooks, 1991, p. 150).

[16] Collins, in *Black Feminist Thought*, places African-American knowledge, experience and consciousness at the centre of her analysis to develop an epistemological framework that is subjective as well as objective. In her discussion of knowledge and African-American feminism she writes: 'An alternative epistemology challenges all certified knowledge and opens up the question of whether what has been taken to be true can stand the test of alternative ways of validating truth. The existence of a self-defined Black women's standpoint using an Afrocentric feminist epistemology calls into question the content of what currently passes as truth and simultaneously challenges the process of arriving at that truth' (Collins, 1991, p. 219).

arguably because of their role as workers, have remained closer to the vagaries of the labour market than their male counterparts and therefore closer to the centre. This raises issues about how we should attribute agency to economically marginalized groups, especially the question as to whether distance from the economic centre promotes a more acute understanding of structures of dominance and, by implication, viable forms of agency and opposition.

Second wave feminists complicated earlier materialist debates on marginality by taking into consideration new perspectives of heterogeneity found in postmodern criticism. Centres of power are now conceived as multiple rather than as singular and monolithic, and marginality assumes many forms that may or may not be related to the central structures of economic power. Agency is not necessarily dependent upon there being a functional yet exploitative relationship between margin and centre; it is rather a force for change to be found in creative acts of re-memory, the recovery of lost language and radical historiographies.[17] To be 'creative' constitutes different forms of socio-political radicalism that, because of their libertarian and celebratory nature, at least appear progressive. Yet within such plurality there exists the temptation to totalize experience under the sign of difference. In *Simians, Cyborgs and Women* Donna Haraway offers an approach that attempts to circumvent bourgeois liberalist versions of postmodernism by calling for a politics of difference 'rooted in a politics of experience that searches for specificity, heterogeneity, and connection *through struggle* not through psychologistic, liberal appeals to each her own endless difference' (Haraway's italics, 1991, p. 109). Haraway recognizes plurality and historical difference, yet also calls for a search for 'affinities' and 'connections' across the 'web' of women's experiences. This manoeuvre offers some resolution to a central problem for feminists in the 1970s and 1980s, namely that in promulgating feminist unity, white feminists failed to recognize the varied social realities of women's existence.

To avoid the inadequacies of an earlier totalizing feminism based on the premise of the common oppression of women, Haraway's argument for an understanding of the specificity of women's experiences draws upon African-American and postcolonial discourse. She is in agreement with Chandra Talpade Mohanty's critique of western feminism which can construct the 'other' as a monolithic category and hence, 'discursively colonize the material

---

[17] In late twentieth-century African-American cultural practices bell hooks identifies the 'struggle in language to recover ourselves, to reconcile, to reunite, to renew' and 'an effort to remember that is expressive of the need to create spaces where one is able to redeem and reclaim the past, legacies of pain, suffering, and triumph in ways that transform present reality' (hooks, 1991, pp. 146, 147).

and historical heterogeneities of the lives of women in the third world, thereby producing/representing a composite, singular "third world woman" – an image which appears arbitrarily constructed, but nevertheless carries with it the authorizing signature of Western humanist discourse' (Mohanty, 1984, p. 53). The implication that feminism in fact repeats the structures of dominance it purports to contest is also apparent in African-American feminist thought, perhaps the most well-known example of this being bell hook's critique of a white middle-class feminism that exclusively serves the interests of dominant white women (hooks, 1984, p. 3). The effect of these criticisms is made clear by the way in which feminists now acknowledge the heterogeneity of women's experience even if this is, as Judith Butler points out in *Bodies that Matter*, little more than 'a list of attributes separated by those proverbial commas (gender, sexuality, race, class), that usually mean that we have not yet figured out how to think the relations we seek to mark' (Butler, 1993, p. 168). In the process of working out the relative importance of questions of gender, race and class the very term 'feminism' is used hesitantly and we now talk about 'feminisms'. It appears, however, that the relationship between women and class has not yet been fully theorized, partly perhaps because so much attention has been turned to issues surrounding the body and identity and across what are sometimes over generalized global networks of power. Hazel Carby has attempted to counter the obscuring of class through a materialist analysis of its place within a century of female black writing. Her work marks a change in the direction of African-American feminist criticism and writers hitherto marginalized within the tradition as bourgeois and urban are now being recovered because they offer a way to historicize African-American class structures (Carby, 1987, p. 17).

As we have seen, in *Sula* Morrison is as much concerned with class as she is with female identity and race. This intersection of gender, race and class perhaps explains Morrison's expressed ambivalence towards the labels 'feminism' and 'feminist'. She has said

> as happened in post slavery days, when suffrage followed abolitionism in the United States, feminism followed the civil rights movement, so that the energies began to be turned away from liberation for black and minority peoples into the women's movement, and it put black women in a peculiar position of having to make choices that were fraudulent: to work for the black movement OR feminism. We are back to these impossible choices. Why should I have to choose between the black movement and women's liberation? (Morrison intv. with Lester, 1988, p. 52)

Her concern is understandable when we consider that a feminist reading of *Sula* could be no more than a celebratory account of sexual freedom as flaunting patriarchal codes. Morrison's awareness of how women's experiences are constructed historically and materially gives her considerations on the culture of gender and the creation of identity a historically specific context. She has said that in writing *Sula* she 'was preoccupied with the culture of gender and the invention of identity, both of which acquired astonishing meaning when placed in a racial context' (Morrison, 1997, p. 9).

Haraway's radical, postmodernist feminism, as an attempt to understand economic and class history and incorporate black and postcolonial feminisms, provides a useful perspective on Morrison's oppositional aesthetic in *Sula*. In 'A Cyborg Manifesto' in *Simians, Cyborgs and Women*, Haraway refers to the links between technology and the underemployment of men and connects these to the condition of postmodernity that embraces everybody living under late capitalism, a condition already familiar to African-American women. 'Black women in the United States have long known what it looks like to face the structural underemployment ('feminization') of black men, as well as their own highly vulnerable position in the wage economy' (Haraway, 1991, p. 168). This is analogous with Morrison's own understanding of postmodernism in relation to the position of black women.

> From a woman's point of view, in terms of confronting the problems of where the world is now, black women had to deal with 'post-modern' problems in the nineteenth century and earlier. These things had to be addressed by black people a long time ago. Certain kinds of dissolution, the loss of and the need to reconstruct certain kinds of stability. Certain kinds of madness, deliberately going mad . . . 'in order not to lose your mind'. These strategies for survival made the truly modern person. They're a response to predatory Western phenomena. You can call it an ideology and an economy, what it is is a pathology. Slavery broke the world in half, it broke it in every way. It broke Europe. It made them into something else, it made them slave masters, it made them crazy. You can't do that for hundreds of years and it not take a toll. They had to dehumanize, not just the slaves but themselves. They had to reconstruct everything in order to make that system appear true. (Morrison intv. with Gilroy, 1993a, p. 178)

Sula's efforts to construct her identity are not simply informed by a feminist impulse, but are rather an attempt at the reconstruction of the self in response to a historical legacy that includes slavery, migration and class differences within the black community. As 'slave masters' justified the oppression of black people through the channels of science, philosophy and literature, so Morrison's denial of the racist codification of African Americans is channelled through her oppositional delineation of Sula's identity as fluid and complex.

Sula, *Their Eyes Were Watching God* and folk discourse

In this regard Morrison takes her place in a tradition of African-American writers concerned to draw on folk culture in their creation of non-reductive black identities. In particular, Zora Neale Hurston, in *Their Eyes Were Watching God* (1937), anticipated Morrison's work in terms of use of language, metaphor and treatment of the community. Importantly, Hurston foreshadows Morrison's recognition of the postmodern 'dissolution' of African-American female identity in modernity's project and the black woman's concomitant efforts towards a 'reconstruction' of that identity. As a supremely African-American modernist text containing the lineaments of what we now call postmodernity, the literary and linguistic innovations of Hurston's novel were derived essentially from the lived experience of African-American women during the 1930s. We are reminded here of Morrison's assertion that black women did indeed encounter postmodernity before others.

These affinities may seem remarkable as nearly 50 years separates their work and yet, as Hortense Spillers argues, it is more profitable to view the black female tradition as one that does not emerge in 'strict sequential order. Ironically, it is exactly the right *not* to accede to the simplifications and mystifications of a strictly historiographical time line that now promises the greatest freedom of discourse to black people, to black women, as critics, teachers, writers, and thinkers' (Spillers, 1990, p. 29). This means freedom from the constraints of Harold Bloom's model of a linear literary tradition and the competitive anxiety of 'improving' upon the work of precursors. Morrison may never have read Hurston's work (Morrison intv. with Naylor, 1994, p. 214) but in a very real sense she did not need to because they find connection across Haraway's 'web' of women's experiences in literary strategies built upon the language of the black community, strategies that traverse time and space; they share a journey that Hurston herself would regard as being 'not so much in time, as in spirit' (Hurston, 1942, p. 97). By articulating and historicizing the experiences of African-American female identity and communal life, Morrison and Hurston politicize this spirit in opposition to America's constructions of black history, culture and language.

For Henry Louis Gates, Zora Neale Hurston was the first black American to write what he calls the

> speakerly text ... a text whose rhetorical strategy is designed to represent an oral literary tradition ... The speakerly text is that text in which all other structural elements seem to be devalued, as important as they remain to the telling of the tale, because the narrative strategy signals attention to its own importance, an importance which would seem to be the privileging of oral speech and its inherent linguistic features. (Gates, 1988, p. 181)

Through the narrative mode of free indirect discourse Hurston produces an innovative text that for the first time gives the African American an authentic voice.[18] For Gates, free indirect discourse is the integration of both the black vernacular and Standard English, and it is Hurston's confident manipulation of language that gives expression to Janie's sense of self-hood in *Their Eyes Were Watching God*.

Janie's story is not, however, a simple quest for identity through language. Although excluded from the 'lying' sessions on the store porch she does speak out against her husband Joe and so creates a voice for herself. Yet, as Barbara Johnson stresses, to do this Janie must become aware of her 'self-difference' rather than her 'self-identity' (Johnson, 1984, p. 212). This knowledge comes after a pivotal confrontation with Jody and her recognition that 'she had an inside and an outside now and suddenly she knew how not to mix them' (Hurston, 1937, pp. 112–13). It is through the use of free indirect discourse – which is, in Bakhtinian terms, 'double voiced' and at times used by both the narrator and the community, as well as by Janie herself – that Hurston expresses her own sense of self-division and displays originality as a writer producing a text which defies, to reiterate Spillers' point, the 'unification and simplification' of a black female experience. Morrison shares this resistance to closure and has expressed the strategies of black literary art in jazz terms. 'I think about what black writers do as having a quality of hunger and disturbance that never ends ... jazz always keeps you on the edge. There is no final chord. There may be a long chord, but no final chord. And it agitates you' (Morrison intv. with McKay, 1994, p. 155). Important as black art forms are to Hurston's and Morrison's aesthetic, the

---

[18] Hazel Carby, in *Reconstructing Womanhood*, opposes critics such as Gates, and more specifically black feminist critics, who place Zora Neale Hurston as a foundational novelist in a tradition of African-American woman writers. Carby argues that such a 'narrative' of a writing tradition presents 'essentialist views of experience' (Carby, 1987, p. 16), in its assumption of 'the rural folk as bearers of Afro-American history and preservers of Afro-American culture' (Carby, 1987, p. 175).

ambivalence and resistance to closure in *Sula* and *Their Eyes Were Watching God* are also informed by the tension inherent in each writer's profound awareness of their position as black female writers moving into the academic and publishing worlds so very distant from the communities they describe.

Sula's and Janie's conflict with the community reflect each writer's problematic relationship with the folk spirit they wish to represent. This appreciation of folk culture allows for the possibility of leaving behind romanticism while retaining a folk perspective that enables resistance. In fact, the concept of the folk becomes a means to explore the changing, often painful experiences of women approaching self-consciousness. In an essay on *Their Eyes Were Watching God*, Hazel Carby suggests that the appropriation of Hurston's work is merely a 'mode of assurance that really the black folk are happy and healthy' and that for some it functions as wish fulfilment for an emerging black middle class and its search for self-hood in an idealized rural past (Carby, 1990, p. 90). This is undoubtedly true of certain valorizations of Hurston's novel and Carby is right to discourage complacent readings of Hurston's work. Carby's earlier *Reconstructing Womanhood* (1987) is also valuable, giving credibility to writers such as Nella Larsen and Jessie Fauset who wrote of an urban, middle-class black female experience, but it is wrong to dismiss Hurston's work simply as a romanticization of a mythical folk past. It is more fruitful to see the impulse behind Hurston's delineation of folk culture as a complex attempt to construct and negotiate a meaningful female identity in the face of urbanization and the possibilities for social mobility for African Americans. Hurston's novel, despite its setting in rural Florida, is as much about the possibilities and limitations of urban existence as experienced by Hurston herself, as is Larsen or Fauset's work. Hurston does not romanticize the folk community, but like Morrison, delineates it as a site of struggle and conflict for women such as Sula and Janie attempting to find their own voice and self; a struggle which in *Their Eyes Were Watching God* occurs primarily through language. Hurston privileges African-American orality not because of its quaint folk elements, but with an awareness of its history in America. During slavery the teaching of literary skills was illegal in certain states, the spoken word therefore gaining especial significance for African Americans.[19] In addition, the diasporic African-American experience could not be expressed or verified in terms sanctioned by the dominant culture and an oral subculture developed, 'functional, collective and direct', the expression of which was sustaining and indeed still sustains (Bell, 1987, p. 9).

---

[19] Henry Louis Gates, Jr, discusses, for example, the '1740 South Carolina statute that attempted to make it almost impossible for black slaves to acquire, let alone master literacy' in his editor's introduction to, *'Race', Writing, and Difference* (Gates, 1986a, p. 9).

Through Janie, Hurston reveals the transformative power of language and the close relationship that exists between voice and action. Hurston knowingly manipulates the oral arts of the folk into a powerful articulation of her protagonist's, and crucially her own, identity at a time of tumultuous change and possibility in the history of African-American women. The men in the novel signify freely but they do so primarily for their own entertainment. Signifying has limited authoritative value and reflects instead their internalization of the economic and cultural thrust of white America. Joe Starks, Janie's husband, wants to be a 'big voice' but he can only achieve this within the incorporated town he helps to establish by becoming the black counterpart to small town America's white civic officials (Hurston, 1937, p. 74). Assuming the bourgeois values of possession and accumulation, Joe declares 'I God amighty!' (Hurston, 1937, p. 121). Yet, paradoxically, his identity is fragile because of this, and in the face of Janie's growing consciousness he is destroyed when she tells Joe the way it really is:

'But Ah'm uh woman every inch of me, and Ah know it. Dat's uh whole lot more'n *you* kin say. You big-bellies round here and put out a lot of brag, but 'tain't nothin' to it but yo' big voice. Humph! Talkin' 'bout *me* lookin' old! When you pull down yo' britches, you look lak de change uh life'. (Hurston's italics, 1937, p. 121)

Hurston's authorial voice now makes a telling intervention, a damning critique of Stark's materialism that opens, crucially, before the eyes of the community:

Then Joe Starks realized all the meanings and his vanity bled like a flood. Janie had robbed him of his illusion of irresistible maleness that all men cherish, which was terrible. The thing that Saul's daughter had done to David. But Janie had done worse, she had cast down his empty armor before men and they had laughed, would keep on laughing. When he paraded his possessions hereafter, they would not consider the two together. They'd look with envy at the things and pity the man that owned them. (Hurston, 1937, p. 123)

As well as emphasizing the devastating power of Janie's newly found voice this passage reveals the central importance of the community in the novel. Joe could survive Janie's verbal attack had the scene taken place within the domestic sphere but under the critical gaze of the store and its porch community Janie's words prove fatal. It is through the community that Hurston preserves black folk oral traditions but, like Morrison, refuses to engage in its idealization at the expense of the individual. As in *Sula*, there exists a conflict between the group and the individual recognized by Janie on her return to the community. Walking back to her house all eyes and discussion are on Janie, 'a mass cruelty. A mood come alive. Words walking without masters; walking altogether like harmony in a song' (Hurston, 1937, p. 10). Hurston's idea of words without masters suggests the choral nature of the community's utterance and reveals that the community, unlike Janie, is not in control of language. In judging Janie, the community, the 'Mouth-Almighty', tries to establish a form of power for itself (Hurston, 1937, p. 16). Having laboured all day long for the white man, when 'Mules and other brutes had occupied their skins', it is now, in the evening, that they can begin to wield this power (Hurston, 1937, p. 156).

Hurston, again like Morrison, is primarily concerned with female consciousness, but a specific awareness of African-American masculinity in relation to the development of each writer's protagonist permeates *Their Eyes Were Watching God* and *Sula*. Janie's growing consciousness is set against her husband's internalization of white male fantasies of civic and corporate power and the agency of her voice operates in stark contrast with the powerless words of the men. It is also telling to consider Morrison's characterization of Sula in relation to her representation of men as either absent, or in Haraway's terms, 'underemployed' and 'feminized'. The Deweys, the small boys adopted by Eva, are preserved in a state of permanent infancy, incapable of physical, emotional and intellectual development; Jude, a victim of racism in the construction industry, cannot gain 'manly' employment building the new tunnel and Ajax, another of Morrison's 'lawless' characters, permanently unemployed and living out projections of black male sexuality.

The Bluest Eye and *Sula* represent a female intervention into Black Power politics whereby Morrison contests both stereotypical representations of black women and monolithic constructions of the community. In terms of the development of her own aesthetic, Morrison moves from the contestatory form of *The Bluest Eye* to a consideration of the complexities of class and gender in *Sula*. Both works are set far from the conventional literary extremes of urban ghetto or the Deep South, recovering instead a history of Midwest African-American experience that goes beyond the political and cultural agenda of the Black Power movement. In the next chapter I examine the progression in Morrison's aesthetic as she moves, in *Song of Solomon* (1977), to a later migratory experience that necessitates a quest for racial identity and history as her characters are dislocated further from the South in both distance and time.

3

Intertextuality and Gender Politics: *Song of Solomon* (1977) and *Tar Baby* (1981)

In *Playing in the Dark* (1992) Toni Morrison describes how nineteenth-century literary America's adaptation of the European romance form made possible the articulation of 'Americans' fear of being outcast, of failing, of powerlessness; their fear of boundarylessness, of Nature unbridled and crouched for attack; their fear of the absence of so-called civilization; their fear of loneliness, of aggression both external and internal' (Morrison, 1992c, p. 37). Importantly, the literary exploration of these fears was shaped by the existence of a black slave population upon which American writers were able to transfer their insecurities and which provided a 'playground' for the expression of terror. A form of Africanism was thus created within American culture, 'a fabricated brew of darkness, otherness, alarm, and desire' against which white America came to define itself as free, rational and civilized (Morrison, 1992c, p. 37).

Morrison's discussion of the romance narrative is a useful starting point for an analysis of her third novel, *Song of Solomon* (1977), an epic work that itself employs many of the techniques of Euro-American romance. This has of course been recognized, but few have focused on the context within which Morrison employs these techniques, that is, with an understanding of the social, historical and political environment in which the American romance narrative was formed.[1] Morrison's non-fiction writing elucidates strategies used by American writers to rationalize exploitation and domination and helps our understanding of how in *Song of Solomon* she uses the romance mode to foreground the concerns of

---

[1] See for example Genevieve Fabre, 'Genealogical Archaeology or the Quest for Legacy in Toni Morrison's *Song of Solomon*' and Gerry Brenner, '*Song of Solomon*: Rejecting Rank's Monomyth and Feminism', (in Mckay, 1988, pp. 105–24). See also Cynthia A. Davis, 'Self, Society and Myth in Toni Morrison's Fiction' (in Harold Bloom, 1990, pp. 7–25).

African Americans. Morrison's novel, however, not only subverts a predominantly white literary genre but also constitutes an important development in her own black aesthetic, one that is 'both print and oral literature'. In *Song of Solomon*, as in *Sula* (1973), she privileges the African-American community, its myths, folklore, history and language from the beginning. As Morrison has explained in 'Unspeakable Things Unspoken', 'The composition of red, white and blue in the opening scene provides the national canvas/flag upon which the narrative works and against which the lives of these black people must be seen, but which must not overwhelm the enterprise the novel is engaged in (Morrison, 1989, p. 225).

Song of Solomon (1977)

Morrison's 'enterprise' in *Song of Solomon* continues the project undertaken in *The Bluest Eye* (1970), to dismantle white America's construction of blackness and explore the significance of the appropriation of white cultural values for black Americans. In *Song of Solomon* and *Tar Baby* (1981), Morrison also maintains her interest, first explored in *Sula*, in the relationship between the individual and the community. She writes in 'Home': 'In *Song of Solomon* and *Tar Baby* I was interested in the impact of race on the romance of community and individuality' (Morrison, 1997, p. 9). In *Song of Solomon*, however, Morrison considers constructions of black masculinity through the development of Macon 'Milkman' Dead and his understanding of racial history. Together with elements of the epic romance narrative, Morrison adopts the form of the *Bildungsroman* for a novel she has described as 'a male story about the rites of passage' (Morrison intv. with Ruas, 1994, p. 109). Morrison's appropriation of traditional narrative strategies is not as straightforward as she implies and, like *Sula*, *Song of Solomon* resists the coherence and closure of the *Bildungsroman* or romance narrative. In *Sula* Morrison subverts the female *Bildungsroman* as it is familiarly known in novels such as *Jane Eyre* (1847) by not introducing her heroine until a third of the way into the novel only to remove her from its centre for a period of ten years. *Song of Solomon* similarly departs from traditional expectations by refusing an overriding narrative voice, revealing instead several truths. Moreover, Milkman's legacy is not money, success and marriage but an understanding of his racial heritage. As Catherine Rainwater puts it: '*Song of Solomon*, like Morrison's other novels, unmoors our confidence in diachronic progression and posits instead a synchronic model of experience that, because of the limitless proliferation of versions, eludes containment within narrative form' (Rainwater, 1991, p. 105). This point in Morrison's aesthetic is evocative of jazz and its lack of closure, the presentation of a multiplicity of truths arising from an understanding of the untruths central to America's constructions of race, underscored by science, philosophy and literature, including the romance narrative form. As a black American, Morrison recognizes the problematic nature of positing a singular monolithic truth and thus undermines the authenticity of a singular perspective in her own appropriations of western narrative strategies. Morrison also makes clear that there is no one version of the black experience from a black perspective as 'black people think differently from one another' (Morrison, 1993, p. xxx).

Form, textuality and orality

Critics of Toni Morrison's fiction have found comparisons with Virginia Woolf and William Faulkner, not least because her Master's thesis (Wofford [Morrison], 1955, cited in Matus, 1988, pp. 61, 178) was a consideration of alienation in the works of Woolf and Faulkner.[2] Certainly, Woolf's modernist sensibilities find reflection in Morrison's engagement with female identity and consciousness in *Sula*. Sula's compulsions arise from her condition of marginality, yet the compressed and lyrical passages of inner consciousness in both *Sula* and *The Bluest Eye* conform to Woolf's idea of how the female novel could take form. Morrison's first two novels are indeed female, feminine and feminist in both content and in their tightly constructed form, a form Morrison has described as 'circular' and 'spiral' (Morrison intv. with Tate, 1983, p. 124). To construct *Song of Solomon* Morrison adapts this circular form to the *Bildungsroman* and creates original literary conventions more appropriate for her exploration of black masculinity. This involves the development of a metaphorical and narrative approach that initially appears more conventional than the form of her previous novels. Sula's quest for identity is an inward one, registered through the use of water imagery and her lovemaking with Ajax is, from her own perspective, the union of earth and water: '*I will water your soil, keep it rich and moist. But how much? How much water to keep the loam moist? And how much loam will I need to keep my water still? And when do the two make mud?*' (Morrison's italics, *S*, p. 131), Sula's sexuality gradually permeates and enriches before becoming

---

[2] See Barbara Christian, 'Layered Rhythms: Virginia Woolf and Toni Morrison' (1997, pp. 19–36) and David Cowart, 'Faulkner and Joyce in Morrison's *Song of Solomon*' (2000, pp. 95–108) and Craig Werner, *Playing the Changes: From Afro-Modernism to the Jazz Impulse* (Werner, 1994).

a destructive effort to possess Ajax in suffocating female domesticity. In *Song of Solomon*, Milkman's quest for 'dominion' assumes the more literal form of a journey from the North to the South of America, the metaphor of flight a central element in Morrison's delineation of his development. As in her use of water imagery to relate Sula's female sexuality, Morrison deploys the flight motif in specifically male sexual terms. Milkman comes to realize the value of his racial heritage and, like his ancestor Solomon, can fly home to Africa,[3] understanding at last that 'If you surrendered to the air, you could *ride* it' (Morrison's italics, *SS*, p. 337). For Morrison, to surrender to the air and ride it at the same time is sexual,

> it's the sexual act, the actual penetration of a woman and having an orgasm; I imagine this is one thing that has the simultaneous feeling that a man at that moment might feel as he is doing both things: a) dominating the woman, b) he's also surrendering to her at the same time. So that the rhythm of the book has this kind of building up, sort of in and out, explosion. (Morrison intv. with Koenen, 1994, p. 76)

Morrison reveals what she acknowledges to be an outmoded belief in inherently masculine characteristics born out of the male will to dominate in the sexual act, but the ending of the novel also suggests the proposal of an alternative masculinity that embraces both 'surrender' and 'domination', that in effect does not erase gender but builds upon difference as a positive force.[4] In this sense the conclusion to the novel, itself the subject of critical debate, is optimistic.[5] To regard Milkman's flight simply as the male abnegation of responsibility for those he abandons overlooks the intent of Morrison's portrayal of a man who takes from both his patrilineage and his matrilineage to construct a new way of being male that valorizes both polarities. Morrison does not suggest the feminization

---

[3] Susan Willis writes in *Specifying: Black Women Writing the American Experience*: 'The confrontation with the reality of slavery, coming at the end of Milkman's penetration into historical process, is liberational because slavery is not portrayed as the origin of history and culture. Instead the novel opens out to Africa, the source, and takes flight on the wings of Milkman's great-grandfather, the original Solomon' (Willis, 1987, pp. 95–6).

[4] In an interview with Rosemarie Lester, Morrison said 'I think that males – maleness – tends to be inherent, and I know that makes me disagree with 80 per cent of the literature on the subject.' However, Morrison also concedes that she is 'willing to be persuaded that they're [male attitudes] not [inherent], and I've read a lot of literature that suggests all of this business is obviously learned' (Morrison intv. with Lester, 1988, p. 48).

[5] Michael Awkward sees Morrison's appropriation of the flying African myth as one that 'divests the narrative of its essential communal impulses' (Awkward, 1995, p. 139). Gerry Brenner regards Milkman's flight as 'but one more gesture of irresponsibility; he flies, indeed, from the burdens of doing something meaningful in life, preferring the sumptuous illusion that he will ride the air' (Brenner' 1988, p. 119).

of African-American masculinity but uses her 'female imagination', 'unruly and let loose', to 'bring things to the surface that men – trained to be men in a certain way – have difficulty getting access to' (Morrison intv. with Lester, 1988, p. 54). As we shall see, Morrison's treatment of masculinity is inflected with the complexities of African-American gender relations in the mid-1970s, a time when African-American women were expected to bolster black masculinity for the sake of the race. At the same time there was an acute awareness among some black women of the attendant dangers for their own liberation struggle and many found themselves in the invidious position of establishing sexual equality for themselves without undermining the struggle for racial equality. It is within this context that Morrison's representation of gender relations and her negotiation of a positive form of masculinity should be understood.

Morrison's entry into concerns of masculinity necessitated new metaphorical constructions and a change in rhythm to 'a kind of building up, sort of in and out explosion'. The circular, or spiral, structure of *Sula* is replaced in *Song of Solomon* by a linear, outward account of Milkman's development (Morrison intv. with Tate, 1983, p. 124). Milkman's quest is a physical journey and Morrison evokes the speech patterns and physicality of black male existence in Chicago. The women in *Song of Solomon* are deeply involved in their domestic worlds, whether in the confinement of the Dead household or in the alternative, informal economy of Pilate's matriarchy. Milkman, by contrast, operates in the street, the pool hall, the barbershop and bars, his mother and sisters mere ciphers of the domestic sphere. Morrison counteracts constructions of African-American masculinity by leading Milkman on a quest, through language and geographical space, to the recognition of racial and filial responsibility. Milkman must understand the ancestral Song of Solomon that heralds his birth, taught to him by Pilate, before he can achieve the freedom that comes with the realization of history. Morrison's novel is, in this sense, double voiced, drawing on but subverting the linear progression of the *Bildungsroman* and engaging, as we shall see, with Faulkner's Southern narrative in order to privilege orality as holding the key to black knowledge and history.

The source of such a synthesis is found in the oral, vernacular forms of expression to which slaves had been confined and the acquisition of literacy as their means to freedom. It is important to understand the novel in the context of a literary tradition in which the acquisition of language and the appropriation of the 'master's tools' were essential. As a child, the slave narrator Frederick Douglass learnt the importance of literacy and language, a lesson ironically seized from his white master. Douglass learns something more valuable than 'ABC', 'to wit, the white man's power to enslave the black man. It was a great achievement, and I prized it highly. From that moment, I understood the pathway from slavery to freedom' (Douglass, 1845, p. 511). He learns to write though secret and meticulous imitation of his young master's handwriting, allowing him to forge a pass in an escape attempt. This literary prowess is matched by a physicality that must, through a prolonged Hegelian struggle for recognition in manly combat with Covey the white 'slave breaker', be acknowledged as equal to that of his master.[6] A century later, Morrison reverses Douglass's journey north because Milkman, although he has civil freedoms and literacy, is 'Dead' in spirit as well as in name as his family assimilate bourgeois values. Milkman heads south and learns the preliterate, oral Song of Solomon as part of the recovery of racial origin and identity, a journey that resonates with the Pan-African 'back to roots' ideologies of the late 1970s. Like Douglass, Milkman becomes embroiled in a fight that marks an important stage in his development as a man, but the function of ritual combat is to now compel an urban, middle-class man to recognize his rural counterpart and racial origins.

Intertextuality

W.E.B. Du Bois stressed the importance of an education in western discourse for African Americans and recognized pre-literate African-American cultural forms as valuable modes of expression. The form of *Song of Solomon* reflects the complexities of African-American writing traditions, including the privileging of orality and the appropriation of western literary forms as a contestatory means of expression. This richly textured novel and its allusions to Joyce and Faulkner invites comparisons to these writers despite Morrison's claim:

> I am not *like* James Joyce; . . . . I am not *like* Faulkner. I am not *like* in that sense. I do not have objections to being compared to such extraordinarily gifted and facile writers, but it does leave me sort of hanging there when I know that my effort is to be *like* something that has probably only been expressed in music. (Morrison's italics, Morrison intv. with McKay, 1994, p. 152)

---

[6] For an analysis of Douglass's physical encounter with Covey see *The Black Atlantic: Modernity and Double Consciousness*. Gilroy sees the conflict as a Hegelian one for recognition that also 'underscored the complicity of civilization and brutality while emphasizing that the order of authority on which the slave plantation relied cannot be undone without recourse to the counter-violence of the oppressed' (Gilroy, 1993b, p. 63).

At issue here is the question of what form literary criticism of Morrison's work should take. She argues in 'Unspeakable Things Unspoken': 'Finding or imposing Western influences in/on Afro-American literature has value, but when its sole purpose is to *place* value only where that influence is located is pernicious' (Morrison's italics, 1989, p. 209). Morrison does not deny the influence of Joyce or Faulkner but suggests that any appropriation of their forms or language needs to be analysed within the context of an evolving and enduring African-American aesthetic, one which derives its form from musical traditions and, to reiterate Ellison's point, from a 'highly developed ability to abstract desirable qualities from those around them, even from their enemies'. Respect for western writers meant Ellison 'could reject bias while appreciating the truth revealed by such art' (Ellison, 1964, p. xx).

David Cowart has claimed Morrison for the wider western literary tradition: 'Her themes of history, identity, and freedom deserve consideration as something more than the self-absorbed, even solipsistic expression of black desire. They deserve consideration as part of a dialogue, or intertextual engagement with certain literary precursors among the most important of whom are Faulkner and Joyce' (Cowart, 2000, p. 95). A valuable analysis of Morrison, Faulkner and Joyce's shared thematic and stylistic devices, Cowart nevertheless overlooks the African-American specificity of Morrison's work despite the influence of modernist writers. Morrison borrows as much from Douglass's slave narrative as she does from Joyce, from Ellison's *Invisible Man* (1952) as from Faulkner and from African-American folklore as from the myth of Daedalus.

Cowart argues that Morrison's engagement with literary precursors has meant the creation of what he calls a 'fiction of universal humanity' that elevates Morrison out of the 'black literary ghetto'. Cowart's notion of universality is contentious, suggesting literary endeavour can only be gauged by the extent to which it builds upon the work of canonical writers, much in the spirit of T. S. Eliot's notion of 'tradition and the individual talent' in which a sense of literary tradition 'compels a man to write not merely with his own generation in his bones, but with a feeling that the whole of the literature of Europe from Homer and within it the whole of the literature of his own country has a simultaneous existence and composes a simultaneous order' (Eliot, 1932, p. 13). If we are to consider Morrison's work as universal it is because of, rather than in spite of, its cultural specificity. Ellison understood this when emphasizing the universality of black American experience. For Morrison, desire for the universal, because it derives from the impulse to explain black lives to white readers, has become a literary burden; universality must arise paradoxically from the local and the specific: 'Faulkner wrote what I suppose could be called regional literature and had it published all over the world. It is good – and universal – because it is specifically about a particular world. That's what I wish to do' (Morrison intv. with LeClair, 1994, p. 124). Morrison's universality encompasses the very personal and, importantly, history, the universal condition made manifest through complex personal histories drawn against particular historical junctures. Joyce's Stephen Dedalus and Morrison's Milkman Dead derive their names from Daedalus, both disaffected young men on the brink of epiphany and yet arriving at self-realization via very different historical and social routes: Dedalus through the realization of his artistic vocation and rejection of his family, nation and church and Milkman's quest one of racial freedom in the recognition of his ancestors and flight to Africa as an expression of commitment to community. Milkman's last name is 'double voiced' in that it refers to the Daedalus myth and is passed to him through his grandfather, himself named in drunken error by a racist clerk after Emancipation. Morrison thus embraces at once Greek mythology and the culturally specific means by which African Americans have been named.

The role of the ancestor is central to both *Song of Solomon* and Morrison's general concerns about what constitutes excellence for black literary writers. Against Harold Bloom's model of the anxiety of influence, Morrison refigures the ancestor as nourishing comforter in a discussion of the novel as a replacement for traditional forms of black expressivity (Morrison, 1984). Writers such as Richard Wright, Ralph Ellison and James Baldwin revealed their ambivalence towards the ancestor figure as contributors to a black literary tradition that has had, for Morrison, an adverse effect on African-American literature written by men (Morrison, 1984, pp. 61–2). Ellison, for example, rejected Richard Wright and Langston Hughes as literary ancestors, choosing instead William Faulkner and Ernest Hemingway, Baldwin's difficult relationship with his father permeates his literary output and Wright's *Native Son* (1940) derives its bleakness from the absence of filial love and a sustaining ancestor figure.[7] Morrison's novel embraces the ancestor as a defining, stabilizing presence that takes on mythical proportions in the character of Pilate as a guiding figure restoring to Milkman Dead his history and the possibility of freedom.

---

[7] Ralph Ellison claimed that Richard Wright did not influence his work: 'But perhaps you will understand when I say he did not influence me if I point out that while one can do nothing about choosing one's relatives, one can, as artist, choose one's "ancestors." Wright was in this sense, a "relative"; Hemingway an "ancestor." Langston Hughes . . . was a "relative"; Eliot . . . and Malraux and Dostoievsky and Faulkner, were "ancestors"' (Ellison, 1964, p. 40). Morrison's essay 'Rootedness' can be read as a direct response to Ellison's ambivalence towards his literary 'relatives'.

Literacy and discourses

In *Song of Solomon* Morrison engages positively with her literary heritage without the anxiety that characterizes her male precursors' relationship with the tradition. As we have seen, on becoming literate Douglass distanced himself from the pre-literate folk culture of his fellow slaves. The Harlem Renaissance writers also had a problematic relationship with language and literacy. Langston Hughes, for example, as discussed in Chapter 1, was very much aware of the chasm between the sensibilities afforded by a bourgeois education and those of the folk (Hughes, 1926, pp. 692–4). In *Sula*, Morrison's ambivalence about the relevance of western education for black Americans is clear, with Sula searching for identity in experience rather than in literacy, the tension between her desires and the folk culture of Bottom explored but never resolved. Milkman, however, in his final, successful flight, reconciles his individuality with commitment to the community. *Song of Solomon* marks an important stage in the development of both the African-American literary tradition and Morrison's own aesthetic in its inclusion of a range of forms, languages, themes and genres that do not jeopardize the purpose of her project to recover black history. Deborah Clarke concludes that Morrison's representation of a variety of discourses constitutes a 'refusal to eradicate either western letters or the black experience. She creates a unique form of non-hierarchical discourse, a language for men and women, for blacks and whites' (Clarke, 1993, pp. 268–70).

As well as appropriating the romance narrative, Morrison draws upon the formal language of the state and again transforms it into an instrument of subversion, pre-empting her concern with language in *The Nobel Lecture in Literature* (1994), discussed in relation to *Paradise* (1998) in Chapter 4. In the *Nobel Lecture* Morrison discusses how language remains innocent, its violence and oppression only realized through manipulation and deployment. The official notice informing the community that Doctor Street is no longer to be called Doctor Street (*SS*, p. 4) but Mains Avenue, the people of Southside establish an alternative means of commemorating their first black doctor by the wilful misinterpretation of this public notice, inverting its legislative intention; everyone comes to know the street as Not Doctor Street. Language, then, may be used as an instrument of control *and* as an oppositional, communal statement of resistance, the intention behind its use more important than the language itself. We see this again in the contrast between the ethereal poetry of Michael-Mary Graham and the sentimentality of Porter's flowery friendship card to Corinthians. The aesthetic qualities of Graham's poetry receive official sanction and admiration –

she is the State Poet Laureate – and yet her poetry lacks the sincerity of Porter's desire to connect with Corinthians. The vulgar verse of the card lacks the taste considered appropriate by Graham and its recipient, her maid Corinthians. It is, however, sincere enough to ignite Corinthians' first meaningful sexual relationship and initiate the breakdown of her bourgeois aspirations (Clarke, 1993, pp. 268–70).

Song of Solomon established Morrison as a writer and its popularity may be attributed partly to its intertextuality.[8] Samuel Allen, for example, recognized Morrison's use of black folklore and 'other accessible cultural resources including a range of classical myths' (Allen, 1988, p. 32). As with Ellison's *Invisible Man*, also rich in African-American *and* Euro-American allusions and which critics in a 1965 *Book Week* poll voted most distinguished novel since World War Two, *Song of Solomon* appealed to white literary establishments – critics, publishers and academics. Morrison was not, however, open to the kind of attacks *Invisible Man* received from proponents of the Black Aesthetic for, despite her use of allusion, she retains a commitment to black culture, the community and the ancestor that is not present in Ellison, whose protagonist remains diffident and cerebral when considering leaving his underground refuge in an act of commitment to his community. His remark, 'there's a possibility that even an invisible man has a socially responsible role to play' (Ellison, 1952, p. 468) can be juxtaposed with Milkman's triumphant leap of commitment at the end of *Song of Solomon*. The invisible man's contribution is expressed only in written testimony, Milkman's reconciliation achieved by understanding the oral narrative of the Song of Solomon and through physical action and experience.

Toni Morrison and William Faulkner

In *The Bluest Eye* we saw a critique of the language of the ideologically loaded Dick and Jane primer. In *Song of Solomon* Morrison's engagement with authoritative white discourse is more subtle and ironic, but no less politically motivated, her appropriations of Faulkner's themes, motifs and symbolism at once both serious and parodic. She shares Faulkner's understanding of the complexity of American history and his preoccupation with familial genealogy and the psychological trauma of America's racial past. They are in fact concerned

---

[8] In 1977 Morrison was awarded the National Book Award for *Song of Solomon* and the novel was a main selection of the Book of the Month Club.

with the same historical tragedy but from their own very different, racially inflected perspectives. Slavery, for Faulkner, was a tragedy white America must understand and repudiate and he employs blackness and its representation as a means for analysing Southern psychology. Ellison recognized this in Faulkner's work, arguing that he and others used blackness or the 'Negro stereotype' to create

> an image of the organized, irrational forces of American life, forces through which, by projecting them in forms of images of an easily dominated minority, the white individual seeks to be at home in the vast unknown world of America. Perhaps the object of the stereotype is not so much to crush the Negro as to console the white man. (Ellison, 1964, p. 41)

To use blackness as a way to comprehend what it means to be American is for Morrison, as for Ellison, an inherent characteristic of American literature, but her purpose in identifying such deployments, especially in later essays, is to complicate and enrich critical interpretations of literary texts rather than simply identify any racism within them. Writers such as Melville, Hemingway and Faulkner represent blackness in ways that 'can be evil *and* protective, rebellious *and* forgiving, fearful *and* desirable – all of the self-contradictory features of the self'. It is often, in fact, whiteness that is problematized in relation to blackness. 'Whiteness, alone, is mute, meaningless, unfathomable, pointless, frozen, veiled, curtained, dreaded, senseless, implacable' (Morrison, 1992c, p. 59). In engaging with Faulknerian themes in *Song of Solomon* Morrison finds expression for the complexities of racial representation in American literature in an approach more nuanced than the direct contestation of racist doctrine she offers in *The Bluest Eye*.

With this in mind the following discussion is concerned with Morrison's intricate engagement with Faulkner's indeterminate, ambivalent treatment of race. This encounter with Faulkner particularly surfaces in Part Two of *Song of Solomon*, where Milkman's mythical journey takes him South to Shalimar, Virginia and Morrison makes an incursion into Faulkner's Southern gothic realism. Faulkner's *Go Down, Moses* (1942) compares with Morrison's novel in its concern with the quest for racial integrity and the return to mythical, pre-literate origins, a return delineated by both writers through the frontier motif of the ritual hunt. Morrison's engagement with Faulkner involves the recovery of different aspects of the same past to complete the black history that is partial and ambivalent in *Go Down, Moses* and expressive of his anxiety about the South's ability to recover from slavery. Fully realized and psychologically detailed black characterization eventually gives way to commonplace racial rhetoric as Faulkner's protagonist, Ike McCaslin, accedes to the fear of miscegenation and ensuing chaos, a form of binarism Faulkner effectively resists in the rest of the novel. As Eric Sundquist writes of *Go Down, Moses*, it 'may be said to represent the extraordinary strain his moral vision and fictional design came under as he drove to the heart of the South's experience, at once casting back to its originating myths and confronting the increasingly intolerable burdens those myths had to bear nearly a century later' (Sundquist, 1983, p. x). Faulkner is concerned to counter the originating myth of segregation upon which the South is founded by depicting American plantation life as one in which racial divisions are broken down through the intermixture of blood and through the equality of the hunter before nature,[9] where men are 'not white nor black nor red but men, hunters, with the will and hardihood to endure and the humility and skill to survive' (Faulkner, 1942, p. 145). Structurally, *Go Down, Moses* is, in part, driven by complications ensuing from this intricate racial history and by Faulkner's attempt to defy the simplistic divisions of racial rhetoric. At times, however, and as James Snead points out, Faulkner disguises the very divisions he wishes to deconstruct: 'Faulkner's "difficult" prose really is a kind of preventive inoculation against the fear of chaos and merging with a threatening tide of blackness' (Snead, 1986, p. 206). The novel's form, impenetrable language and plot reflect the chaos and incoherence of Southern life[10] and, as with Morrison's work, the difficulties in reading and interpreting Faulkner derive less from technical literary innovation than from acute appreciation of the convoluted realties of American history. Moreover, they each privilege representation over any authoritative rhetoric; the reader must share Ike's and Milkman's uncertainty about their origins. This confusion in *Go Down, Moses* is resolved, for the

---

[9] James Snead claims that 'Faulkner's narratives utter a truth of merging across social boundaries that his contemporaries found unspeakable. Faulkner himself set this truth in an elusive, complex discourse of indirection, a literary disfigurement of divisive social figures' (Snead, 1986, p. x).
   Ralph Ellison also recognizes Faulkner's attempts to counter social figures of segregation and division, but sees the impulse to do so as personal and artistic rather than as the direct result of political feeling: 'For not only is the social division forced upon the Negro by the ritualized ethic of discrimination, but upon the white man by the strictly enforced set of anti-Negro taboos. The conflict is always with him. Indeed, so rigidly has the recognition of Negro humanity been tabooed that the white Southerner is apt to associate any form of personal rebellion with the Negro. So that for the southern artist the Negro becomes a symbol of his personal rebellion, his guilt and his repression of it. The Negro is a compelling object of fascination, and this we see very clearly in Faulkner' (Ellison, 1964, p. 42).

[10] Robert Penn Warren argues that Faulkner's technical experiments 'were developed out of – that is, were not merely applied to – an anguishing research into the Southern past and the continuing implications of that past' (Warren, 1966, pp. 1–22).

reader and for Ike, by his discovery of miscegenation and incest in the family ledgers, a discovery that leads to his repudiation of an inheritance built upon the exploitation of slaves. Milkman, conversely, discovers his racial heritage not in the written word but through the orality of the song of Virginia school children, bringing racial integrity and completion.

The quest for racial integrity is expressed metaphorically in Morrison's and Faulkner's different evocations of the wilderness and the ritual of the hunt. In *Go Down, Moses* the primordial territory of the big woods predates man's avarice for land and the racial divisions that became the necessary justification for the plundering of the wilderness. Ike turns repeatedly to the big woods and the hunt in his search for a unity of being that has, after generations of McCaslin exploitation of land, native Americans and slaves, been consumed and degenerated.

> For six years now he had heard the best of all talking. It was of the wilderness, the big woods, bigger and older than any recorded document – of white man fatuous enough to believe he had bought any fragment of it, of Indian ruthless enough to pretend that any fragment of it had been his to convey'. (Faulkner, 1942, p. 145)

Importantly, the woods are associated here with an orality that precedes written language and its power, as in the McCaslin family ledgers, to fix racial identity. Faulkner's preoccupation with the return to an idealized past permeates *Go Down, Moses*, but is especially significant in the hunt as Ike attempts to return to an imaginary wholeness of being in an ultimately retrograde effort to hold on to the past without using it as a means to build the future. His strategy of denial leaves him subsumed by the chaotic racial codes and miscegenation of the South.

In *Song of Solomon* Morrison reverses the darkly comic 'coon hunt' that opens *Go Down, Moses*, the black man as quarry now becomes the hunter of personal integrity and responsibility. Milkman undergoes his personal initiation into the hunt and learns that the woods of the South can transport him to a time before written language. Hearing the Southern hunters communicate with their dogs he concludes:

> No, it was not language; it was what there was before language. Before things were written down. Language in the time when men and animals did talk to one another ... And if they could talk to animals, and the animals could talk to them, what didn't they know about human beings? Or the earth itself, for that matter. (*SS*, p. 278)

Milkman's new understanding of this pre-linguistic sensitivity and its communal qualities is pivotal in his development towards racial and filial responsibility. It is the point from which he is able to make his leap into history, the moment he ceases to concentrate 'on things behind him. Almost as though there were no future to be had' (*SS*, p. 35). This is the point to which Faulkner cannot bring Ike who, being embroiled in the 'was' of history, instead recoils at a present or future of miscegenation and chaos. Faulkner's early moral vision remains unfulfilled even as he distances himself by representing Ike's interior monologue in italics. '*Maybe in a thousand or two thousand years in America*, he thought. *But not now! Not now!*' (Faulkner, 1942, p. 272).

The retreat into the past necessitates the convoluted narrative structure of *Go Down, Moses* as Faulkner continually evokes the past from the position of the present. Morrison shares this complex narrative approach, later extended to new limits in *Beloved*, yet the past she delineates is not an idealized state of innocence but rather partial, ambiguous and open to subjective interpretation. Milkman's growing sensitivity to the multiplicities of truth and his new-found commitment to his own racial history is enabled through an understanding of the past as a necessary precondition for both knowledge of the present and the realization of possibilities for the future. In the ritual of the hunt he comes to understand his father's assertion that, 'if you want to be a whole man, you have to deal with the whole truth' (*SS*, p. 70). Rather than succumb to the oppressions of Southern history Milkman can extract from this intricate past a creative response to the conflict between himself as an individual and his commitment to the community. Such an understanding of history as recovery and interpretation allows Morrison, through Milkman's quest, to articulate new visions of being black, or more specifically, being a black man.

Masculinity

Written in 1977, *Song of Solomon* reflects in many ways the complex nature of gender relations for African Americans at a volatile juncture now encompassing the machismo of the Black Power movement and its feminist critiques of the late 1970s. Susan Willis has argued that Milkman's freedom, his ability to fly, serves to 'reinvent the notion of patrimony that emerges even as Milkman puts together his genealogy' and by extension maintains that Morrison, despite her effort of reconstruction, succeeds only in reinforcing patriarchal codes of irresponsibility and freedom (Willis, 1987, pp. 59–60). Undoubtedly, Milkman's licence to roam Chicago's pool halls, barber shops and bars may be compared to the domesticity of his mother, sisters and lover. While Milkman traverses America in his heroic quest for gold, his lover, Hagar, languishes at home imprisoned by the beauty myth, determined to improve herself in order to win back her man. As a black woman Hagar suffers a double-fold denial. First, she is constrained by an unattainable feminine beauty and secondly, as a woman, denied any possibility for the kind of heroic transformations experienced by Milkman. In presenting this dilemma, however, Morrison in fact interrogates the limits placed upon black women's potential for self-realization and agency even as she documents Milkman's flight. As Michael Awkward argues, '*Song of Solomon*, then, is a record both of transcendent (male) flight and of the immeasurable pain that results for the female who, because she has no access to knowledge, cannot participate in this flight' (Awkward, 1995, p. 152).

Hagar's tragedy is that her love for Milkman, like Sethe's maternal love in *Beloved* (1987), is 'too thick' (*B*, p. 164) and she is condemned to experience the same grief as her slave ancestor, Ryna, whose desolation after Solomon's flight becomes manifest in madness and hysteria. Without appraising male or female behaviour Morrison reflects on damaged gender relationships as a legacy of slavery. The slave-owning class's determination to 'prevent full expression of . . . love' among slaves and concomitant reinforcement of racial inferiority fosters pathological relationships in which love, in all its manifestations, becomes distorted (Morrison intv. with Moyers, 1994, p. 268). Hagar cannot escape internalized notions of romance, her attempts to express love parodic imitations of what love has come to mean. Guitar professes love for his people, but again this love finds violent expression in the vengeful killing of one white person as reprisal for every African American lynched or murdered by racists. Unable to find positive expressions of racial love, he explains to Milkman how a history of racism, oppression and denial has infused the emotional lives of modern African Americans. 'Listen, baby, people do funny things. Specially us. The cards are stacked against us and just trying to stay in the game, stay alive and in the game, makes us do funny things. Things we can't help.' (*SS*, p. 87)

In tracing the origins of the problematical, conflicted nature of contemporary African-American gender relationships, Orlando Patterson has surveyed sociological and historical investigations into the social relations of slavery (Patterson, 1995, pp. 56–104). Patterson acknowledges the scholarship of 1970s revisionist historians who suggest that slavery did not in fact destroy gender relationships nor replace the conventions of the family unit with a destructive 'matriarchy', but finds the approach of feminist counter-revisionists, from the mid-1980s to the mid-1990s, more convincing in their recognition that the slave community was neither 'utopian' nor able to maintain its social structures without the intervention of the slave-owning class.[11] For Patterson, modern African-American gender relations have their origins in a system that reduced the male slave's role to that of 'stud' and worker. The slave, not only unable to protect his wife from sexual exploitation, was redundant in terms of providing food and shelter, further exacerbating an already vulnerable sense of masculinity. Conversely, the institution of slavery – under which women often performed the same physical labour as men, were encouraged to increase slave stock through reproduction and were sensitive to the problematic role of the slave male – compelled slave women to develop forms of autonomy and significantly, as in *Beloved*, to privilege motherhood over marriage as a more fulfilling, attainable role. The modern working-class black male response to a history of 'emasculation' has been,

> to embrace, both defiantly and tomishly, the very role the White aggressor had forced upon them. The resulting anger and self-loathing found expression inwardly in the high incidence of depression among lower-class Black men, both in the rural South and in the modern ghetto, and outwardly in violence against other Black men as well as sexual aggression against women. (Patterson, 1995, p. 88)

Middle-class black men have responded to this legacy in varying ways, either through the inclusion of women as fellow agents in the fight for social equality or, more negatively, by the internalization of white patriarchal codes that found expression in protective, often disciplinarian, male dominance. The findings of counter-revisionists substantiate earlier research such as that of the psychologist John Dollard in the mid-1930s and closer to the period of slavery (Patterson, 1995, p. 88). In his 1937 psycho-ethnographic study *Caste and Class in a Southern Town*, Dollard outlined the ways in which his working-class black male interviewees, many of whom were directly descended from slaves, continued to internalize the sexual role forced upon men under slavery. He concludes, 'the "disproportionate" sex impulse of the Negro' is a 'feature of his permissive slave culture rather than a result of his disproportionate biological desire, as is so often alleged' (Dollard, 1937, p. 420). Dollard then argues that middle-class African Americans, in particular men, 'direct aggression to the real world and

---

[11] Patterson identifies the most convincing counter-revisionist scholarship in the work of: Ann Patton Malone, *Sweet Chariot* (1992); Susan Lebsock, *The Free Women of Petersburg: Status and Culture in a Southern Town, 1784–1860* (1984); and Elizabeth Fox-Genovese, *Within the Plantation Household: Black and White Women of the Old South* (1989).

compete at any cost with the white middle-class group.... They compete for the dominant white values, mastery through skill, prestige, high income, and pride in high personal standards ... and are following the dominant American ideal' (Dollard, 1937, p. 421).

There are similarities between Dollard's findings, counter-revisionist evidence and Zora Neale Hurston's early anthropology of Southern African-American social relations that, as we have seen, informed her literary work. In *Their Eyes Were Watching God* (1937), Joe internalizes white patriarchal codes and places Janie on a 'pedestal' in his efforts to match ideals of masculinity. In contrast, Hurston's first novel, *Jonah's Gourd Vine* (1934) opens with a consideration of lower-class constructions of gender relations among the first generations of freedmen. Amy and Ned Crittenden, mother and stepfather of the protagonist John Buddy Pearson, are poor sharecroppers struggling externally with the residues of an exploitative and dehumanizing institution and internally with the resulting pressures on their marriage. Though never explicitly stated, John is evidently the offspring of a union between Amy and her former slave master, 'Massa' Alf Pearson and this knowledge has a profound, debilitating impact on Ned's image of himself as a man, father and husband. Ned's response is to internalize the prevailing Southern view that 'half-white niggers got de worst part uh bofe de white and de black folks' and to imitate the slave master in his own treatment of his wife and children (Hurston, 1934b, p. 24). 'Ole Marse didn't ast *me* ef hit wuz rainin' uh snowin' uh hot uh col'. When he spoke Ah had tuh move and move quick too, uh git a hick'ry tuh ma back. Dese younguns ain't uh bit better'n me. Let 'em come lak Ah did' (Hurston, 1934b, p. 15). With her taunting, 'Monkey see, monkey do', Amy clearly recognizes Ned's appropriations of the ideology of black racial inferiority, that he can only mimic the slave owner in sadistic expressions of power (Hurston, 1934b, p. 24). Ned's efforts to salvage his masculinity are futile and Amy proves to be his equal as she retaliates physically and with verbal dexterity to the whipping he inflicts upon her. Moreover, and as reflected in Patterson's work, she privileges her role as mother over that of wife. 'But we's free folks now. De big bell done rung! Us chillun is ourn. Ah doan know, mebbe hit'll take some of us generations, but us got tuh' 'gin practise on treasurin' our younguns. Ah loves dese heah already uh whole heap. Ah don't want 'em knocked and 'buked' (Hurston, 1934b, p. 16). Amy encourages her son John to leave the abusive family environment and exploits her relationship with Alf Pearson to establish John as a favoured worker on the plantation. She thereby provides some literary evidence of the relative power of the black woman, a perspective Michelle Wallace in *Black Macho and the Myth of the Superwoman*, finds reflected in Black Power's understanding of men as the true victims of both slavery and contemporary gender relations, not least because of the betrayal of black women sleeping with 'massa' (Wallace, 1978, p. 23).

Wallace's polemic against African-American masculinity was published in 1978, a year after *Song of Solomon*, and helped initiate a new black feminist consciousness formed in reaction to both the Moynihan Report (1965) and machismo excesses of the Black Power movement. Widely vilified for disregarding racism, the Moynihan Report, published in the 1960s, identified a dysfunctional matriarchy as the source of pathological black family relations, coinciding with the self-conscious masculinity of Black Power ideology.[12] Black Power's revolutionary objective to overthrow white modes of power is paradoxically, and fatally, coupled with its subjection of women to the cause of black male freedom. As bell hooks writes: 'Insistence on patriarchal values, on equating black liberation with black men gaining access to male privilege that would enable them to assert power over black women, was one of the most significant forces undermining radical struggle (hooks, 1991, p. 16). It is against the conscious strategy of empowerment, exemplified by the rhetoric of LeRoi Jones and Eldridge Cleaver, which black feminists in the late 1970s began to articulate the means to their own empowerment.[13] Black women, Wallace asserts, had until this point remained isolated from the Women's Movement, preferring instead to support an embattled black masculinity at a time when a black feminist agenda would only serve to undermine the wider struggle for racial equality (Wallace, 1978, p. 11).

---

[12] Daniel Moynihan, *The Negro Family: The Case for National Action*, (1965). For examples of male counter responses to the findings of the Moynihan Report, see Robert Staples, 'The myth of the impotent black male' (1971, pp. 133–45) and 'The myth of the Black Matriarchy' (1970, pp. 174–87). Lynne Segal criticizes Staples' later work, *Black Masculinity: The Black Man's Role in American Society* (1982), for adopting 'essentialist categories of masculinity which lead him to defend the intrinsic masculinity of Black men, rather than to criticize the mechanisms of dominance necessary to establish it in the first place' (Segal, 1997, p. 188). David Marriott also criticizes the sociology of race relations for 'its static, and integrationist model of the state and civic society based on a normative white consensus of what 'good' masculinity is or could be; its unproblematizing of masculinity as a category or concept and consequent misreading of black femininity; its privileging of the phallus as the key signifier of masculinity; its failure to take into account discontinuities, contradictions and fractures within and between men in their relations to patriarchy; and its failure to theorize the relationship between capitalism and racism in anything more than a perfunctory way' (Marriott, 1996, pp. 191–2).

[13] LeRoi Jones's (Amiri Imamu Baraka) infamous declaration, 'The white woman understands that only in the rape sequence [with a black male] is she likely to get cleanly, viciously popped' (Jones, 1965, pp. 216–33). Eldridge Cleaver wrote in *Soul on Ice*, 'We shall have our manhood. We shall have it or the earth will be levelled by our attempts to gain it' Cleaver, 1969, p. 49. Lynne Segal includes both quotations in her study of masculinity, *Slow Motion* (Segal, 1997, p. 198).

Wallace made reference to the 'growing distrust, even hatred between black men and black women' (Wallace, 1978, p. 13), a bleak vision that has sustained, evidenced by the Clarence Thomas and Anita Hill Hearings in 1991. Morrison took great interest in this case, eventually contributing to, and editing, a collection of essays on the proceedings, *Race-ing Justice, Engendering Power* (1992). The Hill-Thomas Hearings, in which Hill accused Thomas, a Supreme Court nominee, of sexual misconduct, prompted renewed debate surrounding black gender relations and led Orlando Patterson to call for the replacement of divisive polemic subsuming gender relations to 'women's issues' with a more open dialogue across the sexes. If not, debate is impoverished and collapses into quantifications of victim-hood and suffering. Importantly, Patterson concludes that black men *and* black women have much to gain by confronting their 'poisoned' relationships, both collectively and individually, in an act of reclamation that involves a return to the past and the original trauma of slavery (Patterson, 1995, p. 95).

It is towards such a confrontation with his past and, by extension, the past of his people, that Morrison takes Milkman Dead. After the epiphany of the hunt Milkman experiences his first genuine, reciprocal relationship with a woman of the South, Sweet, an intimacy impossible in the North where he is geographically, historically and emotionally removed from his Southern ancestry. Until this point Milkman can only duplicate the white patriarchy of the North and his father's accumulation of property and capital. Morrison's concern is the *embourgeoisement* of second-generation migrants to the northern states of America. We have seen how Hurston in *Jonah's Gourd Vine* presents a fictionalized version of a historically transitional moment, the post-bellum period in the South, and how she critiqued the adoption of white patriarchal values by newly liberated black men revelling in their freedom, not least a sexual freedom encompassing the objectification and misuse of women. After leaving the family home and crossing the Big Creek to 'Massa' Pearson's plantation, John Buddy Pearson marries Lucy Potts only to embark on a series of affairs. He does not understand the consequences of his infidelities for his stoical wife and is killed, in ignorance, by the very thing he loves, a train, symbolic of masculine virility and progress. In Hurston's transitional moment, however, the past may have distorted sexual relations but those forms of musical and bodily expression that survived the Middle Passage are still maintained after Emancipation; 'So they danced. They called for the instrument that they had brought to America in their skins – the drum – and they played upon it' (Hurston, 1934b, p. 59).

Milkman exists in a later period of profound change, by which time the effects of two generations of duplication can be overcome only by returning to the past before constructing the future. Unlike John Pearson, Milkman survives long enough to attain self-realization and, in a more nuanced, generously inclusive approach, the question is not one of gender divisions, but rather of the effect American capitalism, and its social relations, have upon the psychology of both black men and women.[14] In her response to the Thomas-Hill Hearings, 'Friday on the Potamac', Morrison bypasses questions of culpability and instead compares Thomas, the right wing Supreme Court nominee, to Daniel Defoe's Man Friday. Again, the point of address is that of language. Thomas and Man Friday are 'rescued' by their white master and in return learn the master's language, forget their own and move 'from speaking *with* to thinking *as*' the master. Morrison concludes that 'both men, black but unrecognizable at home or away, are condemned first to mimic, then to internalize and adore, but never to utter one single sentence understood to be beneficial to their original culture' (Morrison's italics, 1992a, pp. xxv, xxix). The success of men such as Clarence Thomas, Milkman and his father Macon Dead comes at the price of language, idiom and the dislocations ensuing from the ventriloquy of whiteness. Implicit in Morrison's critique of Clarence Thomas, and carried in representations of those characters in *Song of Solomon* who adopt such values, is an acknowledgement of James Baldwin's rhetorical statement in *The Fire Next Time*:

> How can one respect, let alone adopt, the values of a people who do not, on any level whatever, live the way they say they do, or the way they say they should? I cannot accept the proposition that the four-hundred-year travail of the American Negro should result merely in his attainment of the present level of the American civilization.... The only thing white people have that black people need, or should want, is power – and no one holds power for ever. (Baldwin, 1963, p. 82)

Morrison, too, recognizes any claim on power as fragile and transitory. Milkman's grandfather is murdered, his farm confiscated by the land-greedy Butlers, but the power conferred by their whiteness is temporary and ultimately meaningless as the family line dies out, their opulence destined for ruination. Reverend Cooper

---

[14] Doreatha Mbalia, in *Toni Morrison's Developing Class Consciousness*, argues that in *Song of Solomon*, Morrison 'subordinates sexism to both racism and capitalism, realizing that the exploitation of the African woman by the African man is the result of his national and class oppression. That is, sexism is correctly viewed as the consequence of the African's lack of race and class consciousness' (Mbalia, 1991, p. 51).

tells Milkman, 'The ways of God are mysterious, but if you live it out, just live it out, you see that it always works out. Nothing they stole or killed for did 'em a bit a good. Not one bit' (*SS*, p. 232).

Masculinity, Fanon and migration

Morrison's analysis of the Thomas-Hill hearings resonates with Frantz Fanon's theorization of the black man's relationship with language. In *Black Skin, White Masks* (1952) Fanon answers the question 'What does the black man want?' with the reply 'The Black man wants to be white' (Fanon, 1952, pp. 10, 11). Fanon's psychoanalytical approach has its material basis in the economic subjugation of colonial subjects, reinforced as the process of colonization denies the colonial subject his 'local cultural originality'. The subject absorbs ideologies of racial inferiority through which any attempt to prove racial equality is invariably channelled. His mastery of the colonizer's language and the rejection of dialect brings the black man closer to the whiteness and equality he desires; only through the crucial acquisition of language can this be achieved. 'A man who has a language consequently possesses the world expressed and implied by that language' (Fanon, 1952, p. 18). Failure, however, is inevitable, for to speak a language other than one's own amounts, for Fanon, to the 'rupture' of the self, a condition of alienation merely intensified should education take the subject yet further from his cultural originality. Fanon is primarily concerned with language in relation to the Negro of Antilles but includes 'every colonized man' in his considerations on the psychological consequences of migration and the adoption of assimilationist practices. The Antillean Negro's dislocation has its origins in the perceived inferiority of his own language, a dislocation reinforced by his migration to the metropolitan centres of France where he is judged according to the extent to which he has assimilated the language and culture of the 'mother country'.

Morrison is of course concerned with the historical and cultural specificity of African-American experiences rather than with wider colonial encounters. However, it is the experience of migration that generates alienation and dislocation as Morrison's characters are compelled to equate social and political advancement with the adoption of white mores. It is important to remember that the 1960s were without the now familiar notion of diasporic existence as a positive site for resistance and re-invention. The concerns of Black Power proponents were indeed focused upon white modes of domination, but their emphasis on nationalism and the reinvestment of patriarchal convention served to obfuscate the potential of the movement as a transcendent form of political consciousness. In *Paradise* (1998), as we shall see, Morrison articulates her version of positive diasporic existence as 'home', but in *Song of Solomon* her project is the more urgent one of leading Milkman, through the proto-diasporic, guiding figure of Pilate, back to the South and away from the psycho-pathological dislocations of migration. In Fanon's terms, Morrison determines to 'disalienate' Milkman Dead, to liberate 'the man of colour from himself' lest he remains imprisoned by the desire to be white (Fanon, 1952, p. 10). In *The Bluest Eye* (1970) Pecola is destroyed by her desire for the very physicality of whiteness. In *Song of Solomon* this is manifest, for men, not through the acquisition of skin colour, but rather in the privileges and accumulation whiteness confers. Migration north destroys any natural relationship to land or property and, having witnessed the murder of his father and the confiscation of his family's land, Milkman's father, Macon Dead, determines to seal his ownership of Chicago slums in legally sanctioned property transactions, even if this means the eviction of his people. Such practice prompts Mrs. Bains's observation that 'A nigger in business is a terrible thing to see' (*SS*, p. 22) and the price paid by Macon is an unfulfilled marriage to the daughter of the only black doctor in Southside. Their female offspring, Corinthians and Lena, stay home making artificial red velvet roses, metaphors for their detachment from nature and passionate experience.

Milkman's assimilation of whiteness is reflected in his unquestioning adoption of his father's business practices. It is not until he understands the reasons for his father's compulsion to protect what was, in reality, a fragile hold on land and property that Milkman can see the vanity of his own involvement in the family business. He realizes that his father has some justification for his behaviour, knowing how easily land can be taken away. Milkman, however, is unable to take responsibility for what has hitherto been an essentially meaningless existence in imitation of white bourgeois values of social mobility. Milkman's world revolves around upwardly mobile black people who measure their 'racial uplift' in terms of their ability to emulate the social codes of the beach home and the tennis club. He dates white- or light-skinned women even as he retains the black woman Hagar, his 'own private honey pot'. If whiteness is unattainable in actuality, then it is at least Milkman's unconscious desire; he has the 'heart of the white men' (*SS*, p. 266), illustrating Fanon's observations on black male sexuality. As the acquisition of the colonizer's language confers whiteness, so to do sexual relations with the white man's most prized possession, white women. 'By loving me she proves that I am worthy of white love. I am loved like a white man' (Fanon, 1952, p. 63).

For Fanon, ideologies of black inferiority, unlike stereotypes of white persecuted groups, are marked by an awareness of skin colour and the assumption of inherent biological difference between whites and blacks. The black man, 'who is overdetermined from without', is 'fixed' and 'dissected' by the white gaze that associates the black man's corporeality with his sexuality in ways which shatter his conception of wholeness (Fanon, 1952, p. 116). In psychoanalytical terms the black man becomes a symbol of white repressed sexuality.

> The civilized white man retains an irrational longing for unusual eras of sexual license, of orgiastic scenes, of unpunished rapes, of unrepressed incest. In one way these fantasies respond to Freud's life instinct. Projecting his own desires onto the Negro, the white man behaves 'as if' the Negro really had them. (Fanon, 1952, p. 165)

These fantasies are compacted by an '*excess* of symbolization' that positions the white man in anxious relationship with both his own masculinity and black sexuality. The identification of power with the phallus is threatened by positing the black man as penis; an anxiety finding extreme expression in the lynching and castration of black American men throughout the Southern states (Marriott, 1996, p. 194). In *Song of Solomon*, Morrison records the brutal consequences such projection and overdetermination have meant for the black male by referring to the murder of Emmett Till.[15] Significantly, it is in the exclusively male barbershop that the news of Till's murder is first heard and discussed by the Southside men.

The black man's absorption of fantasies about his own un-licensed sexuality has, ironically, granted room for parody and allowed for the projection of this image back on to white society. The dissident masculinity of Black Power, for example, derived much from defiant internalization of the white 'nightmare' of black male sexuality and this, to reiterate bell hooks' argument, was to have unfortunate consequences for the movement's radicalism in that such constructions were still defined by white perceptions rather than being rooted in a genuine desire for social change. The deflection of the myth of 'blackness' back to the white oppressor finds earlier literary representation in Richard Wright's creation of Bigger Thomas in *Native Son*. Bigger is the

---

[15] In 1955, Emmett Till, a 14-year-old Northerner visiting the South, was murdered by whites for allegedly whistling or making remarks at a white woman. Morrison's play, *Dreaming Emmett* (1985, unpublished) is based on the Till murder. Morrison said that the play arose out of her considerations of 'the contradictions of black people, the relationships between black men and women, between blacks and whites, the differences between 1955 and 1985' (Morrison intv. with Croyden, 1994, p. 220).

victim of external forces, including the construction of the African-American male as sexual aggressor and his only means of existence is to fulfil white expectations. As Fanon writes: 'In the end, Bigger Thomas acts. To put an end to his tension, he acts, he responds to the world's anticipation' (Fanon, 1952, p. 139). Baldwin found Wright's characterization problematic precisely because Bigger embodies the myth of the African American, and he warns, in *Notes of a Native Son*, of the danger inherent in attempts to deflect the American image of the black male:

> [T]here exists among the intolerably degraded the perverse and powerful desire to force into the arena of the actual those fantastic crimes of which they have been accused, achieving their vengeance and their own destruction through making the nightmare real. The American image of the Negro lives also in the Negro's heart; and when he has surrendered to this image life has no other possible reality. (Baldwin, 1964, p. 41)

It is probable that Baldwin's assessment of *Native Son*, like Ralph Ellison's, is influenced by his problematic relationship with Wright as a literary precursor and by his antipathy towards the communist impulse of 1940s 'protest' fiction generally. Nevertheless, in the light of Morrison's work, Baldwin's observation that *Native Son* fails to acknowledge the existence of alternative realities for Bigger Thomas or convey a sense of the sustaining traditions developed to ensure integrity and survival, is relevant.[16] Morrison illuminates African-American traditions of music, folklore and literature and in so doing makes clear that African Americans are not simply victims of oppression without choice or power. Unlike Bigger Thomas, Milkman draws on traditions born of his ancestors' struggle for survival and freedom.

James Baldwin shares Fanon's understanding of how constructions of black male sexuality served to justify brutality and effect the transferral of white sexual fantasy onto a black population: 'The white man's unadmitted – and apparently, to him, unspeakable – private fears and longings are projected onto the Negro' (Baldwin, 1963, p. 82). The construction of a mythical black sexuality was linked in the 1950s with certain forms of white social rebellion. For Norman Mailer, the white hipster was expressive of a new form of American existentialism that drew on the history, culture and psychopathy of the black male. The white hipster is 'the white Negro' who identifies with the outlawed

---

[16] Ralph Ellison succinctly summarizes the same point as Baldwin, that Wright essentialized Bigger in his failure to articulate any alternative possibilities for the character: 'Wright could imagine Bigger, but Bigger could not possibly imagine Wright' (Ellison, 1953/1964, p. 114).

black man, living for the moment in spontaneous creation beyond social codes and boundaries.

> Knowing in the cells of his existence that life was war, nothing but war, the Negro (all exceptions admitted) could rarely afford the sophisticated inhibitions of civilization, and so he kept for his survival the art of the primitive, he lived in the enormous present, he subsisted for his Saturday night kicks, relinquishing the pleasures of the mind for the more obligatory pleasures of the body, and in his music he gave voice to the character and quality of his existence, to his rage and the infinite variations of joy, lust, languor, growl, cramp, pinch, scream and despair of his orgasm. (Mailer, 1957, p. 273)

The black man as exemplary antidote to the technological, capitalist decadence of America is also found in Jack Kerouac's *On The Road* (1957): 'I walked with every muscle aching among the lights of 27th and Welton in the Denver colored section, wishing I were a Negro, feeling that the best the white world had offered was not enough ecstasy for me, not enough life, joy, kicks, darkness, music, not enough night' (Kerouac, 1957, p. 169). For Baldwin, identification with blackness is not simply born from the intellectual white man's awareness that too much 'civilisation' means a loss of natural feeling, but rather from an anxiety marking his relationship with power and which fosters the desire 'to become a part of that suffering and dancing country that he now watches wistfully from the heights of his lonely power, and armed with spiritual traveller's cheques, visits surreptitiously after dark' (Baldwin, 1963, p. 82).

Appropriations of blackness resonate with the primitivism of 1920s modernism discussed in Chapter 1. Such projections are promulgated against the realities of black experience, which were in fact far removed from the jazz moment sentimentalized by the Beats and Mailer, who were expressing a solipsist existentialism very much part of the American odyssey of individual freedom.[17] Mailer, for example, is very aware that the root of black 'psychopathy' can be found in the encounter with white oppression and yet he wants to build upon such 'pathology' in order to become the hipster. In her literature Morrison has created characters to convey the complexities of African-American experience, serving as reminders against Mailer's kind of overdetermination. In one sense, Cholly Breedlove in *The Bluest Eye* is indeed 'dangerously free', one of Mailer's sexual outlaws, but Morrison traces the painful intricacies

---

[17] Adam Lively, in *Masks: Blackness, Race and the Imagination,* identifies a 'power-crazed version of existentialism' and a 'narcissistic vision of a self in love with itself' in Mailer's conception of the essence of Hip. (Lively, 1998, pp. 264, 265).

that such freedom can bring. In the character of Mr MacTeer, she presents a form of black masculinity without interest for Mailer and Kerouac, marked by tough, patriarchal love and sacrifice necessary to maintain arduous existence. In *Sula* Morrison undercuts psychological projections of black sexuality and the African-American man's view of himself as victim of white oppression. Nel's husband, Jude, returns from his work as a waiter in the expectation that his wife will massage his injured masculinity with 'milkwarm commiseration'. Instead, Sula interjects:

> I mean, I don't know what the fuss is about. I mean, everything in the world loves you. White men love you. They spend so much time worrying about your penis they forget their own. The only thing they want to do is cut off a nigger's privates. And if that ain't love and respect I don't know what is. And white women? They chase you all to every corner of the earth, feel for you under every bed. I knew a white woman wouldn't leave the house after 6 o'clock for fear one of you would snatch her. Now ain't that love? They think rape soon's they see you, and if they don't get the rape they looking for, they scream it anyway just so the search won't be in vain. Colored women worry themselves into bad health just trying to hang on to your cuffs. (S, pp. 103–4)

It is against this confluence of fantasy, fear and complex gender relationships that Morrison casts Milkman Dead, steering him clear of all projections and internalizations of what it means to be a black man. These, as we have seen, include the deflection of the 'bad nigger' back upon society as a warning, the absorption of white patriarchal values and, not least, the romanticization of black male sexuality as a site of freedom. Morrison achieves this ironically enough through the Tiresian figure of Pilate who, without a navel and not quite woman, bypasses the literal maternal tie and is thus able to be the ancestral mother to everyone. Pilate gives the young Milkman his first lesson – on how to boil an egg – in an apparently insignificant scene, its importance only understood at the culmination of Milkman's quest. 'Now, the water and the egg have to meet each other on a kind of equal standing. One can't get the upper hand over the other. So the temperature has to be the same for both' (*SS*, p. 39). This is Morrison's opening for restructured gender relations as the equilibrium of opposites, its political function to heal, at least in some part, the psycho-pathological repetitions of slavery exacerbated by the dislocations of migration and the mutual antagonisms of Black Power and black feminism.

Migration touches everyone in *Song of Solomon*. Pilate's marginal existence as a bootlegger living in a house of song and laughter is not romanticized by

Morrison, the female space created here by Pilate, her daughter Reba and granddaughter Hagar having degenerated without the presence of a man. Hagar, spoilt, weak and prey to the superficialities of womanhood is a very long way from her Southern origins and unable to form effective emotional relationships. Morrison in 'Rootedness' writes:

> Pilate had a dozen years of close, nurturing relationships with two males – her father and her brother. And that intimacy and support was in her and made her fierce and loving because she had that experience. Her daughter Reba had less of that and related to men in a very shallow way. Her daughter had even less of an association with men as a child, so that the progression is really a diminishing of their abilities because of the absence of men in a nourishing way in their lives. Pilate is the apogee of all that: of the best of that which is female and the best of that which is male, and that balance is disturbed if it is not nurtured, and if it is not counted on and if it is not reproduced. (Morrison, 1984, p. 63)

Pilate's power, then, as mythical ancestral figure, lies in wisdom accumulated from both her matrilineage and her patrilineage, enabling her to retain a sense of history, racial consciousness and cultural origin. Pilate can resist the psychological dislocations of migration as her ancestral knowledge remains intact throughout her travels across America, protecting her from ideologies of accumulation and inferiority. For Morrison, physical displacement need not necessarily mean the alienation of millions of black Americans. As Pilate shows, it is possible to maintain knowledge, to carry everywhere the forest, the site of pre-linguistic being. Pilate smells like a forest (SS, p. 27) and enjoys a sensuous symbolic relationship with the natural world that reconnects her with her racial past, allows her to fly 'Without ever leaving the ground'(SS, p. 336). Having lost such sensibilities, and because he is a man, Milkman's journey South and his flight back to Africa must be realized geographically and physically.

Tar Baby (1981)

Deleuze and Guattari: Linguistics and a minor literature

In *Song of Solomon*, Morrison constructs an oppositional form of literary expression that draws upon the language and conventions of a dominant aesthetic to re-appropriate and re-invent individual and collective African-American identities hitherto in American literature. Through the parodic use of a range of discourses – the language of the state, the American romance and Faulkner's Southern narrative – Morrison privileges African-American orality, history and experience. She contributes to what Gilles Deleuze and Félix Guattari, in their study *Kafka: Towards a Minor Literature*, have termed a 'minor literature' as *Song of Solomon* fulfils their criteria that a work must be political, collective and 'deterritorializing', the process by which a major language can, once dismantled and reconstructed, become subsumed as a minor language.[18] Deleuze and Guattari describe this process as an act of theft from within for the conversion of a language imposed from without. As a writer 'in the margins', Morrison's use of American English and African-American orality in the construction of an aesthetic 'within the heart of what is called great (or established) literature' allows her 'the possibility to express another possible community and to forge the means for another consciousness and another sensibility' (Deleuze and Guattari, 1975, pp. 17, 18 and 17).

Deleuze and Guattari's companion volumes *Anti-Oedipus* (1972) and *A Thousand Plateaus* (1980) encompass studies of aesthetics, political theory, psychoanalysis and linguistics. Their ideas are important for informing literary theory generally, but it is their work on language and 'minority literature' that is most useful for any practical criticism of texts. Their opposition to the universal categories of 'lack' and 'negation' in psychoanalysis (a feature of their work to which I return in the next chapter) and their critique of 'traditional' linguistics encourages an approach that can accommodate the politics of Morrison's writing. Without extracting a model of literary criticism from what is an extremely diverse range of concepts, it is useful to appropriate certain of Deleuze's and Guattari's conceptual 'tools' to avoid what they would themselves conceive as a totalizing theory of literature (Grisham, 1991, p. 44).

An analysis of the *rhizome*, a concept borrowed from botany and central to Deleuze and Guattari's work, demonstrates the extent of their departure from the linguistic and ideological linearity underpinning western knowledge. They consider this knowledge to have always been conceived within an 'arborescent culture', appearing in different forms, and indeed assuming multiplicity, but ultimately returning to a tree-like structure 'defined by a set of points and positions, with binary relations between the points and biunivocal relationships between the positions' (Deleuze and Guattari, 1980, p. 21). By contrast, in

---

[18] In *Kafka: Towards a Minor Literature*, 'The three characteristics of minor literature are the deterritorialization of language, the connection of the individual to a political immediacy, and the collective assemblage of enunciation' (Deleuze and Guattari, 1975, p. 18).

its truly abstract and multiplicitous nature, the rhizome sets us free from the binarisms of the arborescent model.

> Any point of a rhizome can be connected to anything other, and must be. This is very different from the tree or root, which plots a point, fixes an order. The linguistic tree on the Chomsky model still begins at a point S and proceeds by dichotomy. On the contrary not every trait in a rhizome is necessarily linked to a linguistic feature: semiotic chains of every nature are connected to very diverse modes of coding (biological, political, economic, etc.) that bring into play not only different regimes of signs but also states of things of differing status. (Deleuze and Guattari, 1980, p. 7)

In the rhizomatic model, language has become important only as an element within a regime of signs, a disavowal of treatments of language by linguists such as Saussure and Chomsky who rely on the existence of linguistic constants or universals in their work. Ultimately, linguists assume the existence of a standard, stable language against which all fluctuations must be measured. For Deleuze and Guattari, however, 'There is no language in itself, nor are there any linguistic universals, only a throng of dialects, patois, slangs, and specialized languages . . . There is no mother tongue, only a power takeover by a dominant language within a political multiplicity' (Deleuze and Guattari, 1980, p. 7). To accept the existence of a Standard English, or in their case, French, is to deny the political and social processes through which dialects come to be treated as sub-standard. Linguistics should be a *pragmatics* in which language is analysed politically in relation to specific historical situations because '. . . politics works language from within, causing not only the vocabulary, but also the structure and all of the phrasal elements to vary as the *order words* change' (Deleuze and Guattari, 1980, p. 83). Language is driven by *abstract machines* which function as a 'diagram of power' rather than as power itself, machinic assemblages of *content* and *expression*. With other linguists, Deleuze and Guattari agree that content and expression are interconnected, but of entirely different orders. Where they depart is in their conception of content as being made up of social technological machines – the prison, the ship, the hospital – and expression as being the *order words* – that is the condition of language as always being indirect discourse and its function, in terms of power, to impose a collective order.

It should be stressed that the elements of content and expression are variable and that because abstract machines are built around them they themselves are also in flux, operating in *continuous variation*. This is to say that the structure of a language is characterized by virtual lines of variation rather than constants.

Using the example of the statement 'I swear', Deleuze and Guattari show how it is not a linguistic constant as it means different things in different situations – in the courtroom or to a lover, for instance. 'I swear' may appear to be the same in each case, but this is an illusion achieved by the statements' variability being controlled and regulated by a linguistic power structure (Deleuze and Guattari, 1980, p. 94).

In effect, Deleuze and Guattari depart from a model of language as a signifying system and from language as the model of signifying systems. Rather than analysing language in terms of signifiers and signified they see it in terms of regimes of signs or acts that produce *incorporeal transformations* through signs. This refers to the effect that expression, or an act, has of making an event actual. Deleuze and Guattari use the example of an air plane hijacker who, through his threat of physical violence, transforms the passengers into hostages and the plane itself into a prison in an 'instantaneous incorporeal transformation' (Deleuze and Guattari, 1980, p. 81). This concurs with Judith Butler's analysis of language and its possibilities as a bodily performative act and Morrison too recognizes the violence of language as well as its redemptive and regenerative potential (Butler, 1997, p. 9 and Morrison, 1993, p. 16). In a further break with signification, subjectification is produced *by*, rather than *in* language, which in its state of variation allows for 'lines of change or creation' but only on the condition that they are 'fully and directly a part of the abstract machine' (Deleuze and Guattari, 1980, p. 99).

Artists, paradoxically, create the abstract machine at the same time as following its lines of continuous variation. As we have seen, Deleuze and Guattari differentiate between *major* and *minor* usages of language. In its major use language restricts variation, but in its minor mode the major language is deterritorialized and opened up to allow for a *becoming*. By *becoming* they mean that process by which the major language becomes minor through its deterritorialization. The major language must become minor rather than vice versa. In this sense 'Black Americans do not oppose Black to English, they transform the American English that is their own language into Black English. Minor languages do not exist in themselves: they exist only in relation to a major language and are also investments of that language for the purpose of making it minor' (Deleuze and Guattari, 1980, pp. 104–5). The key to *becoming* is in following lines of continuous variation to make the figure of minoritarian consciousness the 'becoming of everybody': 'It is certainly not by using a minor language as a dialect, by regionalizing or ghettoizing, that one becomes revolutionary; rather, by using a number of minority elements, by connecting, conjugating them, one invents a specific, unforeseen, autonomous becoming' (Deleuze and Guattari, 1980, p. 106). Using dialect does not in itself necessarily constitute a minor language, or literature, as dialect can be used for reactionary ends (Deleuze and Guattari, 1975, p. 24). Morrison has stressed that to incorporate the aesthetic sensibilities of black experience in the novel form means moving beyond the simple appropriation of dialect, that 'certain mode of language in which you just sort of drop *g*'s' (Morrison, 1984, p. 60).

Deleuze's and Guattari's understanding of a minor literature is usefully summarized by Ronald Bogue as being 'the focus of an ethnic group's collective life' which offers 'a medium in which conflicts may be articulated', if not resolved (Bogue, 1989, p. 116). The concept of a minor literature and the notion of a 'minoritarian becoming' present possibilities for examining Morrison as a 'minor' writer avoiding conventional or de-politicized interpretations in which the African-American tradition, as a 'sub canon', can only exist in relation to the major canon. It is certainly useful to approach Morrison as a writer capable of achieving individual and collective autonomy through her deterritorialization of 'major' language. She has said, 'I know the standard English. I want to use it to help restore the other language, the lingua franca' (Morrison intv. with LeClair, 1994, p. 124). In Deleuze's and Guattari's terms, Morrison wants 'to use the minor language to *send the major language racing*' (Deleuze and Guattari, 1980, p. 105).

Morrison has explored how African-Americans relate to an alienating language. In *The Bluest Eye*, as we have seen, an authoritative text is subverted by Morrison to provide an ironic backdrop to the lives of her characters. Morrison's omission of grammar subverts a linguistic standard, and yet in Deleuze and Guattari's terms, it is more than this, being an atypical expression that produces 'the placing-in-variation of the correct forms, uprooting them from their state as constants' (Deleuze and Guattari, 1980, p. 105). Morrison disturbs the equilibrium of the major language, assisted by her privileging of black expressions of cosmology, philosophy and idiom. Morrison is not concerned to reproduce black speech patterns as this would be to essentialize black art. Deleuze and Guattari advocate a minor literature 'without even a dialect or patois', as this would mean the ghettoization of black experience and Morrison, like Zora Neale Hurston before her, manipulates language through the integration of both the black vernacular and Standard English. Again, like writers of the Harlem Renaissance confronted by misappropriations of dialect in the minstrel tradition while simultaneously wishing to reclaim that dialect, Morrison resolves this tension through her continuations and extensions of a minor literature. Hurston and Morrison's *becoming* is marked by their ability to stretch and bend orality and the standard forms of language to create literature that can, like music, exist somewhere between the major and the minor key, unresolved (Deleuze and Guattari, 1980, pp. 95–7). Morrison has made a similar analogy in relation to the influence of jazz on her work: 'Classical music satisfies and closes. Black music does not do that. Jazz always keeps you on the edge' (Morrison intv. with McKay, 1994, p. 155).

Deleuze's and Guattari's concept of a minor literature is, then, useful as a key to understanding Morrison's subversive and political deterritorialization of language. Such a deterritorialization is essential given the appropriation and commodification of black cultural forms throughout the twentieth century. It may be argued that this process – from the primitivism of the modernists, through the white hipster existentialism of the 1950s to the ubiquitous reterritorialization of hip-hop – is, in many ways, the aesthetic impulse of the last century. As these cultural forms are folded into the hegemonic structure of worldwide media they lose any deterritorializing functions they may have originally possessed and, in the face of this, the 'minor' artist must extend their critique if they are to express collective forms of becoming that can successfully resist subsumption by the dominant language. On the role of the novelist confronted by this impasse, Morrison has written:

> For a long time, the art form that was healing for Black people was music. That music is no longer *exclusively* ours; we don't have exclusive rights to it. Other people sing it and play it; it is the mode of contemporary music everywhere. So another form has to take that place, and it seems to me that the novel is needed by African-Americans now in a way that it was not needed before. (Morrison, 1984, p. 58)

This act of theft, or reterritorialization is, then, no more or less than the commodification of emotion, the exploitation of artistic expression born out of a traumatic past and present and, once appropriated, reduced to a benign multiculturalism. The challenge is to follow lines of continuous variation in creative acts, leading not to essentializations of blackness, but to a perpetual state of becoming evading reification and commodification. Essential to the creation of a minor literature is the refusal of the rhetoric of 'oppositional nationalism', as nationalism inevitably duplicates western hegemonic forms. Lloyd writes:

> Nationalisms reterritorialize dislocated identities historically and, despite their initially progressive intents, continue thereby to acquiesce in imperial hegemony

even after 'independence'. An alternative response is that represented by what we are terming minor literature, which refuses to reterritorialize identity, preferring to extend the critique of those developmental narratives which perpetuate hegemonic culture. (Lloyd, 1987, p. 174)

Kwame Anthony Appiah similarly critiques cultural nationalism in African literature as the unknowing repetition of western literature's ideology of nationhood. Even in rejecting hegemonic western culture, African writers with a nationalist agenda

> enact a conflict that is *interior* to the same nationalist ideology that provided the category of "literature" its conditions of emergence: defiance is determined less by "indigenous" notions of resistance than by the dictates of the West's own Herderian legacy – its highly elaborated ideologies of national autonomy, of language and literature as their cultural substrate. (Appiah, 1992, p. 95)

In the next chapter, we shall see how in *Paradise* Morrison extends post nationalist formulations in evocation of a new politics of the diaspora for the twenty-first century that transcends racial and national boundaries and answers Appiah's call for a new 'humanism' that 'can be provisional, historically contingent, anti-essentialist (in other words, postmodern) and still be demanding' (Appiah, 1992, p. 250).

Deleuze and Guattari's ideas are useful for an examination of African-American black literature in a context of the wider domain of American ideology and language. If we accept their contention that the black vernacular constitutes an autonomous language, existing in its own right rather than as the sub-standard expression of the major language, and that there is 'a power takeover by a dominant language', then Morrison's project assumes an immediate political function. She engages at the site of conflict perceived by Deleuze and Guattari as operating at the level of the abstract machine and does so without losing sight of the fact that African Americans have had to establish themselves within the rational confines of the major language. This theme is explored in *Tar Baby* in Morrison's representation of the black manservant, Sydney whose assimilation of his white employer's value system is clearly seen when he confronts Son. He defines himself as 'a Phil-a-delphia Negro mentioned in the book of the very same name. My people owned drugstores and taught school while yours where still cutting their faces open so as to be able to tell one of you from the other' (*TB*, p. 164). Rejecting what he regards as Son's African primitivism, Sydney aligns himself with the order words of the dominant culture which function as a collective enunciation of African Americans in works such as Du Bois' sociological study *The Philadelphia Negro* (1899). His people have helped maintain the dominant social system as school teachers promoting the use of language in its major mode in direct opposition to the art of scarification, the inscription of minor literature on to the body itself. Morrison's reference to Du Bois's work as a sociologist indicates her ambivalence towards preoccupations with 'racial uplift'; her characterization of Sydney implies admiration for his loyalty and discipline, but is nevertheless critical of his aspirations despite their historical and social construction. Du Bois, in *The Philadelphia Negro*, adheres to late nineteenth-century notions of propriety and measures the weaknesses of black Philadelphians against them.[19]

Myth and indeterminacy

The structural and thematic impulse of *Tar Baby* is to reclaim, and attribute new meanings to, the original tar baby myth. This African-American folk story has been appropriated, for example, in the ideologically charged plantation narrative of Joel Chandler Harris's *Uncle Remus* but in *Tar Baby* Morrison 'apprehends myth both as a tool of Euro-American power and as a reservoir of historical knowledge capable of resisting that power' (Werner, 1988, p. 151).[20] As in *Song of Solomon*, in which Morrison invests the slave tale of the flying African with new possibilities for the creation of masculine identity, *Tar Baby* draws on myth and oral narrative to articulate ever more complex issues of identity and, significantly, class. Morrison again follows the 'lines of variation', here of the tar baby myth, and creates an intricate rhizomatic web in which the main characters variously assume the identity of both tar baby and Briar Rabbit. There are many versions of the tar baby myth but that appropriated by Morrison tells of a white farmer, troubled by Briar Rabbit's stealing, making a baby from sticky tar to trap him (Morrison intv. with Ruas, 1994, p. 102). Once stuck fast

---

[19] See Adolph L. Reed, Jr, for an analysis of Du Bois, *The Philadelphia Negro* in, *W.E.B. Du Bois and American Political Thought: Fabianism and the Color Line* (Reed, 1997, pp. 27–41). Reed points out that Du Bois's model for African–American social organization emphasizes: '(1) monogamous nuclear family organization; (2) temperance and orderliness as behavioral principles, including thrift and internalization of disciplined work habits; (3) favorable disposition toward formal education and training in the ways of urban civilization; and (4) legitimation of class hierarchy within the racial community.' (Reed, 1997a p. 28).

[20] For a comprehensive analysis of Morrison's use of folklore see Trudier Harris, *Fiction and Folklore: The Novels of Toni Morrison*. Harris makes the important point that Morrison 'is able to show folklore in *process* rather than as the static force many other works picture it as being' (Harris, 1991, p. 11).

to the tar baby, Briar Rabbit relies on his trickster cunning to escape, begging the farmer not to throw him into the deathly briar patch. The gullible farmer, unaware that the briar patch is where the rabbit is most at home, decides to throw him to his doom from which, of course, Briar Rabbit makes his escape. Morrison transfers this myth to a contemporary setting in which the figure of the farmer becomes Valerian Street, a white confectionary magnate in retirement on the French Caribbean island of Isle des Chevaliers and where he pursues his horticultural interests. Jadine, the niece of his black servants Sidney and Ondine, has a European education, financed by Valerian and who thus contributes to her construction as the tar baby ensnaring the trickster Son, a lawless fugitive from American justice. As *Song of Solomon* ends with Milkman's flight to Africa so *Tar Baby* begins with Son's rebirth in the feminized current, 'like the hand of an insistent woman', guiding him to the island. These journeys are endowed with the language of myth and both novels share a structure in which the motifs of flying and birth-by-water are repeated at the beginning and the end. Beginning *Song of Solomon*, Robert Smith's prosaic suicidal dive from the rooftop of No Mercy Hospital serves as a prototype for the exalted transcendence of Milkman's flight into a future of possibilities at the book's end; in *Tar Baby*, Son's arrival by water prefigures his intense rebirth as 'a certain kind of man' guided by the ancestor Thérèse. The novel begins ambiguously, 'He believed he was safe', doubtful of whether Son really is safe, 'because safety itself is the desire of each person in the novel. Locating it, creating it, losing it' (Morrison, 1990, p. 227). Moreover, the opening words evoke the indeterminacy and ambiguity underlying *Tar Baby* as Morrison refines the use of minoritarian language in order to convey new possibilities for African Americans at a postcolonial, global juncture in which questions of race and gender now intersect with issues of class. In *Tar Baby* it is primarily class that problematizes the return to the ancestor and its sustaining properties. Faith in racial or cultural origin was appropriate for *Song of Solomon*, a novel concerned with the rise of a black middle class that could be reminded of a not too distant racial past, but Jadine is far removed from any clearly defined cultural identity. She is in fact a literal and 'cultural orphan' far from America, her Sorbonne education and success as a model allowing self-assured reinventions as a black woman in the 1980s. Marilyn Sanders Mobley explains that:

> Morrison's dilemma in *Tar Baby* is how to narrate the quest of a contemporary African-American female hero who happens to be a cultural orphan, one whose sense of self is based on a denial of her own cultural heritage and an identification with one other than her own. (Mobley, 1991, p. 135)

Jadine understands black art and politics but consciously aligns herself with the western aesthetic: 'Picasso *is* better than an Itumba mask. The fact that he was intrigued by them is proof of *his* genius, not the mask-makers' (*TB*, p. 72). To return holds no promise of freedom for Jadine; nothing is to be found there that may be judged by the conventional criteria for success and, for her, Son's search for something more than money is a poor apology for failure (*TB*, p. 172).

Cultural heritage

The orphaned Jadine is without a past to which she can return for sustenance, without Son's roots, allowing her to make herself as she feels she should be made but also leaving her vulnerable to exploitation as exotic 'copper Venus' on the cover of French *Elle*. Her Art History education fails to provide her with any significant insight into her own cultural history, wilfully blind to the realities that surround her. Jadine's inability to connect with her racial self contrasts with the blind ancestor Thérèse's searing insight. It is Thérèse, invisible and uneducated, who alone provides an accurate, reliable narrative for the events that unfold in *Tar Baby*. She recognizes Son as redemptive bearer of culture, herself a descendant of the blind horsemen, who were originally slaves blinded by their first sight of Dominique and who have now come to represent the ancestral community. Jadine's refusal to recognize Thérèse as anything other than nameless servant exemplifies her rootlessness, and yet she is troubled by the presence of female ancestor figures who make her feel 'inauthentic' (*TB*, p. 45), reminders of the 'ancient properties' (*TB*, p. 308) she could possess. At the height of her career she encounters one such ancestral figure, an African woman in Paris who, dressed in canary yellow and with tribal markings scored into her cheeks, appears again and again in her consciousness. The African woman becomes a fantastical figure in the mundane setting of a French supermarket, possessed of transcendent beauty and grace that speak, as she disappears from Jadine's view, of 'a moment before the cataclysm, when all loveliness and life and breath in the world was about to disappear' (*TB*, p. 43). The woman has 'skin like tar', Morrison reclaiming the tar baby myth, transposing a racial slur into one in which tar is invested with sacred racial properties, but the African woman's essentialized identity also threatens to trap Jadine (Goulimari, 2011, p. 77). She struggles to resist contact with her racial past, fearful of sticking to it and losing 'the person she had worked hard to become' (*TB*, p. 264). Trapped in the tar swamp she again, through force of will, resists the permanent embrace of the ancestor, represented this time by the tree women of the swamp.

> This girl was fighting to get away from them. The women hanging from the trees were quiet now, but arrogant – mindful as they were of their value, their exceptional femaleness; knowing as they did that the first world of the world had been built with their sacred properties; that they alone could hold together the stones of pyramids and the rushes of Moses's crib; knowing their steady consistency, their pace of glaciers, their permanent embrace, they wondered at the girl's desperate struggle down below to be free, to be something other than they were. (*TB*, p. 184)

Like Milkman Dead, Jadine has the opportunity for epiphany in the primordial space of the woods. Unlike Milkman, however, Jadine, an ambitious and progressive young woman, resists engagement with history. Morrison intensifies this ambivalence in order to take into account the experience of black women shaping their individual, rather than their group, identity. She does this not without sympathy for women like Jadine who find themselves successful members of a new black middle class confronted by tensions of individual and collective responsibility that leave the contemporary black woman trying to be 'both ship and safe harbour' (Morrison intv. with Ruas, 1994, p. 102). In *Tar Baby* Morrison returns to concerns raised in *Sula* about the anxiety engendered by the social mobility of certain black women, and her characterization of Jadine warns against the abandonment of African-American female epistemology and advocates the balancing of 'nurturing sensibilities' with 'ambition'. In 1979 Morrison delivered the commencement address to black female students at Barnard College:

> I am suggesting that we pay as much attention to our nurturing sensibilities as to our ambition. You are moving in the direction of freedom and the function of freedom is to free somebody else. You are moving toward self-fulfilment, and the consequences of that fulfilment should be to discover that there is something just as important as you are. . . . in your rainbow journey toward the realization of personal goals, don't make choices based only on your security and your safety. . . . Let your might and your power emanate from that place in you that is nurturing and caring. (Cited in Mobley, 1991, p. 139)

Identification with a black, mystical female identity is nevertheless problematized in *Tar Baby*. As Elliott Butler-Evans argues: 'The reader who insists on placing Jade's behavior within the realm of some mystical racial politics runs the risk of missing a serious Black feminist issue: the need for Black women to construct their own identities without having to submit to a dominant myth of racial authenticity'

(Butler-Evans, 1989, p. 157). Morrison makes clear that Jadine's alienation is not only the result of her immersion in a certain educational and social environment but also stems from her desire to create an identity separate from black manhood. She rebukes Son for 'pulling that black-woman-white-woman shit on me. . . . If you think you can get away with telling me what a black woman is or ought to be . . .' (*TB*, p. 121). Moreover, Jadine is aware that African-American culture has been co-opted by white counterculture. Valerian's son, Michael, offsets his traumatic childhood with well-meaning benevolence towards African Americans, even daring to tell Jadine how to be black. Michael's consciousness-raising is typical of 1970s radicalism, but his plans for establishing Sydney and Ondine as practitioners of African handicrafts belie his insensitivity to the reality of their lives as elderly servants to his millionaire father. This youthful compulsion for assisting racial progress is the means by which Michael can rebel, heal and define himself as a white man who suffered as an abused child, another form of the projection of suffering onto blackness.

Jadine is in many ways Sula's 1980s counterpart. Jadine has, however, advantages of education, travel and money but still her dilemma is Sula's dilemma, namely to resolve the crisis of self-expression and commitment to family and community. Son, initially, has no such problem, being from the all black town of Eloe, Florida and fully committed to its world. He invests the realities of an environment characterized by poverty and mental illness with romanticized memories that fade only when he sees Jadine's photographs of the women in his hometown. 'Beatrice, pretty Beatrice, soldier's daughter. She looked stupid. Ellen, sweet cookie faced Ellen, the one always thought so pretty. She looked stupid. They all looked stupid, backwoodsy, dumb, dead' (*TB*, p. 275). His wistful dreams about 'yellow houses with white doors which women opened and shouted Come on in, you honey you! And the fat black ladies in white dresses minding the pie table in the basement of the church' (*TB*, p. 119), all that Jadine rejects, are the fantasies of a homesick man. Neither Son's valorization of black womanhood or of the South, or Jadine's dismissal of the town as 'rotten' and 'boring' (*TB*, p. 262) are accurate, mere delusions serving to widen the class divide between them. Son and Jadine are oblivious to the strength of the women and the community as a whole; Son blinded by romanticism, Jadine by her cosmopolitan sensibilities. Son is, however, the chosen one, but must divest himself of idealized notions of blackness and respect black women's need for independence and autonomy.

Unlike Milkman Dead, Son is very aware of his origins in a storytelling African-American culture. This alone, however, does not bring self-realization and that he too must embark on a quest in spite of his commitment to the community reveals how, for Morrison, the search for meaningful racial identity is never ending. Importantly, in *Tar Baby* the quest motif is extended beyond the nation state of America and the implication that Son may join the island's ancestral community gives his journey a global significance, linking his destiny to the history of the world's dispossessed.

Tar Baby as postcolonial narrative

The setting of Isle des Chevaliers widens the concern with racial identity to include a consideration of imperialist geo-politics as an environment against which the complexities of class, gender and race can be traced. The island, like the woods in *Song of Solomon*, offers a return to pre-linguistic origins, a place in which elements of the natural world, clouds, rivers and forests, communicate as a chorus witnessing the events of the story (*TB*, p. 7). As in *Go Down, Moses* the wilderness is being destroyed by the territorializations of expansionism. *Tar Baby* and *Go Down, Moses* are structured thematically around the process by which nature becomes commercial land, providing a conceptual framework for understanding the American frontier psyche that must, to fulfil its manifest destiny, always mark nature and subjugate man. Again like Faulkner, Morrison uses the life of the river as history's witness to illustrate the extent to which man has inscribed himself on the natural world.[21] The river in *Tar Baby* is a repository for the psychosis of colonial and imperialist history; 'Poor insulted, brokenhearted river. Poor demented stream. Now it sat in one place like a grandmother and became a swamp the Haitians called Sein de Vielles. And witch's tit it was: a shrivelled fog bound oval seeping with a thick black substance that even mosquitoes could not live near' (*TB*, p. 8).

The river is as female as the sea it feeds, the sea guiding Son to his destiny. Despite its near destruction the river retains its essence as the site of pre-historical origin and ancestral knowledge, reduced to the thick black substance that is tar, the maternal essence Jadine resists. At once female and elusive, the river survives as a figure for the endurance of racial origin in the face of a history

---

[21] Faulkner fictionalizes the Mississippi as the 'River' in *Go Down, Moses* and in the penultimate section of the novel links its geography with that of the wilderness: 'He had watched it, [the wilderness] not being conquered, destroyed, so much as retreating since its purpose was served now and its time an outmoded time, retreating southward through this inverted-apex, this V-shaped section of earth between hills and River until what was left of it seemed now to be gathered and for the time arrested in one tremendous destiny of brooding and inscrutable impenetrability at the ultimate funnelling tip.' (Faulkner, 1942, p. 259). Graham Clarke points out that, 'the river's presence suggests the very nervous system of a continent upon which that "western" spirit hacks and scratches' (Clarke, 1990, p. 159).

encompassing the colonization of Dominique, the transportation of slaves as labour and the latest appropriations of land by wealthy Americans. Valerian Street creates a rationalized version of paradise that involves the exploitation Haitian labourers and the destruction of the island's eco-system, a palimpsest on which the narrative of the natural world is overwritten by his efforts to civilize and limit its fecundity. In cultivating plants alien to the habitat, Street ignores the natural language of the island, joining a long tradition of natural scientists who have, since the eighteenth century, classified nature within a narrative claiming the natural world for the European. As Mary Louise Pratt writes in *Imperial Eyes*, 'natural history asserted an urban, lettered, male authority over the whole of the planet; it elaborated a rationalizing, extractive, dissociative understanding which overlaid functional, experimental relations among people, plants, and animals' (Pratt, 1992, p. 38). The ideology of naturalist science, Pratt maintains, remains today, resonating with Morrison's evocation of the island as a microcosm of modern colonial relations. Valerian's form of control is what Pratt terms 'anti-conquest', the process by which Europeans asserted hegemony through the 'innocent' codification of the natural environment. This may be distinguished from geographic, bureaucratic conquest of the colonized and constitutes 'a utopian, innocent vision of European global authority' (Pratt, 1992, p. 39). Valerian, his imperious 'head-on-a-coin profile', is convinced of his innocence, oblivious to the destruction of the natural world in his determination to impose his language – of seed catalogues and international horticulture – upon the island, a monological language in opposition to the language of books which have, for him, become 'stained with rivulets of disorder and meaninglessness' (*TB*, p. 12). The will to impose 'order words' effecting linguistic and literal power by establishing a mail service to the island is, however, disturbed and his colonial text is one of 'undecidability' as identified by Homi Bhabha in *The Location of Culture* (1994, pp. 112–13). Valerian's transpositions of order and rationality become futile acts as he occupies himself with the 'construction of the world and its inhabitants' (*TB*, p. 245), 'whispering first to his wrist, then to the ceiling the messages he has received that need telling. And when he has got it straight – the exact wording, even the spelling of the crucial words – he is happy and laughs lightly like a sweet boy' (*TB*, p. 40). Although able to articulate the 'exact spelling' of the message, Valerian's 'order words' are uprooted 'from their state as constants' and the message underlying his manifest destiny, '*These iceboxes are brown broken perspective v-i-o-l-i-a-x is something more and can't be coal note*' (Morrison's italics *TB*, p. 47), is rendered ideologically useless and belies the disorder of his existence. Valerian's confidence in rationality and his innocence as 'normal', 'decent', 'fair' and 'generous', 'always rational and humane' (*TB*, p. 51), are in fact refusals to confront his part in an exploitative history. His family's confectionary empire, established upon the labour of slaves on the cocoa and sugar plantations of the Caribbean and America, provides the capital allowing the Streets to purchase the island under the illusion such appropriation is benign. Morrison returns here to a trope in *Song of Solomon* in which sugar is a figure for the pathology of oppression, Guitar's hatred of anything sweet originating in the death of his father in an industrial accident and the paltry gift of a box of candy offered by way of compensation by his father's employer (*SS*, p. 61). Valerian is convinced that he is within his rights to dismiss Gideon and Thérèse for stealing apples he has imported to the island and in this conviction denies centuries of theft and appropriation in the name of legally sanctioned, commercial enterprises. As Son notes, Valerian

> had been able to dismiss with a flutter of the fingers the people whose sugar and cocoa had allowed him to grow old in regal comfort; although he had taken the sugar and cocoa and paid for it as though it had no value, as though the cutting of cane and picking of beans was child's play and had no value; but he turned it into candy, the invention of which was really child's play, and sold it to other children and made a fortune in order to move near, but not in the midst of, the jungle where the sugar came from and build a palace with more of their labour and then hire them to do more of the work he was not capable of and pay them again according to some scale that would outrage Satan himself and when those people wanted a little of what he wanted, some apples for *their* Christmas, and took some, he dismissed them with a flutter of the fingers, because they were thieves, and nobody knew thieves and thievery better than he did and he probably thought he was a law abiding man. (*TB*, pp. 203–4)

Son reveals his knowledge of Valerian and the system of subjugation that he supports, insight not possessed by Valerian himself. As James Baldwin and others have observed, African Americans on the receiving end of oppression and racism have come to understand whites more than whites understand themselves.[22]

---

[22] James Baldwin writes in *Notes of a Native Son*, 'it is one of the ironies of black–white relations that, by means of what the white man imagines the black man to be, the black man is enabled to know who the white man is' (Baldwin, 1964, p. 158). W.E.B. Du Bois claims in 'Criteria of Negro Art' that: 'Once in a while through all of us there flashes some clairvoyance, some clear idea, of what America really is. We who are dark can see America in a way that Americans cannot' (Du Bois, 1926c, pp. 60–1).

Whiteness and 'Innocence'

Valerian's delusions shatter as Ondine reveals how his wife Margaret had cut and burnt their son Michael when a child. Valerian reflects: 'He was guilty, therefore, of innocence. Was there anything so loathsome as a wilfully innocent man?'(*TB*, p. 245). Morrison's delineation of this family trauma reflects a concern with the wide sweep of a history of 'innocent' white patriarchy and racism.[23] Valerian's efforts to define and control his wife's identity, efforts resulting in the abuse of their child, are symptomatic of a patriarchal benevolence; he is, he believes, merely instructing Margaret on how to be a wealthy man's wife. Similarly, Valerian fails to see how his reshaping and civilizing of Isle des Chevaliers precludes the destruction of the land and the exploitation of people. He realizes the ramifications his crime have for his family relationships, but Morrison is unable to bring him to an encounter with his wider responsibility as an agent of history. In this sense, Valerian is one of James Baldwin's 'innocents', an epithet for white Americans 'still trapped in a history which they do not understand', having failed to accept responsibility for the destruction of 'hundreds of thousands of lives'; it is this 'innocence which constitutes the crime' (Baldwin, 1963, p. 16). Morrison is engaging here with Baldwin's open letter to his brother's son in *The Fire Next Time* (1963). Baldwin writes:

> I said that it was intended that you should perish in the ghetto, perish by never being allowed to go behind the white man's definitions, by never being allowed to spell your proper name. You have, and many of us have, defeated this intention; and, by a terrible law, a terrible paradox, those innocents who believe that your imprisonment made them safe are losing their grasp of reality. But these men are your brothers – your lost younger brothers. And if the word *integration* means anything, this is what it means: that we, with love, shall force our brother to see themselves as they are, to cease fleeing from reality and begin to change it. (Baldwin's italics, 1963, p. 17)

Morrison does not share Baldwin's preoccupation with blackness as having redemptive possibilities for white America, yet she considers whiteness very much within his terms. Morrison's characters are defined by 'innocent' naming: Jadine/Copper Venus, Gideon/Yardman, Thérèse/Mary, Sydney/Kingfish, Ondine/

---

[23] Terry Otten in *The Crime of Innocence in the Fiction of Toni Morrison* offers a different reading in which he interprets Valerian's 'innocence' in biblical terms. *Tar Baby*, 'like her [Morrison's] other novels, describes the passage from innocence to experience with biblical and theological overtones – garden images, references to the serpent, expressions of guilt and lost innocence, a yearning to return to the garden.' (Otten, 1989, p. 80). See also Bessie W. Jones 'Garden Metaphor and Christian Symbolism in *Tar Baby*' (Jones, 1985, pp. 116–17).

Beulah and Son's many pseudonyms reflect a history of ownership and control that may be overcome through the reclamation of real names and other identities. Baldwin's faith in the possibility of reclamation to disrupt the securities of power and ideology resonates within the thematic structure of *Tar Baby*. 'He believed he was safe' establishes Son's insecurity, but also prefigures Valerian's realization that his hold on paradise is spurious and fragile. Morrison problematizes normative and invisible whiteness in ways which pre-empt theorizations of academic enquiry into whiteness, and which often take Baldwin as a starting point.[24] Her purpose, in common with proponents of 'White Studies', is to deconstruct the architecture of race, to turn racial theory inside out.[25] In a study of whiteness, Richard Dyer writes: 'White power . . . reproduces itself regardless of intention, power differences and goodwill, and overwhelmingly because it is not seen as whiteness, but as normal. White people need to learn to see themselves as white, to see their particularity. In other words, whiteness needs to be made strange' (Dyer, 1997, p. 10).

In *Tar Baby* the pathologies of expansionism are beginning to come home. Valerian's codes and 'message' break down, his safety jeopardized as the mechanisms and consequences of his power are exposed. He becomes visible, the mask removed at last, his descent contrasting markedly with Son's ascent towards the recognition of the sensibilities offered by his own diasporic legacy. Son's escape as the trickster figure is possible because he encounters his history and the island becomes his natural home, his briar patch. Jadine refuses to confront history and thus the island cannot offer the safety desired. Without such understanding paradise is unreachable. In *Paradise* (1997) Morrison provides a more realized version of paradise, one in which the particular history of each character's quest is made more explicit than the esoteric notions of return to the ancestor that end both *Song of Solomon* and *Tar Baby*. In the development of her aesthetic Morrison herself returns to origins, giving them substance in the corporeal form of the ghost, Beloved. Moreover, she reverses the quest motif by propelling the violence of the original trauma, slavery, directly into the present as the unwanted intruder, the ancestor made real.

---

[24] Crispin Sartwell, *Act Like You Know: African–American Autobiography and White Identity* (1998, pp. 80–4). See also *Mike Hill, Whiteness: A Critical Reader* (1997).

[25] Morrison is apparently in accord with Hazel Carby's claim in 'The Multicultural Wars', that 'We need to recognize that we live in a society in which systems of domination and subordination are structured through processes of racialization that continuously interact with all other forms of socialization. Theoretically, we should be arguing that everyone in this social order has been constructed in our political imagination as a racialized subject. In this sense, it is important to think about the invention of the category of whiteness as well as that of blackness, to make visible what is rendered invisible when viewed as the normative state of existence: the (white) point in space from which we tend to identify difference' (Carby, 1992, p. 193).

4

Repetition, Memory and the End of Race: *Beloved* (1987), *Jazz* (1992) and *Paradise* (1998)

In charting black history from the 1920s to the early 1980s, Morrison has confronted the pathologies engendered by ideology in *The Bluest Eye* (1970), the essentialization of black women in *Sula* (1973) and African-American masculinity in *Song of Solomon* (1977). *Tar Baby* represents an aesthetic transition from which she reaches further back into history in order to understand the present and negotiate the future. The past, and especially slavery, permeates all Morrison's novels, but in *Tar Baby* its true nature is obfuscated by a mystical quest for an undefined racial authenticity. To go beyond this uncertainty, this stage in Morrison's work necessitates a more direct reclamation of the past in a radical, fragmentary historiography that retells the story of slavery in new and potent language. Thus, in *Beloved* (1987), as the first part of a trilogy, Morrison extends her aesthetic to reopen history and time and to map the discontinuities of history within the discontinuities of her own narrative structure. Morrison embarks here on a project of recovery that extends from *Beloved* to the 1920s in *Jazz* (1992) and culminates in the articulation of possibilities for the twenty-first century in *Paradise* (1998).

The Trilogy: *Beloved*, *Jazz* and *Paradise*

As early as 1985 Morrison made a clear link between the concerns of *Beloved* and those of its sequel, *Jazz*, published in 1992, novels inspired by fragments of true stories in which Morrison found the connections she articulates.[1] The inspiration for *Beloved* was a newspaper clipping from 1856 about a slave, Margaret Garner, who killed her child rather than see her 'live how I have lived',[2] for *Jazz* a 1920s photograph, taken by the Harlem photographer James Van der Zee, of a girl who died refusing to identify the ex-lover who had shot her. *Beloved* and *Jazz*, both involving a woman who 'loved something other than herself so much. She had placed all of the value of her life in something outside herself' (Morrison intv. with Naylor, 1994, p. 207), are explorations of identity and ask what a sense of self might mean for African-American women in particular historical circumstances, specifically slavery after Emancipation and Harlem in the 1920s. The ghost of Sethe's murdered daughter, Beloved, connects the two novels, operating as the 'mirror' of the self and as an extended presence whose 'quest' can be articulated 'all the way through as long as I care to go, into the twenties where it switches to this other girl. Therefore, I have a New York uptown-Harlem milieu in which to put this love story, but Beloved will be there also' (Morrison intv. with Naylor, 1994, pp. 208–9). In their own ways, each work recovers and re-writes the history of slavery and its aftermath from the perspective of those misrepresented in, or excluded from, archival accounts. More than social history, Morrison performs a feat of imaginative power that exposes the psychosis of the self hitherto obscured by history. In this sense *Beloved* and *Jazz* can be seen, in psychoanalytical terms, as literary embodiments of the *return of the repressed* (Freud, 1914–16, p. 154).

The third part of the trilogy, *Paradise*, also has its origin in recorded history, an 1890s newspaper notice inviting freedmen with sufficient capital, to '[c]ome prepared or not at all', to a new life in an Oklahoma black township (Morrison intv. with Denard, 2008a, p. 190). Without any obvious connection to either *Beloved* or *Jazz*, *Paradise* retains the ghost as the repository for trauma, memory and recovery, corporeal menace now refigured as the benevolence of Dovey's 'Friend', heralded by butterflies (*P*, pp. 90–3), 'the walking man' leading the migrant community to the site of their new town (*P*, pp. 97–8), and as Consolata's green-eyed male companion with 'tea-colored' hair whose visit inaugurates her commitment to the Convent women's redemption (*P*, pp. 251–2). In this imaginative scheme, the ancestral presence is never ethereal or ghostly but

---

[1] Justine Tally in 'The Morrison Trilogy' notes that there has been 'a curious critical silence concerning what the author herself [Morrison] has described as a trilogy' (Tally, 2007, p. 75). Tally then reads the trilogy in relation to Foucault, Bakhtin and French Feminism (Tally, 2007, pp. 75–91).

[2] For an analysis of Margaret Garner's story in relation to *Beloved* see Paul Gilroy, *The Black Atlantic* (Gilroy, 1993b, pp. 64–8).

always bodily, real and human. Like Ralph Ellison's invisible man, the ghost is not the 'spook' of Edgar Allan Poe's gothic but rather, in all its manifestations, a human of 'substance, flesh and bone, fibre and liquids' (Ellison, 1952, p. 7),[3] employed to foreground an African-American presence as yet 'unspeakable' and 'unspoken' (*B*, p. 199). As noted in Chapter 3, Morrison has emphasized how the white literary imagination represses this presence only for it to erupt from its unconscious as the dead or impotent counterpoint to striking, intense images of whiteness. *Beloved* reverses this trope and it is whiteness that now finds its representation as a ghostly presence in the 'men' or 'ghosts without skin' (*B*, p. 241).

Repression of African-American experience has been economic, political, historical and, as Morrison stresses in her non-fiction work, artistic. In 'Unspeakable Things Unspoken' (1989) Morrison discusses 'race' as the 'unspeakable' presence in American literature shaped, paradoxically, by its 'great, ornamental, prescribed absence'. She calls for literary enquiry into 'the ways in which the presence of Afro-Americans has shaped the choices, the language, the structure – the meaning of so much American literature. A search, in other words, for the ghost in the machine' (Morrison, 1989, p. 210). She suggests that this search could utilize critiques of colonial literature and in the collection of essays *Playing in the Dark* engages with postcolonial discourse and its intersection with psychoanalysis. Again, Morrison describes how an African presence has shaped American identity, but here it has become 'a dark, abiding, signing Africanist presence', 'Africanism' as the 'fetishising of color in the transference of blackness to the power of illicit sexuality, chaos, madness, impropriety, anarchy, strangeness and helpless, hapless desire' (Morrison, 1992c, pp. 80–1).[4] The transference, in fact, through the condensation and displacement of metaphor and metonymy, of everything prohibited by the rational codifications of the Enlightenment. As with Freud, 'fetishisation' is associated here with repulsion and attraction, as

---

[3] The opening sentences of *Invisible Man* are: 'I am an invisible man. No, I am not a spook like those who haunted Edgar Allan Poe; nor am I one of your Hollywood movie ectoplasms. I am a man of substance, of flesh and bone, fibre and liquids – and I might even be said to possess a mind. I am invisible, understand, simply because people refuse to see me' (Ellison, 1952, p. 7). In *Playing in the Dark* Morrison analyses Edgar Allan Poe's *The Narrative of Gordon Pym*. In this, as in other American texts, an invented African presence serves as 'both antidote for and meditation on' the black presence in America, 'the shadow . . . that moves the hearts and texts of American literature with fear and longing' (Morrison, 1992c, p. 33).

[4] By 'Africanism', or more accurately 'American Africanism', Morrison is referring to what she regards as the invention and employment of a black persona 'as well as the entire range of views, assumptions, readings, and misreadings that accompany Eurocentric learning about these people' (Morrison, 1992, p. 7). The term bears a resemblance to Said's 'Orientalism' as denoting those discursive and ideological constructs that have helped to define western civilization. See Edward Said, *Orientalism* (Said, 1978, pp. 1–9).

Morrison puts it, 'the language of dread and love'. *Playing in the Dark* pre-empts the work of the postcolonial critic Homi Bhabha, whose analysis, in *The Location of Culture*, of how the colonial subject is constructed in discourse reveals the significance of the unconscious for colonial relations. Using the psychoanalytic concept of ambivalence, Bhabha elucidates 'Otherness' in terms of existing simultaneously as the 'object of desire and derision'. Stereotyping, for instance, is a complex psychological construction that involves 'projection and introjection, a fusion of the conscious and unconscious' that renders the colonial subject as at once 'substitute' and 'shadow' (Bhabha, 1994, pp. 66–84).

Beloved (1987)

Deleuze and Guattari: Materialist psychiatry

Bhabha emphasizes the role of language, rather than that of violent geographical and economic appropriation, at the site of colonial relations. The work of Deleuze and Guattari is again useful for examining both the operations of colonial discourse *and* the geo-politics of domination. Their materialist psychiatry provides a means to examine Morrison's work as a form of oppositional resistance to 'American Africanism' in its re-appropriations of the 'shadow', the 'ghost in the machine' of American literature. Against traditional psychoanalysis, Deleuze and Guattari reject desire as originating in a lack created as the subject enters the symbolic order and represses desire for the mother. Instead, desire, or what they call the *desiring machine*, is always socially produced.

> Lack is created, planned, and organised in and through social production . . . The deliberate creation of lack as a function of market economy is the art of a dominant class. This involves deliberately organising wants and needs amid an abundance of production; making all of desire teeter and fall victim to the great fear of not having one's needs satisfied; and making the object dependent upon a real production that is supposedly exterior to desire (the demands of rationality), while at the same time production of desire is categorized as fantasy and nothing but fantasy. (Deleuze and Guattari, 1972, p. 28)

For Deleuze and Guattari the classical concept of desire as rooted in lack is a capitalist construct, articulated through the mechanism of the Oedipus complex. Here, repression becomes 'massive social repression' and desire is always *group fantasy*. Robert Young has connected these ideas with colonial discourse in general, and racism in particular, as an example of group fantasy (Young, 1995, pp. 166–74). The Oedipus complex serves capitalism by attributing the origin of neurosis to the family triad of mummy-daddy-me and functions as one more means by which to police the world. Desire, for Deleuze and Guattari, is *a flow* 'that exists before the opposition between subject and object, before representation and production'. Desiring machines, or the interconnected flow of energies, 'do not recognize distinctions between persons, organs, material flows, and semiotic flows' (Guattari intv. with Stambolian and Marks, 1979, p. 57). Hence, the distinction between materiality and consciousness is broken down, made possible by their concept of the *body without organs*. By this they mean everything – the social body, capital, desire and the earth itself – that has not yet been codified into separate units. This is not a simple process by which capitalism controls desire. Whereas the *socius* (their term for society or community), as a body *with* organs, functions to codify the flows of desire, capitalism must first destroy (deterritorialize) existing cultures and institutions (socius) 'in order to make it a body without organs and unleash the flows of desire on this body as a deterritorialized field'. This functions to extract surplus value from the labour of the now deterritorialized worker. Capitalism then reterritorializes by creating 'residual and artificial, or symbolic territorialities' such as the state, the family, religion and education (Deleuze and Guattari, 1972, pp. 33–4). As Young points out, these ideas can assist an understanding of colonial relations that takes account of discursive, ideological operations as well as the physical, geographical and economic apparatus imposed, usually with violence, by capitalism (Young, 1995, pp. 166–74).

As we have seen, the notion of the Oedipalized subject assists the reterritorializing proclivities of capitalism by situating neurosis exclusively at the level of the family. This is inadequate for analysis at the scene of colonial struggle where the Oedipal triangle is 'exploded', open, and its members grappling with outside agents – the 'missionary', the 'tax collector', the 'white man'. 'Extreme situations of war trauma, of colonization, of dire poverty, and so on, are unfavorable to the construction of the Oedipal apparatus' (Deleuze and Guattari, 1972, p. 96).[5]

Instead of distorting desire by the imposition of an Oedipal complex, Deleuze and Guattari want to liberate it through a schizoanalysis that constructs an unconscious where desire is fluid, unrestrained and able to break through systems of territorialization. Literature has the potential for positive forms of

---

[5] In this context Deleuze and Guattari cite the work of Frantz Fanon who was very aware, when treating psychosis in the colonial subject, of the effects of the violence of deculturation and acculturation.

deterritorialization, especially when released from an Oedipalized analysis that is inadequate in its 'reduction of literature to an object of consumption conforming to the established order, and incapable of causing anyone harm'. Although such a reading concedes that 'a little neurosis is good for the work of art', it fails to recognize the radical potential of a schizoanalytic reading because it treats literature 'As if the great voices which were capable of performing a breakthrough in grammar and syntax, and of making all language a desire, were not speaking from the depths of psychosis, and as if they were not demonstrating for our benefit an eminently psychotic and revolutionary means of escape' (Deleuze, 1972, pp. 133–4). Elizabeth Wright notes how, for Deleuze and Guattari, writing 'is like schizophrenia' as literature offers potential to break open an imposed Oedipal system. She continues: 'But the author cannot do it without some help. So now yet another type of reader is required, the desire liberating reader, the schizoanalyst, whose task it is to convert the text into a desiring-machine, or better still, into a revolutionary machine' (Wright, 1987, p. 165). This implies a politicized, Bakhtinian dialogical relationship between reader and text that bestows responsibility upon the reader of a 'minor' writer to disengage from the ideological assumptions of Oedipalized literary criticism. In *Beloved* Morrison extends this relationship to new limits in a narrative that necessitates the reader's participation in its construction. Although set in 1873, the pivotal event of *Beloved* – Sethe's infanticide 18 years earlier, shortly after escaping from slavery – is not fully revealed until half way through the novel and from the perspective of the white slave master, a narrative device demanding the reader's contribution to the history unfolding in each character's 'rememory' and storytelling. Morrison has said how her 'clean' and 'lean' technique requires a 'complex and rich response from the reader'.

> They always say that my writing is rich. It's not – what's rich, if there is any richness, is what the reader gets and brings him or herself. That's part of the way in which the tale is told. The folk tales are told in such a way that whoever is listening is in it and can shape it and figure it out. It's not over just because it stops. It lingers and it's passed on. It's passed on and somebody else can alter it later. You can even end it if you want'. (Morrison intv. with Darling, 1994, p. 253)

Beloved, *Jazz* and *Paradise* fulfil Deleuze and Guattari's criteria for minor literature as the expression of a collective consciousness that can embrace the unconscious past as a never-ending story to be communally told. Slavery, like the folk tale, is 'not over just because it stops' but a story to be passed on in imaginative reconstruction, reclamation and retelling to contest the determinism of history. The teller/listener has the agency to end the story and so, in effect, end the psychological damage of slavery.

The release of desire

The ambiguous conclusions of *Song of Solomon* and *Tar Baby* force a participatory response from the reader, but the ending of *Beloved*, 'This is not a story to pass on' (*B*, p. 275), requires politicized engagement with the dialectic of liberation or repression that it offers. The repression engendered by capitalism's reterritorialization is forced asunder through the breaking of the codes of language. Elizabeth Wright summarizes this aspect of schizoanalysis: 'The work of the unconscious endeavours to ensure that the fantasy of subjugation (the ideology that has kept desire under constraint) is transformed into one of revolutionary potential for a "subject group" (the power to liberate those so oppressed)' (Wright, 1987, p. 166). Works of art deemed minor literature contain, in a complex dialectic analogous to Bakhtin's dialogism, articulations of subjugation and repression and the means for breaking out of repression through the expression of desire. 'This is not a story to pass on' encapsulates this dialectic in its implication that the traumatic events Morrison describes in *Beloved* can be *passed* on – that is, ignored/repressed, or passed *on* and transmitted as part of the healing and liberation of racial unconsciousness. Thus, Morrison engages closely with the working of the unconscious at a collective, historical level. The psychosis brought to bear on the present by the past must be confronted, and made real, through the bodily manifestation of the ghost and, although it should not consume or debilitate the present or the future, as it almost does at the end of *Beloved*, it should never be repressed because it enables the liberation of desire and the awakening of feeling. Freedom is not to be found in the legal documentation of freedom papers or the flight north, but in the realization of repressed desire and psychological reclamation. As Sethe says, 'Freeing yourself was one thing; claiming ownership of that freed self was another' (*B*, p. 95). This finds echo in Frederick Douglass's *Narrative* (1845) and his use of the chiastic phrase 'You have seen how a man was made a slave; you shall see how a slave was made a man.' (Douglass, 1845, p. 533). Douglass's struggle for manhood is a philosophical one expressed in very physical terms, a bodily test of strength against Covey the slave-breaker in which psychological conflict is latent, rather than explicit. Morrison's neo-slave narrative, however, reclaims the psychology of the master/slave dialectic for a modern, post Civil Rights America where everyone is now free before the law. Through the figure of Beloved, Morrison appropriates the past and unleashing, rather than repressing, desire as part of a project to claim ownership of the self. To despatch the repressed to whence it came is to return to a state of subjugation, to accept a position within an Oedipal apparatus constructed by capitalism as a form of social and ideological control. Beloved's touch is 'loaded with desire' (*B*, p. 58) and her arrival propels the numb, traumatized inhabitants of number 124 into a world of feeling. Sethe, for example, comes to appreciate colour and the power of storytelling and in their sexual union Beloved escorts Paul D 'To some ocean-deep place he once belonged to' (*B*, p. 264).[6]

For Morrison, the repression of slavery is 'fruitless' and her return to history is marked by an understanding of an American national psyche

> where the past is always erased and America is the innocent future in which immigrants can come and start over, where the slate is clean. The past is absent or it's romanticized. This culture doesn't encourage dwelling on, let alone coming to terms with, the truth about the past. That memory is much more in danger now than it was thirty years ago. (Morrison intv. with Gilroy, 1993a, p. 179)

By the late 1980s, African Americans risked being subsumed within America's language of forgetting by refusing to confront their past as commodities in America's purest form of deterritorialized racial capitalism, slavery. To repress this past may have once been necessary for the reconstruction of 'certain kinds of stability', but in the 1980s African Americans, without the leadership of Martin Luther King and Malcolm X, needed to re-inhabit the past to avoid reterritorialization by Reaganomics and new waves of consumer capitalism, either as the rural poor and the dispossessed of the urban ghetto or, as Morrison puts it, the 'I have made it people', complicit in their own subjugation through their assumption of values that may imply choice and freedom but which once, in their deterritorialized form, served to exploit and dehumanize.

Beloved: A communally authored text

Morrison bears witness to such a past not to enshrine or memorialize, but to create something 'usable' from the 'unusable' with, and for, the community (Levy, 1991,

---

[6] See David Lawrence's 'Fleshly Ghosts and Ghostly Flesh: The Word and the Body in *Beloved*', for an analysis of Beloved's exorcism and her function as a catalyst for the release of desire. 'The exorcism of Beloved, an embodiment of resurgent desire, opens the way to a rewording of the codes that have enforced the silencing of the body's story, making possible a remembering of the cultural heritage that has haunted the characters so destructively' (Lawrence, 2000, p. 232).

p. 179). Like Baby Suggs's preaching in *Beloved*, Morrison's narrative technique, eschewing control and authority, devolves this responsibility to the reader, or in Baby Suggs's case, those who gather to hear her. Baby Suggs's alternative, non-prescriptive and non-authoritarian form of worship, like Reverend Misner's in *Paradise*, does not 'tell them to clean up their lives or to go and sin no more. She did not tell them they were the blessed of the earth, its inheriting meek or its glorybound pure.' Instead she tells them 'that the only grace they could have was the grace they could imagine. That if they could not see it, they would not have it' (*B*, p. 88). Baby Suggs's call for her congregation to imagine their liberated selves reflects Morrison's narrative that also, in withholding the unspeakable, requires the reader to imagine a communal narrative that can be either ignored or passed on in an act of liberation or grace.

In his discussion of *Beloved,* Andrew Levy problematizes Morrison's narrative strategy:

> The fact that Morrison distances herself, however slightly, from even her own telling of *Beloved*, also suggests the depths of her understanding of the limits of narrative. It also suggests her awareness that *Beloved* is, in a sense, a sinful text: if the novel risks overstepping anything, it is Morrison's own standards for narrative, her own faith that the self-definition sought with difficulty by individuals might be found by many individuals acting in concert – the project that the multivocal but singly authored *Beloved* both fulfils and repudiates. (Levy, 1991, p. 121)

Levy's suggestion that Morrison knows the limits of narrative perhaps underestimates the extent to which the purpose of her aesthetic is to take the novel beyond convention to create an unwritten history and a community hitherto unmade. The content of *Beloved*, the experience of motherhood under the economy of slavery, is unspoken partly because of the forgivable amnesia of African Americans and the wilful forgetting of American culture. Moreover, to articulate the unspeakability of an atrocity requires a new form of narrative, one communally constructed with the reader.

As Levy says, Baby Suggs's call for the imagining of grace fails in the first instance, the community 'angry at her because she had overstepped, given too much, offended them by excess' (*B*, p. 139). They fail to warn her, and Sethe, of Schoolteacher's arrival and are thus indirectly responsible for Sethe's infanticide. Levy relates Baby Suggs's preaching to Morrison's project and suggests that she, too, is aware her novel may 'give too much, or offend by excess' (Levy, 1991, p. 121). Here Levy misses the progression implied by Morrison's aesthetic undertaking in *Beloved*. After all, the community eventually comes to Sethe's assistance under Ella's practical guidance, acting as one to dispel Beloved before her embodiment as the past consumes her mother. Ella is herself guilty of infanticide having refused to nurse the baby she conceived after being raped by her young white master and his father but, unlike Sethe, she rejects 'the idea of past errors taking possession of the present' (*B*, p. 256). Ella and the other women of the community, however, are able to assimilate the excess of Sethe's crime and Beloved's return, if only to despatch the ghost back 'to the other side' and 'stomp' out the past. Beloved's return threatens Sethe's very existence and so she must be exorcized by the community. Their repression of the past, although 'practical' and necessary for survival in 1870s America, is in psychoanalytic terms unsuccessful and, Morrison suggests, ultimately damaging for the emotional and spiritual condition of the self. In the coda to the novel we assume that Beloved, and the personal and historical trauma associated with her presence, has been forgotten as 'remembering seemed unwise' and yet the past is always present in the community's unconscious dream world, dormant but always ready to return. 'So they forgot her. Like an unpleasant dream during a troubling sleep. Occasionally, however, the rustle of a skirt hushes when they wake, and the knuckles brushing a cheek in sleep seem to belong to the sleeper' (*B*, p. 275). For the reader of the late 1980s to forget is dangerous, perhaps impossible, and the past is to be embraced, not in horrific repetitions of history, 'of past errors taking possession of the present', but in an active form of shared mourning. The ghost of Beloved should not be repudiated but assimilated in new and positive ways, including its articulation in the novel form, for the reconstruction of the future. The end of the novel, the single word 'Beloved', implies its use in both the past tense of the funeral sermon, as in 'dearly beloved', and in the active, progressive tense of two separate words, 'be loved'.

Morrison and the slave narratives

If the past is not assimilated and spoken it will return to haunt the future. This is made clear in Morrison's lecture 'The Site of Memory' (1987) in which she refers to the slave narratives of the eighteenth and nineteenth centuries and the experience that such accounts could not address. Constrained by the possibility that their work would be considered 'inflammatory' or 'improbable', and by notions of good taste, the narrators omitted the portrayal of their interior lives (Morrison, 1987a, p. 67).

> But whatever the level of eloquence or the form, popular taste discouraged the writers from dwelling too long or too carefully on the more sordid details of their experience. Whenever there was an unusually violent incident, or a scatological one, or something 'excessive', one finds the writer taking refuge in the literary conventions of the day. . . . Over and over, the writers pull the narratives up short with a phrase such as, 'But let us drop a veil over these proceedings too terrible to relate.' In shaping the experience to make it palatable to those who were in a position to alleviate it, they were silent about many things, and they 'forgot' many other things. . . .
>
> But most importantly – at least for me – there was no mention of their interior life. (Morrison, 1987a, pp. 69–70)

Things unspoken in the eighteenth and nineteenth centuries demand articulation, a connection made between the interior psychological trauma of slavery and its external, material realities. 'For me, a writer in the last quarter of the twentieth century, not much more than a hundred years after Emancipation, a writer who is black and a woman – the exercise is very different. My job becomes how to rip that veil drawn over "proceedings too terrible to relate" (Morrison, 1987a, p. 70). The trauma of slavery not represented directly by the slave narrators only returns a century later as the repressed, repeated as individual and collective rememory. Mae Henderson reads *Beloved* as an articulation of the repressed experiences of the slave narrators. She argues that Morrison 'aims to restore a dimension of the repressed personal in a manifestly political discourse. In some ways, the texts of the slave narratives can be regarded as classic examples of the "return of the repressed," primarily because the events relating to violence and violation (which are self-censored or edited out) return again and again in "veiled allusions"' (Henderson, 1991, p. 63).

Memory and the sublime

The ghost Beloved is more than the embodiment of Sethe's murdered daughter. Her memory extends backwards beyond her birth in Kentucky to the slave hold of the Middle Passage, a figure for the eruption of repressed, collective memory and one of the 'Sixty Million and more' of Morrison's dedication. The violence of this eruption is contained in the first two sentences of the novel, '124 was spiteful. Full of a baby's venom' (*B*, p. 3), the reader forced into a traumatic space – not, this time, the hold of the slave ship, but a house in which the original trauma is repeated. Without warning, we are thrown into confusion and propelled, even if subliminally, back to the slave hold, the structure of the original trauma repeating as memory and operating without the need for Morrison to delineate actual events of the Middle Passage.[7] In effect, she is addressing the question of the un-representable and of how the terror of the Middle Passage may be received in the imagination of the reader. As we have seen, Levy has identified the risk of using a narrative strategy so dependent upon the engagement of the reader, a risk that lies in Morrison's articulation of terror and its aesthetic representation as the sublime. Following Edmund Burke, Jean-François Lyotard defines this aspect of the sublime as the pleasure to be taken from pain suspended, 'kept at bay, held back' (Lyotard, 1984, p. 204).[8] To reproduce the sublime, art, by distancing menace, must intensify feeling, agitate the soul into a return to that state somewhere between life and death, otherwise the soul is dead (Lyotard, 1984, p. 205). In *Beloved*, the house at 124 is this 'agitated zone', in which Sethe, concerned with 'keeping the past at bay' (*B*, p. 42), resists the un-representable past she cannot yet confront. Morrison, in producing the sublime, complicates aesthetic judgement through the inversion of beauty and terror; the scars on Sethe's back assume the shape of a chokecherry tree (*B*, p. 17) and Sweet Home, the site of torture and psychological annihilation, is remembered as a 'pretty place' (*B*, p. 6).[9] The reader, in Lyotard's conceptualization of the sublime, is alone in judging a text to which conventional aesthetic standards cannot be applied.

> With the idea of the sublime, the feeling when faced with a work of art is no longer the feeling of pleasure, or not simply one of pleasure. It is a contradictory feeling, because it is a feeling of both pleasure and displeasure, together . . . With the sublime, there is no criterion for assessing the role of taste, and so everybody is alone when it comes to judging. The question then becomes: how can we share with others a feeling which is so deep and unexchangeable? (Lyotard, 1989, p. 22)

---

[7] In Morrison's own analysis of the opening sentences of *Beloved* she writes: 'The reader is snatched, yanked, thrown into an environment completely foreign, and I want it as the first stroke of the shared experience that might be possible between the reader and the novel's population. Snatched just as the slaves were from one place to another, from any place to another, without preparation and without defense' (Morrison, 1989, p. 228).

[8] For Lyotard, in Burke's lexicon 'Terrors are linked to privation: privation of light, terror of darkness; privation of other, terror of solitude; privation of language, terror of silence; privation of objects, terror of emptiness; privation of life, terror of death. What is terrifying is that the *It happens that* does not happen, that it stops happening.

Burke wrote that for this terror to mingle with pleasure and with it to produce the feeling of the sublime, it is also necessary that the terror-causing threat be suspended, kept at bay, held back. This suspense, this lessening of a threat or a danger, provokes a kind of pleasure that is certainly not that of positive satisfaction, but is, rather that of relief. This is still privation, but is privation at one remove' (Lyotard's italics, 1984, p. 204).

[9] For a discussion of *Beloved* in relation to Kant's conceptualization of the sublime, see Barbara Freeman, *The Feminine Sublime: Gender and Excess in Women's Fiction* (Freeman, 1995, pp. 105–48).

As we have seen, in a non-prescriptive and communally authored text concerned to represent the un-representable, Morrison's answer as to how trauma may be shared is for the community to call upon their own grace and take hold of their freedom. Morrison, as a writer and, Lyotard would claim, a philosopher, enters the realm of the postmodern in that she does not 'supply reality but invents allusions to the conceivable which cannot be presented' (Lyotard, 1982, p. 81). Non-realist, experimental acts of imaginative reconstruction as a strategy for survival are a response to the postmodern dissolution of the self-engendered originally by slavery.[10]

The postmodern, time and repetition

The dialogues of postmodernism and the theoretical language in which they are often expressed are attractive and promote what Marshall Berman describes as the 'mystique of postmodernism, which strives to cultivate ignorance of modern history and culture' (Berman, 1983, p. 33). Morrison's conception of the postmodern is, however, a deeply historical one onto which she maps notions of race, culture and gender to problematize postmodern discourse itself and, as in Peter Nicholls' 'alternative' understanding of postmodernism, disrupt the linearity of history and project the margin into the centre (Nicholls, 1996, p. 52).[11] In Nicholls's psychoanalytical reading of *Beloved*, which takes into account the historicity of postmodernism, the concept of the return of the repressed assumes a complexity that elucidates Morrison's engagement with history, time, memory and mourning.[12] The risk with any reading of *Beloved* as the return of the repressed is 'that we begin to think of the repressed as

---

[10] Toni Morrison believes that black people, and more specifically black women, have been negotiating the postmodern condition since slavery. Postmodernism has its origins in the modernity project and slavery was central to that project (Morrison intv. with Gilroy, 1993a, p. 178). See also Gilroy's *The Black Atlantic* and Homi K. Bhabha's recognition of an eighteenth and nineteenth-century 'colonial contra-modernity' that 'anticipated, *avant la lettre*, many of the problematics of signification in contemporary theory – aporia, ambivalence, indeterminacy, the question of discursive closure, the threat to agency, the status of intentionality, the challenge to totalizing concepts to name but a few' (Bhabha, 1994, p. 173).

[11] Referring to Lyotard, Nicholls argues in 'The Belated Postmodern: History, Phantoms, and Toni Morrison', that the modern and the postmodern coexist, 'inhabiting the same conceptual and historical space, and producing a tension which rends History from within' (Nicholls, 1996, p. 52). In *Postmodern Literature* Ian Gregson writes: 'Morrison is routinely discussed as a postmodernist writer, and it is true that she deploys a number of postmodernist narrative strategies and engages with characteristically postmodernist philosophical, and especially ontological, questions. Yet her preoccupation with African-American history challenges a number of key postmodernist tenets. Far from confirming the loss of the historical referent, Morrison's novels are determined acts of imaginative retrieval' (Gregson, 2004, p. 88).

[12] Nicholls adopts Jacques Derrida's distinction between 'history', which in Derrida's words is the 'unfolding of presence', and 'historicity', which Nicholls summarizes as 'the movement of temporal difference' (Nicholls, 1996, p. 55).

simply a lost fact or datum, a link which once restored will return us to a form of historical continuity' (Nicholls, 1996, p. 58). Nicholls invokes postmodern theory in conjunction with the concept of *Nachträglichkeit* (belatedness), developed by Freud in the Wolf Man (1914) case study for his analysis of trauma. Memory is not necessarily the recurrence of the past as it was, but rather the effect of the repetition of a structure; the trauma of an event is such that it only becomes present after the fact, and even then as reconstructed memory, not as direct experience. Thus, the trauma of an event can never be said to be present; the past is always present, but never in its original form, and cannot be clearly articulated in memory. The past, therefore, disrupts linear time as it erupts into the present and compels the traumatized subject to be inhabited by the past. This disruption is reflected in the narrative structure of *Beloved* as Morrison represents the un-representable and, as Nicholls says, evokes 'the traumatic force of a historicity which splits the subject, compelling it to live in different times rather than in a secure, metaphysical present' (Nicholls, 1996, p. 58).

In this sense, Morrison's understanding of history is synchronic rather than diachronic; through the figure of Beloved and Sethe's rememories, Morrison merges the past and the present in opposition to memorializing historical accounts that merely record events as serial moments to be concluded and forgotten. It is a 'psychic history' that recognizes, in accord with Freud, that the unconscious has no temporality (Bhabha, 1994, p. 11).[13] Freud writes: 'The processes of the system *Ucs.* [unconscious] are *timeless*; i.e. they are not ordered temporally, are not altered by the passage of time; they have no reference to time at all' (Freud, 1914–16, p. 187). Consumed by the past, Sethe can no longer believe in time itself, clock time being meaningless to her: 'I was talking about time. It's so hard for me to believe in it' (*B*, p. 35). Illiterate, unable to 'read clock time very well' (*B*, p. 189), Sethe is disassociated from western temporality, slavery disrupting her ability to conceive of, and exist in, linear and progressive time.

Sethe is effectively trapped in repetition, a pattern that is psychologically debilitating, even life threatening, as she attempts, at the end of *Beloved*, to repeat the act of murder in an effort to save her daughter from the community's exorcism. If, as Morrison suggests, the release of desire repressed by slavery is important, it is also crucial that the return of such desire does not take the form of 'past errors taking possession of the present' (*B*, p. 256). In other

---

[13] Bhabbha, in *The Location of Culture*, describes *Beloved* as a 'psychic history'. 'Beloved, the child murdered by her own mother, Sethe, is a daemonic, belated repetition of the violent history of black infant deaths, during slavery' (Bhabha, 1994, p. 11).

words, *Beloved* obliquely engages in debates about beneficial and detrimental forms of repetition. At the wider level of the repetitions of history, Morrison understands history as cyclical, as occurring more than once, as Marx wrote in *The Eighteenth Brumaire of Louis Bonaparte* (1852), first as tragedy and again as farce. History here is overdetermined: 'Men make their own history, but they do not make it just as they please; they do not make it under circumstances chosen by themselves, but under circumstances directly encountered, given and transmitted from the past. The tradition of all the dead generations weighs like a nightmare on the brain of the living' (Marx, 1852, p. 10). Marx's evocation of the past working on the unconscious dream world of present generations, compelling them to destructive repetition is perhaps the source of postmodern understandings of history. History is no longer fated to occur twice but is in fact re-enacted in endless, atemporal repetition. The intersection of postmodernism and psychoanalysis suggests ways to escape repetition. The repetition of trauma is debilitating but, paradoxically, repetition or 'working through' and sublimation, also enables the release of the traumatized subject.[14] Through the retrieval and reconstruction of history Morrison breaks its determinism, not through the repression of trauma, but through the creation of a community engaged in collective memory as crucial for the reclamation of the self. Creative narration of the past can indeed change that past, which is in fact never present in its original form and only has life as psychological recollection; and, of course, if the past can be changed so can its effect on the future.

Motherhood and identity

Morrison's epistemology deconstructs and reconstructs African-American experience in order to delineate unrecorded histories. Her alternative narrative affirms the humanity of African Americans under slavery in opposition to the racist rhetoric of nineteenth-century science. This is figured mainly through Sethe's experience as both a slave and a mother; her infanticide is in fact a choice made to spite the classifications of science. She kills her child because 'nobody on this earth, would list her daughter's characteristics on the animal

---

[14] See Robert Young's examination of history and psychoanalysis in *Torn Halves: Political Conflict in Literary and Cultural Theory*. Young addresses the question: 'Does psychoanalysis challenge linear and progressive narratives of history?' and concludes, 'as long as there are good and bad forms of repetition, then history can still be coerced and transformed: we do not have to resign ourselves to inevitability, to the assumption that any particular bad repetition will always go on repeating. We need to recognize that, as psychoanalysis intimates, history works in a complex dialectic of linear movements and repetition' (Young, 1996, pp. 145–7).

side of the paper' (*B*, p. 251). *Beloved* is a powerful narrative of motherhood exploring the loss of self engendered by maternity within the context of a system in which people, including babies, are stock and motherhood merely the means to the accumulation of property. By the economic rationale of slavery, Sethe's infanticide is nothing more than the destruction of private property; for Sethe, it means killing the one good thing, the best of herself, her identity split between womanhood and motherhood. Julia Kristeva, in 'Women's Time', refers to the 'radical ordeal' (Kristeva, 1979, p. 206) of the splitting of the subject that is pregnancy and motherhood, and in an attempt to construct a post-Virginal, secular discourse of maternity she writes in 'Stabat Mater':

> My body is no longer mine, it doubles up, suffers, bleeds, catches cold, puts its teeth in, slobbers, coughs, is covered with pimples, and it laughs. And yet, when its own joy, my child's, returns, its smile washes only my eyes. But the pain, its pain – it comes from inside, never remains apart, other, it inflames me at once, without a second's respite. As if that was what I had given birth to and, not willing to part from me, insisted on coming back, dwelled in me permanently. One does not give birth in pain, one gives birth to pain: . . . a mother is always branded by pain. . . . (Kristeva, 1977, p. 167)

Kristeva's concern with the psychological dimensions of motherhood resonates clearly with Sethe's maternal experience. Beloved inhabits Sethe as the pain that cannot be dispelled and, further, Kristeva's account mirrors the splitting of the self experienced by Sethe who, in recounting her maternal feelings to her daughter, remarks: 'You asleep on my back. Denver sleep in my stomach. Felt like I was split in two' (*B*, p. 202). Yet she and Beloved also fantasize their shared totality, 'I am Beloved and she is mine' (*B*, p. 214). In this triad of Sethe, Beloved and Denver, 'us three', the 'hand holding shadows', identities of mother, daughter and sister intersect and, in poetic passages, the women speak in a communal semiotic space, 'in between', claiming and naming each other (*B*, pp. 215–17). Sethe asserts her humanity through motherhood, the bond between mother and child powerful enough to override the economic and social relations of the slave system. The connection between mother and child is essentially a relationship that exists in a semiotic zone, one that, for Kristeva, places motherhood into the contestatory realm of poetry. 'Let us call 'maternal' the ambivalent principle that is bound to the species, on the one hand, and on the other stems from an identity catastrophe that cause the Name to topple over into the unnameable that one imagines as femininity, non-language or body' (Kristeva, 1977, pp. 161–2).

The poetic language used to convey each character's claiming and naming of others is appropriate for articulating the mother/daughter dyad. In these passages, however, Morrison alludes to the un-representable that transcends the mother/child relationship as characters move backwards into history and remember, and indeed become, the dead pushed into the sea in an evocation of the passage from Africa to America. Although true that, in Kristeva's terms, Beloved takes possession of her mother as the pain that never leaves, it is clear Sethe's pain is the deeper pain of history. Sethe, and her mother before her, are not branded metaphorically but physically, like animals, as commodities to be owned, enumerated and exploited.

As an alternative Marian discourse, Kristeva's analysis is open to the charge of placing the maternal body before culture and its construction and of building a universal and naturalistic version of motherhood from her own, very personal, experience. In her critique of Kristeva, Judith Butler claims that: 'Her naturalistic descriptions of the maternal body effectively reify motherhood and preclude an analysis of its cultural construction and variability' (Butler, 1990, p. 80).[15] Butler also questions Kristeva's claims for the subversive qualities of poetic language as expressive of the recovery of the maternal body. In Kristeva's schema, poetic language disrupts the Symbolic, paternal law, but as Butler points out this relies, first, upon the assumption of a unitary and stable paternal law and, secondly, if poetic language is taken to exist in relation to this law, its subversive function nonetheless remains secondary to it. Moreover, it is a temporary and unsustainable condition, the subject inevitably returning to the language of the Symbolic in order to avoid the psychosis that poetic language ultimately engenders (Butler, 1990, p. 80). Butler identifies in Kristeva the tension that also ends *Beloved*; to repress the past or to exist with it in an atemporal and chaotic state. This returns us to the problem of good and bad forms of repetition and to the question of whether, in Deleuzian terms, the flow of desire should be in permanent release as the subversion of Oedipalized constructions, whether the past should be passed *on* or *passed* on, remembered or forgotten.

Beloved's possession of her mother is a detrimental form of repetition and, although repressed desire needs to find expression, it must return in affirming ways to enable the construction of the future. Denver realizes and comes to terms with this and she comes to embody possibilities for the future. She wants to know her

---

[15] Helen Carr in 'Motherhood and Apple Pie' recognizes that maternal feeling is 'historically constructed' and argues that feminist discourses of motherhood must rethink 'the Western based assumptions into which so much "old" as well as "new" feminist thinking was and is locked' (Carr, 1998, p. 287).

past and, having assimilated this past, reinvents herself in the world beyond the house at number 124 in order to ensure her family's survival. In 'Women's Time', Kristeva discusses second-generation feminists interested in female psychology and its symbolic realization and concerned to establish women's discourse that gives voice to 'the intrasubjective and corporeal experiences left mute by culture in the past' (Kristeva, 1979, p. 194). 'Reproduction', 'life and death', 'the body', sex and symbol are heard as feminists assert their position outside linear time. It is in artistic creation, and especially literature, that Kristeva finds the scope for women to affirm themselves through a playful subversion of the Symbolic Order, 'a space of fantasy and pleasure, out of the abstract and frustrating order of social signs'. Kristeva wants to 'nourish our societies with a more flexible and free discourse, one able to name what has thus far never been an object of circulation in the community: the enigmas of the body, the dreams, secret joys, shames, hatreds of the second sex' (Kristeva, 1979, p. 207). The task facing feminists is to engage in literary creation and criticism that combines 'Women's', or 'maternal' time with linear, or historical and political, time. Morrison achieves this by combining imaginary poetic creativity with historical facts about slavery, making passing reference to certain legislature and topical issues of the time, 'the Fugitive Bill, the Settlement Fee, God's Ways and Negro pews' (*B*, p. 173). These establish exactly where we are in 'real' historical and political time. A chronology is thus established, albeit one temporally disrupted as it takes its poetic, aesthetic and psychological form. Denver joins linear time having assimilated maternal, women's time, recognizes the repetition of the Sethe/Beloved dyad and is aware of the destructive possibilities of mother love. Denver breaks away from her mother, proving that she is 'Her father's daughter' (*B*, p. 252). She 'step[s] off the edge of the world' (*B*, p. 243), resumes her education and finds employment, thus joining the order of social signs to survive and support her mother and sister. Until she does this, Denver risks losing herself in the repetitions of the past, her autonomy threatened by her mother and the weight of history.

In the context of 1870s post-bellum America such a response is a necessary act of survival and represents a radical form of self re-invention under the historical conditions of slavery. Sethe, too, learns of the possibilities the future may hold as she is led to the realization that identity as a woman is separate from that as a mother; she becomes, as Paul D says, her own 'best thing' (*B*, p. 273). The imagining of 'some kind of tomorrow' (*B*, p. 273) is, however, constructed upon an engagement with the past and an acknowledgment of its place in the present and the future. Sethe's renewed relationship with Paul D is based on his need to 'put his story next to' (*B*, p. 273) hers, a life together in which they will share, through storytelling, a narrative of the past. As in the narrative of *Beloved*, which insists on possibilities for spiritual freedom through the imaginative and communal retelling of slavery, Sethe can gather 'the pieces' of Paul D's identity, and return them 'in all the right order' (*B*, pp. 272–3) in a shared story that can overcome the determinism and repetitions of history.

Jazz (1992)

The concern to effect change through a communally constructed history is extended in *Jazz* as Morrison offers an explicit invitation to participate in its narration through the use of a structural device which, like jazz itself, requires a creative response from the audience. Jazz achieves the same illusion of effortless creation that Morrison wants to bring to her writing, but as she points out, 'The power of the word is not music', jazz being for her 'the mirror that gives me the necessary clarity' as a recorded, aural working through of African-American experience and memory (Morrison intv. with Gilroy, 1993a, p. 181).[16] To map Morrison's aesthetic against the technical properties of jazz music, as critics have done, is to isolate the form and style of her texts from the historical and political intent of her project.[17] Jazz is often taken as both an authentic standard against which the 'blackness' of a literary text must be measured and as a homogeneous entity without development.[18] Morrison draws upon music in the same way she draws upon the work of her literary precursors, in a spirit of evocation and

---

[16] For a discussion of the illusion of effortlessness in jazz music and an examination of the cultural, social and political complexities of jazz performance see, Ingrid Monson, 'Doubleness and Jazz Improvisation: Irony, Parody, and Ethnomusicology'. Monson views jazz improvisation as a conscious 'mode of social action that musicians selectively employ in their process of communicating' (Monson, 1994, p. 285).

[17] See for example, Alan J. Rice, 'Jazzing It up a Storm: The Execution and Meaning of Toni Morrison's Jazzy Prose Style.' Rice makes an illuminating point in relation to the influence of jazz on the structure of Morrison's novels when he refers to the non-linear, circuitous constructions of both her novels and jazz music. (Rice, 1994, p. 424). Less convincing, however, are Rice's attempts to interpret individual passages from Morrison's work as 'stylistic' duplications of jazz's 'riffs' and 'repetitions' (Rice, 1994, pp. 426–32). Eusebio L. Rodrigues in 'Experiencing Jazz' reads *Jazz* as a 'musical score' and like Rice focuses on what he perceives to be Morrison's formal use of jazz through a close reading of particular passages (Rodrigues, 1997, pp. 245–66). I wish to argue that Morrison's deployment of repetition is thematic and related to the development of African-American history rather than emphasize any stylistic use of a jazz mode.

[18] In his critique of commentators such as Rice and Rodrigues, 'Misreading Morrison, Mishearing Jazz: A Response to Toni Morrison's Jazz Critics', Alan Munton questions the accuracy of their understanding of the complexity and history of the 'riff' or 'repetition' and concludes that it 'would be very difficult matter indeed to establish a relationship between jazz and prose fiction on the essential similarity between the riff and instances of repetition in prose' (Munton, 1997, p. 241). For Munton, a 'jazzy prose style' cannot be said to exist and attempts to identify one reveal the workings of 'an ideology of authenticity' (Munton, 1997, p. 235).

intertextuality rather than in formal duplication. Her evocations of the rhythms and repetitions of jazz are constructed, I shall argue, as thematic devices for the exploration of trauma, memory and history.

The repetition of history

Jazz, as the second part of Morrison's trilogy, outlines a later, migratory history of African Americans living in 1920s Harlem and the un-gendered narrative voice, or simply the 'voice' as she prefers to call it, at first evokes a modernist confidence in the possibilities the City offers for the invention of self and identity.[19] In Harlem, the voice claims, 'The way everybody was then and there' has ended and 'History is over, you all, and everything's ahead at last' (*J*, p. 7). It becomes evident, however, that such optimism is unfounded as the reader, together with the intimate narrative voice, learns of the unresolved trauma of Joe and Violet's past lives. The voice's triumphant description of the City landscape and the end of history is in fact premature and belies the darker truth of how Joe and Violet inhabit pasts that limit their ability to either live in the present or imagine a future.

The narrative voice also proves to be unreliable in its depiction of the triangular relationship at the centre of *Jazz*. Joe has shot his young lover, Dorcas and his wife Violet has assaulted the young girl's body as it lies in the funeral coffin. The voice predicts the duplication of this tragedy in the 'scandalizing threesome' of Joe, Violet and Dorcas's friend Felice, claiming that the only difference will lie in 'who shot whom' (*J*, p. 6). The voice is, however, deluded in assuming that Joe's shooting of Dorcas, and Violet's attack on her corpse, are the defining traumas of their story. This urban tragedy indeed unfolds as a figure for the pattern of repetitions unique to the disassociation of the self brought by urban migration and which keeps Harlem 'bound to the track', caught in the repetitions of the City's rhythms which pull Joe 'like a needle through the groove of a Bluebird record' (*J*, p. 120); and yet it also serves to obscure the deeper, unresolved traumas originating in slavery.

Dorcas, Joe and Violet's tragedy is the repetition of history erupting, to reiterate Nicholls's point, as a 'traumatic force of a historicity which splits the subject'. Violet's identity is split partly because of the unresolved traumas of her childhood in the post Reconstruction South, the family abandoned by her father

---

[19] Morrison points out that she consciously created a narrator 'without sex, gender or age' (Morrison intv. with Carabi, 1995, p. 42 cited in Matus, 1998, f.n.2, p. 185).

and her mother, Rose Dear, commits suicide to escape dispossession and racial violence. Having internalized ideologies of whiteness, represented by Golden Gray, Violet is temporally and psychologically fractured. Joe's identity splits as he reinvents himself in efforts to find his place in post First World War America, a period of race riots as African-American anticipations of new equalities dissipated. Joe feels he has 'changed once too often', that he has 'been a new Negro all [his] life' (*J*, p. 129). Morrison, like Ralph Ellison, reveals the inventive improvisations of African Americans in the face of change determined from without, and yet exposes the psychological impact of constant re-invention.[20] Abandoned by his mother Wild, Joe, like Violet, is yet another motherless child of Morrison's fiction, orphaned by history and beyond the Oedipal triad. Hunters Hunter, Golden Gray's black father, believes Wild's rejection of Joe is really the effect of her hunger for Golden Gray, for his 'yellow hair' (*J*, p. 167).

Joe and Violet's separate pasts, then, merge to form a single history that is mapped out against the figure of Golden Gray. As with Pecola in *The Bluest Eye*, beauty is denied, their identity subsumed by the whiteness embodied in Gray's golden hair. Morrison signifies here on Faulkner's preoccupation with the doomed mulatto, locked in tragic racial destiny and the genealogical convolutions of the South. In an inverted Southern narrative, Morrison figures Golden Gray as the whiteness touching the lives of both Joe and Violet, and as the body upon which, in projecting their own neuroses, they lose something beautiful in themselves. Until Joe and Violet confront the legacy of slavery, all relations remain distorted and the flows of desire displaced. All love is invested, but lost, in the golden boy; Joe hunts the City for Dorcas but he is really looking for 'Wild's chamber of Gold', the mother love he lost to Golden Gray (*J*, p. 221) and Violet is looking for the 'golden boy' in Joe (*J*, p. 97). In *Jazz*, Morrison refigures Beloved, slavery's ghost, as Dorcas within a female genealogy that extends to Joe's mother Wild. Dorcas and Wild are quarry, eruptions of the past hunted by Joe in the City and the South. They are repositories for, and bear witness to, an original trauma now finding repetition in the Harlem of the 1920s, history a record repeating at the scratch in the groove until confronted and set free to reinvent the rhythms of the City. The inevitability of history is challenged as the voice in *Jazz* relinquishes omniscience and concedes agency to the characters beyond the repetitions of its own narrative. Joe and Violet do repeat past traumas; Joe shoots Dorcas and

---

[20] African-American creativity and inventiveness is exemplified, for Ellison, in jazz musicians: 'that joint creation of artistically free and exuberantly creative adventurers, of artists who had stumbled upon the freedom lying within the restrictions of their musical tradition as within the limitations of their social background' (Ellison, 1964, p. xiii).

Violet stabs her corpse, but they do not repeat the tragedy in their relationship with Felice and there is no repetition of violence.

History, in the specific sense of a Harlem love triangle and in the wider context of slavery, need not be 'an abused record with no choice but to repeat itself at the crack' (*J*, p. 220). African Americans can, once the past has been 'figure[d] in' and 'figure[d] out' (*J*, p. 228), 'lift the arm that holds the needle' and change the record (*J*, p. 220). The novel recreates history as the recurrence of trauma, and yet Morrison's sensibility allows for improvisation on the repetitions of the racial past as a means to disrupt the sequence and determinism of history. The narrative voice is that of the jazz soloist employing the 'cut' to temporarily break away from the original musical phrase in a flight of playful improvisation and transcendence that nonetheless retains the trace of, and always returns to, a central motif.[21] The central motif for Morrison is, of course, the original trauma of slavery, the source to which, as Ralph Ellison claims, African-American musical expression constantly returns in an impulse to 'keep the painful details and episodes of a brutal experience alive in one's aching consciousness, to finger its jagged grain, and to transcend it' (Ellison, 1964, p. 78).

Jazz music as a motif for repetition

Morrison's embellishment of this central experience is reflected in the structure of *Jazz* as the essence of the story is revealed in the opening paragraph, only to be subsequently retold from different viewpoints. Morrison extends and elucidates these retellings rather as the musician responds to the rhythms and punctuations of the ensemble using narrative structure that evokes the inflections and repetitions of jazz. Very slowly, Morrison unravels her characters' histories in order to reveal the hold of the past on the present. The narrative voice is forced, through constant readjustment and improvisation, to reinvent its understanding of Joe and Violet's past lives. Morrison has commented on the narrative in *Jazz*:

> [W]hen I was thinking who was going to tell this story, the idea of 'who owns jazz' or who knows about it, came up. . . . I decided that the voice would be one of assumed knowledge, the voice says 'I know everything'. . . . Because the

---

[21] James Snead in 'Repetition as a Figure of Black Culture' provides a useful definition of the 'cut': 'In jazz improvisation, the "cut" . . . is the unexpectedness with which the soloist will depart from the "head" or theme and from its normal harmonic sequence or the drummer from the tune's accepted and familiar primary beat. One of the most perfect exemplars of this type of improvisation is John Coltrane whose mastery of melody and rhythm was so complete that he and Elvin Jones, his drummer, often traded roles, Coltrane making rhythmic as well as melodic statements and "cutting" away from the initial mode of playing' (Snead, 1984, p. 69).

voice has to actually imagine the story it's telling ... the story ... turns out to be entirely different from what is predicted because the characters are evolving.... It reminded me of a jazz performance ... Somebody takes off from the basic pattern, then the others have to accommodate themselves. (Morrison intv. with Carabi, cited in Matus, 1998, p. 123)

As a literary reflection of a jazz performance, the novel works on two levels. First, the narrative voice has to respond to the stories that unfold and, secondly, the reader's response to this ambivalent, non-linear narrative must itself be improvised to negotiate the spaces in the text. Novelist, narrative voice and the reader/audience work together in a collective engagement with the recovery of the past. The novel's thematic and historical repetitions are the constant rhythmical narrative beat upon which the improvisations of the ensemble are constructed in a collective process of revelation and becoming.

Repetition, considered in the context of African-American cultural expression, assumes positive possibilities. James Snead stresses how, 'Without an organising principle of repetition, true improvisation would be impossible, as an improvisator relies upon the ongoing recurrence of the beat' (Snead, 1984, p. 68). Change can thus only be affected by recognizing its points of departure from the repetitions preceding it and it is the structural repetitions of *Jazz*, or rather the spaces between them, that allow Morrison to articulate possibilities for the future of history. Gilles Deleuze, in *Difference and Repetition*, theorizes repetition and difference in terms of music and rhythm, distinguishing between two kinds of repetition; 'cadence-repetition' as the abstract, regular and identical division of time and 'rhythm-repetition', the poly-rhythmic, irregular eruption of difference, or gaps in time, expressed musically in jazz through the accented beat or note (Deleuze, 1968, p. 21). Deleuze views 'cadence-repetition' as being merely the homogeneous 'envelope' to which the more profound accents and unequal inflections of 'rhythm-repetition' are related as dissonant, yet positive, expressions of creative difference (Deleuze, 1968, p. 21). In *Jazz*, Joe and Violet improvise on the negative repetitions of history to create a future from which the past can be imagined creatively, transforming repetition into a positive, dissonant event that can effect change.

Constructing the future

At the end of *Jazz*, Morrison asks the reader to assume a participatory role in the making of history, to bring their own improvisations. This dialogical relationship bestows responsibility upon the reader of Morrison's work, once again, to disengage from the ideological assumptions of Oedipalized literary criticism. Morrison stretches this relationship further than in *Beloved* when the narrative voice of *Jazz* assumes the physicality of the book itself and demands a political response from the reader. The book, as voice, says:

> *That I have loved only you, surrendered my whole self reckless to you and nobody else. That I want you to love me back and show it to me. That I love the way you hold me, how close you let me be to you. I like your fingers on and on, lifting, turning. I have watched your face for a long time now, and missed your eyes when you went away from me. Talking to you and hearing you answer – that's the kick*
>
> But I can't say that aloud; I can't tell anyone that I have been waiting for this all my life and that being chosen to wait is the reason I can. If I were able I'd say it. Say make me, remake me. You are free to do it and I am free to let you because look, look. Look where your hands are. Now. (Morrison's italics, *J*, p. 229)

The word 'Now', the last word, demands immediate and positive response to the plea 'make me, remake me', suggesting that recovery from the psychic trauma of American history is possible. Deleuze and Guattari's *schizoanalysis* allows for a complex dialectic of the expression of liberated desire and the repression of desire. In *Jazz* this dialectic is in operation, in that the unconscious transforms the narrative from one of apparent subjugation within a dominant ideology, to one of liberation. The radical historiography of both *Beloved* and *Jazz* is not preoccupied solely with the miserable legacy of slavery, but stands instead as testament to the redemptive powers of the self and, importantly for Morrison, of the community. In this sense Morrison's work, despite its grotesque violence, becomes more than 'atrocity literature', or as Stanley Crouch puts it with reference to *Beloved*, 'black face holocaust' literature (Crouch, 1990, p. 205). To view Morrison's work in this way is to overlook the progression, across the body of her work, that mirrors the movement of black Americans from slavery to freedom and from the rural South to the urban centres. For example, the ghost of Beloved assumes a destructive physical manifestation which, in the 1920s Harlem of *Jazz*, becomes 'the shade', a much more benign presence 'Pushed away into certain streets, restricted from others, making it possible for the inhabitants to sigh and sleep in relief, the shade stretches – just there – at the edge of the dream, or slips into the crevices of a chuckle' (*J*, p. 227). As Joe's adopted name suggests, there are 'traces' of a vicious past in *Jazz*, and yet they are overcome as Violet achieves a complete sense of self and with it the freedom and strength to make the world as she wants it and to abandon her wish to be 'White. Light. Young again'; to conform to limiting, standardized notions of beauty (*J*, p. 208).

To become 'Me' she has to 'kill' the consuming figure of Golden Gray. Violet says to Felice: 'My grandmother fed me stories about a little blond child. He was a boy, but I thought of him as a girl sometimes, as a brother, sometimes as a boyfriend. He lived inside my mind. Quiet as a mole. But I didn't know it till I got here. The two of us. Had to get rid of it' (J, p. 208). Golden Gray's presence prevents Violet's liberation because, as Felice reminds us, he is like the ring her mother steals from Tiffany's, 'a present taken from white folks given to me when I was too young to say No thank you' (J, p. 211). By allowing him to possess her Violet places herself within a sterile, destructive Oedipal triangle in which Golden Gray replaces the mother she lost.

Violet's liberation from racial construction and the repetitions of history takes form in an assertion of 'Me', a progression from Sethe's tentative, questioning 'Me? Me?' that closes *Beloved*. In *Sula* we saw how the tension between the expression of individual identity and commitment to the community is never fully resolved, but Violet's new sense of identity represents possibilities for assertion without losing commitment to community and, as an improvisator within the narrative of *Jazz*, her characterization may be considered in the context of Ellison's claim that

> [T]rue jazz is an art of individual assertion within and against the group. Each true jazz moment ... springs from a contest in which each artist challenges all the rest; each solo flight or improvisation, represents (like the successive canvases of a painter) a definition of his identity: as individual, as member of the collectivity and as a link in the chain of tradition. (Ellison, 1964, p. 234)

In telling her story to Felice, Violet becomes a link in this chain, transferring valuable knowledge to those who follow. Morrison refigures Ellison's conception of the individual by removing his emphasis on competition and attributing positive values to the individual's relationship with both community and 'ancestor'. In her next novel Morrison extends her concept of the community to accommodate individual, racial and class differences in a literary creation of a diasporic, non-nationalist collectivity that she names 'paradise'.

Paradise (1998)

Addressing the Race Matters Conference in the 1990s Morrison talked about how she wishes to contest, and at the same time 'domesticate', the architecture of racialized discourse (Morrison, 1997, pp. 3–12). Using the metaphor of 'home', she envisages what may be called 'the end of race', where 'home' comes to mean a space from which it is recognized that the promises of twentieth-century discourse remain unrealized and that, as antinomies of modernity's rationalisms, they have evaporated along with the grand narratives themselves. Language, music and the idiom of counterculture are being rapidly subsumed by a process of commodification and reification that has brought us to what Paul Gilroy has called 'the crisis of race', a moment of liberatory potential and yet which, like Morrison's concept of 'home', needs careful, pragmatic construction if it is to be realized (Gilroy, 2000, pp. 11–53). 'Home', for Morrison, means 'to sign race while designing racelessness', a double-stepped reformulation of racial theory for the twenty-first century that has at its centre a profound and strategic understanding of the postmodern condition as the traumatized fragmentation of the self as pre-figured by Du Bois's notion of double consciousness, not as weak aesthetic representations of linguistic games, pastiche and irony so evident in post Second World War American fiction.[22] This is not to say that even in its more meaningful representations 'postmodernism' necessarily now provides a ready panacea for the theorization of anti-racism. This form of postmodern discourse importantly recognized the excesses of racial history and, in Donna Haraway's terms, looked for affinities across identities of race, gender, class and nationality that need closer interrogation (Haraway, 1991, pp. 149–81). Gilroy's critique of identity politics constitutes such an analysis in that he recognizes the reterritorialization and branding of identity and the danger of exclusionist notions of pure, unadulterated identity that can flourish from within the politics of victimization and in which suffering, or at least the memory of suffering, becomes accredited and measured on a scale of trauma (Gilroy, 2000, pp. 112–13).[23] This kind of identity politics can, at best, provide vapid ideologies of sameness within difference or, at worst, allow for the possibility of new forms of fascism within the nationalisms of Black Atlantic cultures. Instead, Gilroy locates the meaningful contestation of 'race' and the progressive maintenance of the memory within a politics of the diaspora.

[22] Morrison rarely uses the term 'postmodern'. In her interview with Paul Gilroy, she does, however, make it clear that her understanding of the postmodern is fully historical. For Morrison, contemporary black writers are more concerned with historical issues than their white 'postmodern' counterparts. She says: 'History has become impossible for them [postmodern white writers]. They're so busy being innocents and skipping from adolescence into old age. Their Literature and art reveals this great rent in the psyche, the spirit' (Morrison intv. with Gilroy, 1993a, p.179).
[23] Gilroy's discussion of the commodification of blackness: 'Layer upon layer of easily commodified exotica have culminated in a racialized glamour and contributed an extra cachet to some degree of nonspecific, somatic difference' (Gilroy, 2000, p. 21).

> By embracing diaspora, theories of identity turn instead towards contingency, indeterminacy, and conflict. With the idea of valuing diaspora more highly than the coercive unanimity of the nation, the concept becomes explicitly antinational. This shift is connected with transforming the familiar unidirectional idea of diaspora as a form of catastrophic but simple dispersal that enjoys an identifiable and reversible originary moment – the site of trauma – into something far more complex. Diaspora can be used to instantiate a 'chaotic' model in which shifting 'strange attractors' are the only visible points of fragile stability amid social and cultural turbulence. (Gilroy, 2000, p. 128)

The notion of a non-linear diaspora as a contestatory 'web' transcending nationalist identity formations and the trauma of history, as well as inviting creativity and resistance, resonates with Morrison's conceptualization of a 'race-specific yet non-racist' home that has potential for Gilroy's 'fragile stability' in its offer of a 'social space that is psychically and physically safe' (Morrison, 1997, pp. 5, 10). Morrison recognizes literary and academic discourses on race, including her own, as discourses about home and homelessness, 'creative responses to exile, the devastations, pleasures, and imperatives of homelessness as it is manifested in discussions on feminism, globalism, the diaspora, migrations, hybridity, contingency, interventions, assimilations, exclusions' (Morrison, 1997, p. 5). Morrison's notion of home is therefore diasporic, a place where race matters, but one that must be constructed beyond racialized discourse. Importantly, as for Gilroy, this includes resisting nationalism and spurious notions of identity that 'are frequently as raced themselves as the originating racial house that defined them' (Morrison, 1997, pp. 10–11).

Morrison's remarks at the Race Matters Conference reveal the extent to which her literary endeavours are closely linked with her work as an academic and public intellectual. Morrison politicizes her aesthetic in subtle engagement with the intellectual and political efforts of African Americans to establish freedom, equality and a sense of identity.[24] In *The Bluest Eye*, Morrison narrates the victimization of a young black child in 1940s Ohio, but she also contributes to the debates about notions of black beauty and the pathology of the black family prevalent among proponents of the Black Aesthetic and Black Power in the late 1960s. Again, in *Sula* she engages with themes of female identity, migration and

---

[24] In 'Rootedness', Morrison writes: 'I am not interested in indulging myself in some private, closed exercise of my imagination that fulfils only the obligation of my personal dreams – which is to say yes, the work must be political. It must have that as its thrust. . . . It seems to me that the best art is political and you ought to be able to make it unquestionably political and irrevocably beautiful at the same time' (Morrison, 1984, p. 64).

the loss of community that were as relevant in the 1970s as in the 1920s and 30s, and the treatment of masculinity and *embourgeoisement* in 1940s Chicago in *Song of Solomon* draws on debates within African-American feminism towards the end of the 1970s. *Paradise*, the third part of her trilogy, marks a further step in Morrison's genealogical recovery and exploration of African-American history as she moves to the 1970s. Again, Morrison goes further than an imaginative and aesthetic recovery of forgotten African-American experiences in her encounter with racial theory at the end of the twentieth century. Without polemic, *Paradise*, as Morrison's millennium novel, forces us to reformulate race for the twenty-first century.

Language, agency and the responsibility of interpretation

In doing this, Morrison extends her aesthetic through the construction of de-raced language to resist those forms of 'language that can powerfully evoke and enforce hidden signs of racial superiority, cultural hegemony, and dismissive "othering" of people and language' (Morrison, 1992c, pp. xii–xiii). This is also addressed in the 1993 Nobel Lecture in which Morrison discusses how language, as the medium of ideology, has socially concrete functions, how 'Oppressive language does more than represent violence; it is violence' (Morrison, 1993, p. 16), therefore having a material function as well as a representational role. As Judith Butler points out, oppressive language in all its guises has the potential for a future act of violence. A speech act, even though it may not be directly physically threatening, 'presages and inaugurates a subsequent force' (Butler, 1997, p. 9). Language is here a bodily performative act with material as well as representational functions. Morrison is aware, however, of the possibilities in language for contesting representations, 'as agency – as an act with consequences' (Morrison, 1993, p. 13) and throughout her work she does this by rejecting, altering and exposing ideologies in language.[25] *The Bluest Eye*, for example, offers a profound critique of the language of education in her subversion of a school primer that privileges whiteness. In her rejection of the exclusionary language of education, culture and religion, Morrison instead emphasizes the language, idiom and cultural forms of the black community. For Butler, the contestatory

---

[25] Butler makes a further point regarding language and agency in a comment that is directly related to Morrison's remark in the Nobel Lecture about language 'as agency': 'Because this formulation is offered *in* language, the "agency" of language is not only the theme of the formulation, but its very action. This positing as well as this figuring appear to exemplify the agency at issue' (Butler, 1997, p. 7).

language employed in opposition to linguistic power structures is enabled precisely by those very power structures to which it is opposed; 'within political discourse, the very terms of resistance and insurgency are spawned in part by the powers they oppose' (Butler, 1997, p. 40). Therefore the effectiveness of Morrison's language derives from the existence of an oppressive language and its codes. Again, in *The Bluest Eye*, Morrison's privileging of the language and idiom of the community achieves authority in contrast with the hegemonic codes of the school primer extracts at the head of each chapter.

That language has possibilities 'as agency' conveys an important distinction between language itself as a form of agency and the potential within language as an instrument for agency. She implies a particular form of agency that 'shifts attention away from assertions of power to the instrument through which that power is exercised' (Morrison, 1993, p. 12). Morrison does not want to achieve 'control' through language, as this is precisely the effect of oppressive language. The power of contestatory language, for Morrison, lies in the refusal to use language to define and limit. In fact its 'force, its felicity, is in its reach towards the ineffable' (Morrison, 1993, p. 21). As Butler points out, when it seeks to 'encapsulate' or 'capture', 'language not only loses its vitality, but acquires its own violent force' (Butler, 1997, p. 9).

In *Paradise*, Morrison intensifies this effort to decontaminate language while simultaneously and paradoxically making this language race-specific. Her intention is 'to sign race while designing racelessness', a difficult but more immediately realizable ambition than the wider utopian ideals of the liberation movement (Morrison, 1997, p. 8). The new century marked a juncture at which critical work began to interrogate blackness transnationally, national boundaries being violently contested in postcolonial conflict and identities globally reformulated. Although there is a wariness of nationalism, Frantz Fanon's concern in the 1960s that the newly decolonizing states should not duplicate western systems of power and expansion again finds relevance as the new century begins to confront the dislocations of slavery, colonialism and global capitalism (Fanon, 1961, pp. 252–4). The twenty-first century has brought new movements of people and profound re-conceptualizations of race and difference in which skin colour may or may not be relevant.

The opening sentence of *Paradise*, 'They shoot the white girl first' (*P*, p. 3), is a strategic reversal of racial codes that agitates the reader into immediate confrontation with conventional understandings of the racial terrain. Morrison's representations of difference and the intolerance of difference confound racial expectations and we are forced to 'step outside established boundaries of the racial imaginary' (Morrison, 1997, p. 9). In *Paradise* Morrison is returning to a technique, first experimented with in her 1983 short story 'Recitatif', in which the relationship between two abandoned children, Roberta and Twyla, is explored over a 30-year period (Morrison, 1983, pp. 243–61). As in *Paradise* there are no visual markers in 'Recitatif'; instead, the text plays upon the expectations of the reader confronting that the story possessed only of his or her own cultural knowledge. 'Recitatif' begins with Roberta and Twyla's first meeting as roommates in the St Bonaventure children's shelter and from the outset it is clear that the girls are of different racial origin and yet the reader has no definitive evidence of which girl belongs to which race. Instead, Morrison provides cultural signposts that may or may not suggest that, in fact, Twyla is white, Roberta is black or vice versa. This ambiguity is maintained throughout the text, the reader left to construct the 'truth' according to their assumptions.

By 'de-racing' race, Morrison is able to amplify class and its complex intersection with race as in, for example, how Roberta's middle-class status as an adult tells us nothing but that which we assume about her race. When the girls meet in the 1970s Roberta is married to a wealthy IBM executive, a cultural marker that could indicate whiteness. Morrison herself points out, however, that IBM made efforts to recruit black executives during this period. Similarly, Twyla's marriage to a fireman and her lower status indicates blackness, but again Morrison has remarked on the racially exclusionary practices of the firemen's union.[26] Morrison creates such ambiguity from the very specificity of her cultural references that sociological, psychological and political readings of 'Recitatif' can yield very different, dialogically formed, interpretations (Abel, 1993, pp. 243–61). In the Nobel Lecture, Morrison draws on folklore and positions herself as griot in order to illustrate metaphorically both the oppressions of language and as a source of resistance. The old blind woman in the folk story Morrison relates can be read, she says, as a black woman writer, perhaps Morrison herself. Two children enter the wise old woman's home, one of them claiming to hold a bird in his or her hands and asks if the bird is dead or alive, an allegory illuminating the devolving of responsibility for language and its interpretation onto the reader. The bird represents language, the children perhaps readers, and to the question posed the old woman replies: 'I don't know whether the bird you are holding is dead or alive, but what I do know is that it is in your hands. It is in your hands' (Morrison, 1993, p. 11). The reader, then, holds responsibility for the life

---

[26] See Elizabeth Abel's reference to her correspondence with Morrison about 'Recitatif' in 'Black Writing, White Reading: Race and the Politics of Feminist Interpretations' (Abel, 1993, p. 476).

or death of language and the blind woman, as writer, 'shifts attention away from assertions of power to the instrument through which that power is exercised' (Morrison, 1993, p. 12). As Butler comments, the writer is blind and cannot predict the use to which her work may be put (Butler, 1997, p. 8).

The indeterminacy characterizing Morrison's work can be more clearly understood in the context of her Nobel Lecture. In *Paradise*, for example, the question as to whether the Convent women survive the massacre or do indeed perish at the hands of the men of Ruby is left open to the philosophical, psychological and political interpretation of the reader, as it is they who attribute meaning. Moreover, Morrison offers the reader the possibility of political engagement in ways that reflect the artistic motifs of black art, particularly the call and response of the sermon and the relationship between audience, soloist and ensemble in jazz (Morrison, 1984, p. 59).

'Recitatif', as its title obliquely suggests, is very much like a talking blues in which the reader must respond to the story's racial indeterminacy. Morrison's removal of racial codes means she cannot go beyond the title to represent the idiom, language or art forms of African-American culture as this would allow definite racial identifications to be made. In *The Bluest Eye*, Morrison contested racial discourse and went on, in subsequent novels, to represent and privilege the art, history and culture of black communities. In 'Recitatif' her concern shifts slightly to retain the essence of the participatory and dialogical functions of black art without representing that art directly. In *Paradise* Morrison can both foreground the concerns of the all black town, Ruby, and extend this experiment through her characterization of the women who occupy the Convent. We never learn which of the four Convent women is 'the white girl', but this is unimportant as the violence perpetrated is of greater significance than her racial identity.

In *Playing in the Dark* Morrison said of 'Recitatif':

> The kind of work I have always wanted to do requires me to learn how to maneuver ways to free up the language from its sometimes sinister, frequently lazy, almost always predictable employment of racially informed and determined chains. (The only short story I have ever written, 'Recitatif', was an experiment in the removal of all racial codes from a narrative about two characters of different races for whom racial identity is crucial.) (Morrison, 1992c, p. xiii)

The elimination of linguistic racial codes in *Paradise* allows Morrison to foreground gender in the same way she privileges class in 'Recitatif'. De-raced language is more appropriate for privileging female experience over race than, say, feminist rhetoric, even when racial identity is central to that female experience. A theme of both 'Recitatif' and *Paradise* is that of the abandonment of the daughter by the mother, the damage done in the absence of mother love. Despite their racial difference, Twyla and Roberta in 'Recitatif' share an understanding of their abandonment that transcends race, though race remains as a repository for the anger and shame their desertion has caused. It is the figure of Maggie, the shelter's kitchen worker, who functions as a repository for this transference of loss. She is described as being of a racially indeterminate sandy colour, a deaf mute who having been raised in the shelter, is much feared by Twyla and Roberta as somebody they might themselves become. Being deaf and dumb, Maggie is a vessel who symbolizes the absence of a mother figure. Moreover, Maggie assumes different racial characteristics, so for Twyla she is white, for Roberta black and it is clear these assumptions about race inflect their desire, as children, to kick her when she falls. When the girls meet for the last time, 30 years after this incident, neither can be really sure whether Maggie was black or not. What is important is their recognition of how they had transferred their pain and loss onto Maggie in racially specific ways and that they are able at last to grieve for their mothers, and for Maggie.

The women of the Convent in *Paradise* share trauma not always directly attributable to race; it is not that of Sethe in *Beloved*, born of slavery, or the pain of remembering in *Jazz*. In *Paradise*, deep, historical trauma has dissipated, its manifestations fragmented and peripheral to the immediate concerns of African-American experience in the 1970s. It is the contemporary world the women are trying to escape; in stark contrast to the inflexible racial codes of Ruby and the town's static commemoration of past trauma, the Convent women live a marginal, diasporic existence above and beyond race. They create a female space through the reterritorialization of what was once an embezzler's palace, complete with suggestive, almost pornographic fixtures that blend with the iconography of Catholicism when the building becomes Christ the King School for Native Girls. Their conversion of this unlikely space allows the women to create 'home' for themselves in which to reconstruct their sexuality against the defining representations of the original decor and where their rituals of exorcism, led by Consolata, replace those of Catholicism. The Convent is a place offering temporary physical and psychological security and the transformation they achieve is an organic one, without structure or possession. Ruby, in its first embodiment as Haven, is founded upon communal, collective principles established to negotiate shared historical trauma, and yet the story of the new town, Ruby, is one of how such values become exclusionary and segregationist in parodic imitation of white, patriarchal civic life. As Peter Widdowson points out, 'Ruby is both a chilling indictment of white America (the failures of the Declaration, Reconstruction, twentieth-century reforms), and a celebration of black resilience, independence and honour (a triumph of the Exoduster spirit). But the latter, as reflexes of the former, come with a price, too' (Widdowson, 2001, p. 324).

Civic and religious versions of paradise

As with Hurston's incorporated town of Eatonville in *Their Eyes Were Watching God* (1937), Ruby's civic success has come at the expense of certain founding ideals. In Ruby these have become too rigid and outmoded to accommodate African-American experience that now incorporates Vietnam, the Civil Rights movement and changing female consciousness. The momentum for the rational codes of accumulation and civic authority is provided by an entrenched patriarchal power, again in mirror image of the very hierarchical structures they were originally meant to replace. In Hurston's Eatonville, Joe Starks' metamorphosis into a black version of the small-town dignitary can only occur if his wife is denied a voice; upon speaking her truth, Joe is destroyed, now a man envied only for what he has, not for what he is. Janie instead finds love and companionship in Tea Cake, a folk figure devoid of Starks' materialist ambitions. Their unlikely relationship reveals Hurston's problem in finding appropriate forms of meaningful agency; the choice is either the assumption of white middle-class values or to exist within a folk sensibility that may provide emotional sustenance and escape, but little practical economic and political agency. Thirty years after Hurston's creation of Janie, Morrison explores this dilemma in Sula's struggle to construct her own identity against the bourgeois aspirations adopted in the community. As with Janie, Sula's choice is either the assimilationist values of 1920s migratory African Americans or the autonomy of a folk existence, a dilemma remaining for professional black women such as Morrison herself as she wrote *Sula* in the early 1970s. To find creative and intellectual refuge through the privileging of the folk and its idiom is now a more problematic alternative, given its progressive reification as a lifestyle. Race is now being highly exoticized for the purposes of marketing intent on selling the promise of identity through difference and individualism, what Gilroy calls 'corporate multiculturalism', an empty promise as culture and identity find representation not as lived existence but as commodities to be bought and owned.

Morrison's conception of 'home' addresses this dilemma by denoting a space beyond racial, sexual or class boundaries and appropriations of blackness, a universal human space to be entered once history is articulated and difference accommodated. As she remarks in her address to the Race Matters Conference, Morrison sees possibilities for a space in which to be black without relinquishing blackness. In personal terms, this means the creation of a safe, but challenging and subversive, space within the academy, her conception of home therefore intellectual and theoretical as well as emotional and visceral. Her ideas also resume an interrupted African-American tradition of intellectual and political activism that came to an end with Martin Luther King's assassination and the move towards the isolationism of Black Power nationalist politics. Morrison has argued that King's death 'came at a moment when it was most useful to the reigning order' as his call for an inclusive politics of liberation gained credence.

> It is interesting that before Martin Luther King died, on his poor people's march, he had been going into small Southern towns, talking to mixed audiences, poor white dirt farmers and poor black people, and he was persuading them that their interests were the same, that the enemy was the same, that the problems were not black liberation or white oppression – it was a class struggle that they were in, and that it was only to benefit the ruling class that they had always responded racially. (Morrison intv. with Lester, 1988, pp. 52–3)

Morrison denotes the 'hopeful language' of King as representative of an unrealistic project to construct 'a-world-in-which-race-does-not-matter' as such a world could only be visualized by King and his followers 'if accompanied by the Messiah' (Morrison, 1997, p. 3).[27] In *Paradise*, however, Morrison revives and revises King's Christian humanism through her characterization of the Reverend Misner, a progressive, liberal minister mindful of Ruby's racial exclusivity and political apathy towards affairs beyond the town's boundaries. Misner's understanding of a 'true home' incorporates his Christianity, but the emphasis is on a spiritual and physical space that is transglobal and transhistorical in its metaphorical reach to the origins of humanity.

> But can't you even imagine what it must feel like to have a true home? I don't mean heaven. I mean a real earthly home. Not some fortress you bought and built up and have to keep everybody locked in or out. A real home. Not some place you claimed, snatched because you got the guns. Not some place you stole from the people living there, but your own home, where if you go back past

---

[27] Paul Gilroy draws on the legacy of King, but attempts to place his 'nonracial humanism' 'upon more stable foundation than those provided by King's open-minded and consistent Christianity' (Gilroy, 2000, p. 15).

your great-great-grandparents, past theirs, and theirs, past the whole of Western history, past the beginning of organized knowledge, past pyramids and poison bows, on back to when rain was new, before plants forgot they could sing and birds thought they were fish, back when God said Good! Good! – there, right where you know your own people were born and lived and died. (*P*, p. 213)

Misner's version of 'home' pre-empts the conceptualization of paradise with which Morrison ends the novel. Crucially, Misner's vision attempts to reverse the 'whole of Western history', whereas paradise for Morrison is a futuristic vision in which the confrontation of history is a necessary precondition for its existence; not a place marking 'the end of history' or looking backwards to an imaginary wholeness before history but one, cleared of 'racist detritus', constituting a space for the future of history in its re-figuring of race 'outside the raced house' (Morrison, 1997, p. 8).

Diaspora as paradise

In Morrison's paradise the ways in which to be black, to be human, are multiplied and possibilities of security exist beyond intolerance. Morrison's vision is indeterminate and again relies, in its resistance to closure, upon the reader's engagement and interpretation. It could be regarded as utopian, a useful novelistic, aesthetic conceit allowing the writer the luxury of two endings. A politicized reading is, however, much more productive in its emphasis upon a diasporic space traversing race, class and sexuality, a reading analogous to Donna Haraway's project of fusing the material and the imaginary in her unreservedly utopian feminist effort to break down conventional distinctions between the natural and the man-made (Haraway, 1991, p. 150).[28] The Convent women's reincarnation and repossession of their own past lives, after their massacre, leads them to the 'paradise' of Morrison's title, and yet this paradise is not a secluded, idyllic island; rather, it includes a worldly detritus that is imbued with a certain shimmering beauty: 'Around them on the beach, sea trash gleams. Discarded bottle tops sparkle near a broken sandal. A small dead radio plays the quiet surf' (*P*, p. 318). To exist in paradise is not to escape from twentieth-century realities of oppression and inequality, ratified by the language of the 'race house'. Those in paradise have attained the knowledge and understanding to recognize,

---

[28] Haraway's 'A Cyborg Manifesto' is 'an effort to contribute to socialist-feminist culture and theory in a postmodernist, non-naturalist mode and in the utopian tradition of imagining a world without gender, which is perhaps a world without genesis, but maybe also a world without end' (Haraway, 1991, p. 150).

'domesticate' and transcend ideologies of western power. The radio, although still playing its message, is disabled in the face of Piedale's, the Black Madonna's singing and redemptive love.[29] Paradise is realizable when responsibility for language and culture is seized, not only in oppositional, but also in genuinely new and imaginative ways that can bypass the malady of culture. Paradise is not fantastical in the sense of other worldly, heavenly existence but, as aesthetically rendered by Morrison for whom narrative is 'one of the principal ways in which we absorb knowledge' (Morrison, 1993, p. 7), it offers possibilities for ways of being in the real world that recognize oppression and yet provide the cognitive and imaginative tools for its transcendence. As Donna Haraway says: 'Liberation rests on the construction of the consciousness, the imaginative apprehension, of oppression, and so of possibility' (Haraway, 1991, p. 149).

Despite its inclusivity, paradise as a home has no room for complacency. In a reversal of Beloved's 'rememory' of the slave ship, Morrison's final images in *Paradise* are of a ship carrying the 'lost and saved' of the twentieth-century 'home', not to the injustices of the New World. Paradise requires 'endless effort', constant reshaping and creativity, for its maintenance. Importantly, as in the image of the ship shows, original trauma is kept alive in new and positive forms. In this sense, Morrison's paradise is analogous to Gilroy's politics of the diaspora that encompasses an appeal towards a universal, or non-racial, humanism that again requires vigilance. Rather than being a liberal, multiculturalist approach to race theory, Gilroy's call for universal humanism is, in its transcendence of western systems of political and economic organization, subversive. He accepts this move towards a non-racial humanism is likely to be received with scepticism by those engaged in long, painful struggle to establish bonds of nationality, culture and racial identity. Without undermining the importance of such struggles, Gilroy's case for abandoning race as a defining trope is compelling. The establishment of 'traditions of politics, ethics, identity, and culture' have of course been crucial for subjugated groups in providing protection against the brutalities of modernity, but they are defensive and, as countercultures of modernity, so closely allied to modernity's workings that their 'defence of communal interests has often mobilized the fantasy of a frozen culture, of arrested cultural development' (Gilroy, 2000, p. 13).

Morrison's title, *Paradise*, has multiple meanings. It denotes the meaning of home but at the same time is used with irony as an epithet for Ruby's failure to either progress from, or to maintain, the spirit of the town's original ideals. In

---

[29] See Bouson's *Quiet as It's Kept: Shame, Trauma, and Race in the Novels of Toni Morrison* for a brief discussion of Piedale as Black Madonna (Bouson, 2000, p. 241, f.n. 6).

Gilroy's terms Ruby is 'frozen' in its repetition of cultural and religious ritual and in its stories of endless struggle.

> Over and over with the least provocation, they pulled from their stock of stories tales about the old folks, their grands and great-grands; their fathers and mothers. Dangerous confrontations, clever maneuvers. Testimonies to endurance, wit, skill and strength. Tales of luck and outrage. But why were there no stories to tell of themselves? About their own lives they shut up. Had nothing to say, pass on. As though past heroism was enough of a future to live by. As though, rather than children, they wanted duplicates. (*P*, p. 161)

This isolationist patriarchy mimics, as we have seen, the civic, nationalist patriarchy of its white counterpart. In a fully incorporated town like Ruby, where the emphasis is on maintaining sameness and protecting pure lines of blood, the impact of nation building ideology, especially upon women, may be more severe than in white civic life.

> Gender differences become important in nation-building activity because they are a sign of an irresistible natural hierarchy that belongs at the center of civic life. The unholy forces of nationalist biopolitics intersect on the bodies of women charged with the reproduction of absolute ethnic difference and the continuance of blood lines. The integrity of the nation becomes the integrity of its masculinity. (Gilroy, 2000, p. 127)

It is the fear of losing hard won 'integrity of masculinity' that prompts the men of Ruby to attack the women of the Convent. As the barely tolerated and only woman of mixed race in Ruby, Patricia Best recognizes the purity of blackness as integral to the town's existence and the New Fathers' nationalistic version of paradise. Of course, the preservation of blackness entails both the worship of a particular form of femininity that will perpetuate the purity of bloodlines and a suspicion of women who appear to threaten such purity. As Patricia is perceived as a contaminating presence she consequently possesses an acute awareness of Ruby's sexual politics. 'Unadulterated and unadulterated 8-rock blood held its magic as long as it resided in Ruby. That was their recipe. That was their deal. For Immortality. Pat's smile was crooked. In that case, she thought, everything that worries them must come from women' (*P*, p. 217). The Convent women are the snakes in Ruby's Eden, temptresses threatening the racial purity very much equated by the men with God's own purity. They exist as the repository for all fear, guilt and sexual frustration arising from the drive to statehood and order, rationalisms that contain woman only as virgin or whore. They pose no real threat to anyone, their only sin being the ability to live without men outside the structures of Ruby. In their outsiderness, the women represent the 'stranger' as theorized by Zygmunt Bauman, the 'stranger' as the 'bane of modernity' whose existence as a figure of 'ambivalence' and 'incongruity' challenges codes of order, rationality and cleanliness.

> The stranger disturbs the resonance between physical and psychical distance: he is *physically close* while remaining *spiritually remote*. He brings into the inner circle of proximity the kind of difference and otherness that are anticipated and tolerated only at a distance – where they can be either dismissed as irrelevant or repelled as hostile. . . . His presence is a challenge to the reliability of orthodox landmarks and the universal tools of order making. (Bauman, 1991, p. 60)

The 'stranger' gradually transforms the temporary abode into 'home' but, unlike indigenous residents, has the freedom to leave at any point, enabling the stranger 'to view local conditions with an equanimity the native residents can hardly afford. Hence another incongruous synthesis – this time between involvement and indifference, partisanship and neutrality, detachment and participation' (Bauman, 1991, p. 60).

All the women reach the Convent as a temporary refuge and, though it does in fact become home, they all intend to leave. In contrast, Patricia Best is confined to Ruby, her internalization of its codes duplicated in her treatment of her daughter Billie Delia, itself expressive of how she lacks the equanimity of vision enjoyed by the stranger. Lone DuPres, an orphan adopted by the founding families on their journey across Oklahoma, is a stranger within the community and, as midwife, endowed with the gifts of second sight and the ability to bring the dead back to life. It is Lone, the true stranger within, who foresees the violence inflicted on the Convent women. As strangers, Lone and the mythical figure of Consolata – also an orphan with special gifts – experience a particular form of loneliness, as Lone's name suggests, that in Bauman's terms is engendered by their ambivalence. The loneliness of such ambivalence is, however, the source of their creative, critical insight and the vantage point from which profound and reflective understanding of modern human experience arises (Bauman, 1991, p. 149). The condition of marginality or strangerhood constitutes a 'postmodern' awareness, a condition, Morrison and Gilroy have argued, first experienced by minority groups in their encounters with modernity's brutality. For Morrison, the dissolution of the self has in fact been countered by strategies for survival that include reconstructions of 'certain kinds of stability' (Morrison intv. with Gilroy, 1993a, p. 178). In *Paradise* it is the insight of the diasporic stranger, existing at the margin regardless of race, that provides the security necessary for the construction of home. Under the influence of Consolata, the 'new and revised Reverend Mother' (*P*, p. 265), the women re-enact episodes of infanticide, motherlessness, racial murder and rape as a means to empowerment through the understanding of each other's pain and shame. They discover 'the beloved' inside, the 'unbridled, authentic self' (*P*, p. 177) and emerge somehow to exist beyond their massacre. By contrast, in their efforts to construct home the people of Ruby have failed to confront racism and exclusion, the town constructed upon a reaction to shame, not upon its redemption.[30]

Language and paradise

The families of Ruby are 'haunted' by a secret history of humiliations, too shameful to be recorded in the Old Fathers' narrative of the town's origins, and by the latest of its adulteries, illegitimacy and failed abortions. The ritual of exorcism in which the Convent women engage constitutes an alternative path to redemption that not only contrasts with Ruby's attempts at paradise but also is more successful than the benevolent Catholicism of the nuns who ran the Convent as a school for 'native girls'. The nuns' version of a redemptive paradise is achievable only through the inculcation of shame. For the nuns, the establishment of the Convent

> was an opportunity to intervene at the heart of the problem: to bring God and language to natives who were assumed to have neither; to alter their diets, their clothes, their minds; to help them despise everything that had once made their lives worthwhile and to offer them instead the privilege of knowing the one and only God and a chance, thereby, for redemption. (*P*, p. 227)

Consolata's awareness of the inadequacy of a monolithic Catholicism founded upon such shame commits her to the salvation of the Convent women and the creation of a transcendent language, 'the loud dreaming', taking them beyond the 'raced house' soaring 'high above guttering candles, shifting dust from crates and bottles.' (*P*, p. 264) The existence of 'the one and only God' is challenged through Consolata's revival of Piedale, the Black Madonna, an alternative figure of redemption whose 'song without words' is non-prescriptive and non-defining. It offers new kinds of solace that move 'towards the ineffable' and beyond the

---

[30] For an analysis of the role of shame in *Paradise* see *Quiet as It's Kept* (Bouson, 2000, pp. 191–216).

unity of language. Piedale, 'who sang but never said a word' (*P*, p. 264), does not attempt to encapsulate or delimit the multiplicities and particularities of women's histories, narratives and languages. This resonates with Donna Haraway's socialist feminism that establishes affinities across the range of women's experiences and yet denies a common language that would essentialize those experiences. 'The feminist dream of a common language, like all dreams for a perfectly true language, of perfectly faithful naming of experience, is a totalising and imperialist one' (Haraway, 1991, p. 173). Consolata's evocation of Piedale's song and her appropriations of the African-Brazilian religion of Candomblé are diasporic as they have their origins in, but are in opposition to, the modes of power found in the Catholicism encountered in Brazil, the country of her birth, and in her education at the Convent in Oklahoma. Consolata's adaptation of Candomblé practices reveals an understanding of her origins of dispossession and dislocation, a realization that African diasporic traditions are empowering and redemptive.[31]

The desire to imbue tradition and history with new relevance is at the heart of the conflict in Ruby over the construction of paradise. The conflict finds focus in language as the people of Ruby contest the meaning of the inscription on the Oven, built by the Old Fathers in 1890 as a monument to symbolize and commemorate a safe place they could regard as home or, as the town was originally named, Haven. The decline of Haven after the Second World War drives its people further into Oklahoma where they establish Ruby and reassemble the Oven as a shrine to the endurance of the freedmen who had founded Haven. By the mid-1970s, however, Ruby has a generation very aware of the intense struggles for civil rights that take place beyond the town boundary and they claim the Oven as a site for the celebration of Africanism and Black Power. With Reverend Misner's encouragement, the young people contest their elders' interpretation of the Oven's inscription, part of which is now missing, arguing that it should be read as 'Be the Furrow of His Brow', not 'Beware the Furrow of His Brow' as remembered by the older generation. The imperious command, 'Beware the Furrow . . .' evokes an all-powerful and fearful God whose will is to be obeyed, a faith the elders regard as profound affirmation of their attempts to maintain Ruby's racial and political insularity. For Misner and the young 'Be

---

[31] Bouson points out Consolata's Brazilian origins and notes that Toni Morrison travelled to Brazil to carry out research on the African-Brazilian religion of Candomblé. For Bouson this suggests a link between the occult practices of the Convent women and Candomblé. See Bouson's detailed footnote on the history and function of Candomblé, in *Quiet as It's Kept* (Bouson, 2000, pp. 238–9, f.n.5).

the Furrow . . .' implies a form of worship that encompasses and encourages involvement in the world beyond Ruby. Misner teaches a 'message of God as a permanent interior engine that, once ignited, roared, purred and moved you to do your own work as well as His – but, if idle, rusted, immobilizing the soul like a frozen clutch' (*P*, p. 142).

Situating *Paradise* in African-American intellectual traditions

It is through the debate over the meaning of the missing words in the Oven's inscription that Morrison contributes to an intellectual tradition that has attempted to articulate effective channels of progression for black people. In effect, she replays the oppositions of Booker T. Washington's segregationist position and W.E.B. Du Bois' advocacy of integration based on equality, a debate traced in Reverend Misner's adoption of Martin Luther King's Christian humanism and the militant separatism of the youth of Ruby. In 'The Atlanta Exposition Address' (1895) Washington articulated a model of paradise, 'a new heaven and a new earth', attainable if African Americans were to consolidate a racial solidarity within the economic rationality of America and the South's structures of legalized segregation: 'In all things that are purely social we can be as separate as the fingers, yet one as the hand in all things essential to mutual progress' (Washington, 1895, pp. 412, 414). Ruby's elders adopt Washington's advocacy of racial self-reliance and separatism and, like him, take American versions of progress and modernity as given and so can only duplicate white forms of social and economic organization. In his famous critique of Washington, Du Bois saw this as 'adjustment and submission', warning of 'triumphant commercialism, and the ideals of material prosperity', and advocating instead higher learning and political activism (Du Bois, 1903, pp. 26, 30). The extremes of racial capitalism have made America 'an ill-harmonized and unmelodious land', its values inappropriate for the spiritual and social advancement of African Americans. Du Bois elevated the African-American arts of 'story and song' believing they could alleviate American materialism and be used politically in a wider project to affirm African-American equality (Du Bois, 1903, p. 163).

Du Bois exposes the fracture in black identity in his concept of double consciousness, the feeling of 'two-ness' black Americans experience because they are both American and African American (Du Bois, 1903, p. 2). The central problem for Du Bois is that of resolving the psychological dilemma of double consciousness not, as do Ruby's elders, by adopting American values and promoting black separatism, but through the realization of this duality of African-American identity. Du Bois writes of the African American:

> He would not Africanize America, for America has too much to teach the world and Africa. He would not bleach his Negro soul in a flood of white Americanism, for he knows that Negro blood has a message for the world. He simply wishes to make it possible for a man to be both a Negro and an American. (Du Bois, 1903, p. 3)

Du Bois does not articulate a finished version of paradise, as it is clear that the reconciliation of double consciousness, as with Morrison's notion of paradise, requires 'endless work' or, as he puts it, 'dogged strength', if it is to be realized (Du Bois, 1903, p. 2). However, if Du Bois and Morrison realize the difficulty in achieving a 'world-in-which-race-does-not matter' they are also aware of the possibilities for negotiating pathologies by exploiting the critical insight that double consciousness can offer. For Morrison, double consciousness becomes a 'strategy rather than a prophecy or a cure', a way of appropriating the rupture in identity and from it creating a space that can accommodate the marginalized without duplication (Morrison, 1997, p. 11).

Reverend Misner knows that for the people of Ruby 'Booker T. solutions trumped Du Bois problems every time' (*P*, p. 212) and understands their refusal to engage with history and politics beyond their own concerns will mean the failure of the town as paradise. In his effort to instil a sense of social and civic responsibility Misner comes into conflict with the Methodist minister Reverend Pulliam who denies the humanity of Christianity by declaring that God 'is only interested in Himself' (*P*, p. 142), and that redemption only comes with unquestioning worship of God as a higher authority. For Misner, inspired by Martin Luther King's message that, 'Love is creative, understanding goodwill for all men', love the foundation of a Christianity that encourages human agency rather than blind faith (King, 1957, p. 47). His Christianity acknowledges global inequities that can only be contested by a form of worship that certainly embraces civil rights activism but also reaches towards profound change in its wide reaching humanism. King's interpretation of the Crucifixion rests on an understanding of its historical, political and trans-global significance.

> So the greatest of all virtues is love. It is here that we find the true meaning of the Christian faith. This is at bottom the meaning of the cross. The great event on Calvary signifies more than a meaningless drama that took place on the stage of history. It is a telescope through which we look out into the long vista of eternity and see the love of God breaking forth into time. It is an eternal reminder to a

power-drunk generation that love is [the] most durable power in the world, and that it is at bottom the heartbeat of the moral cosmos. (King, 1956, p. 36)

Misner's understanding of the Crucifixion resonates with King's in his recognition of love as an enabling force with the power to transcend intolerance based on fear and the desire for power.

This execution made it possible to respect – freely, not in fear – one's self and one another. Which was what love was: unmotivated respect. All of which testified not to a peevish Lord who was His own love but to one who enabled human love. Not for His own glory – never. (*P*, p. 146)

This understanding of love as a conduit for mutual respect and equality crystallizes at the wedding of K.D. and Arnette. Misner presents a divided congregation with a wordless sermon, using the cross to signify not only the suffering and death of Christ but also to communicate through reaching back to the beginning of language – the sign of the cross – and, at the same time, to follow King's call to 'make of this old world a new world' (King, 1957, p. 57). Language cannot convey Misner's humanism and, as with Consolata's 'loud dreaming', he attempts to force the wedding congregation to a confrontation of their secret histories. This effort to move beyond the confines of discourse, however, ultimately fails; Misner still evokes the Messiah and chooses to operate within the Christian faith, thereby allowing Ruby to make a slow kind of progress that reflects, in microcosm, the attritional struggles of the American twentieth century.

American civil life and Ruby are not, then, paradise which cannot be founded upon a Christianity that remains, despite its universality and anti-materialism, reliant upon what Donna Haraway calls the 'blinding illuminations of the god trick', that is to say, omniscient, messianic presence and 'salvation history' (Haraway, 1991, pp. 150, 193). For Haraway, oppositional narratives 'must not be about the Fall, the imagination of a once-upon-a-time wholeness before language, before writing, before Man.' Rather they are to be created anew by the exiled and marginalized and should be 'about the power to survive, not on the basis of original innocence, but on the basis of seizing the tools to mark the world that marked them as other' (Haraway, 1991, p. 175). An overarching Christian faith denies the particularity and rationality necessary for creative freedoms at this fluid historical juncture, now striated by ever more complex movements of people and capital. Hegemonic Christianity, even King's, is unable to contain, let alone direct, this new world that now demands realistic, partial and localized engagement.

Language, however, does not necessarily bring paradise any closer, whether it is the discourse of Christianity or other attempts to understand the complexity of human existence. Patricia Best's written history of Ruby is an effort to articulate the truth of experience in conventional narrative terms. That she eventually burns her 'history book' reveals its inadequacy as truth claim. Lone, as a figure of exile, realizes that conventional narrative fails to reach towards the ineffability of 'the "trick" of life and its "reason"' (P, p. 272). Language obstructs and, as the expression of a transnational culture, must be dismantled, 'cleaned up' and reconstructed. Morrison assumes responsibility for creating de-raced language and in turn passes that responsibility on to the reader to create politicized interpretations of her work. In *Paradise* Morrison's aesthetic operates at times beyond the spoken and written word. Absence, signified by the missing words of the Oven's inscription, is the source of both conflict and change in Ruby as the town's people debate the religious, political and philosophical meaning of something not there, a debate that finds its parallel within the African-American literary tradition itself. To establish a presence in a society that has consistently rendered African Americans absent from its political, economic and social formations, this literary and intellectual tradition has been characterized by positive debate and critical engagement and *Paradise* marks a culmination of these endeavours at the end of the twentieth century and signals new possibilities for the theorization of race at the beginning of the twenty-first century. The novel claims a place for those absent from western discourse, a move that rejects previous efforts towards inclusion in the body politic of America and transcends the contaminations of western rationality and modernity in what is essentially a politics of the diaspora that encompasses understanding of the particularities of experience. Morrison's version of paradise exists beyond the physical boundaries of the nation state and, as a metaphysical space, allows for the construction of affinities of experience that traverse racial, gender and class differences even as they are recognized and accommodated.

5

Reading and Writing: *Love* (2003), *A Mercy* (2008) and *Home* (2012)

In *Paradise* (1998) Toni Morrison suggests new possibilities for the theorization of race in her articulation of diasporic identities that transcend racial distinctions and, in the version of paradise that ends the novel, through the evocation of a space beyond the physical boundaries of the nation state. Morrison's post-realist imaginings of a 'paradise' that can accommodate marginality without duplicating western rationality and inequity resonate with contemporary theorizations of race which seek to replace nationalist ideologies with diasporic, but non-race specific, forms of 'universal humanism'. The development of the 'incorporated' Oklahoma town of Ruby in Paradise is ultimately stultified by the community's efforts to maintain racial purity and its preoccupation with past traumas prevent the possibility of creative and new social formations. It is transcendent love, rather than separatist doctrine, that propels Morrison's millennial version of paradise, a love she politicizes as the Convent women in Paradise subvert racial, gender and class distinctions through the shared confrontation of their individual past lives. From love born of their disparate diasporic experiences, the Convent women forge paradise for the twenty-first century, located beyond Martin Luther King's Christian humanism that is, for Morrison, problematic in its dependence on a messianic presence. At the end of Paradise the alternative, redemptive voice of the black Madonna, Piedale, is privileged over Reverend Misner's vision of a 'paradise' or 'home' predicated on King's liberal and progressive Christianity.

In her next novel, *Love* (2003), Morrison explores further the intricacies of love in an African-American community, this time in the East Coast resort of Cosey. Here, Morrison again refines her literary project for the reconstruction of history to examine the possibilities, distortions and limitations of sexual, filial and racial love within the context of specific African-American experiences in the 1990s. This concern with the universal theme of love may appear to be a distraction from the historically specific and contestatory nature of black American existence within white American culture. However, love itself, or its absence and corruption, is delineated by Morrison as being subject to the economy of marginalized existence in America. In this sense *Love* continues Morrison's engagement with the psychological and spiritual complexities of African-American experience and extends her project to privilege the specificity of African-American knowledge. Morrison also reaffirms her place within the African-American writing tradition as she engages with the intellectual efforts of her literary precursors to establish freedoms and identity. In *Paradise*, as we have seen, Morrison problematizes King's version of Christian humanism through her representation of Misner and his understanding of what paradise might be. The novel also contributes to key debates in African-American intellectual history as Morrison replays the oppositions of Booker T. Washington's segregationist policies and W.E.B. Du Bois' advocacy of integration based on equality, a debate she traces through to Reverend Misner's adoption of Martin Luther King's Christian Humanism and the militant separatism of Ruby's younger generation.

For Morrison the issue has become one of how to define identity and achieve civic and social equality without duplicating modernity's hierarchies of race, gender and class. This effort is especially significant in the context of global, genocidal mechanisms of nationalism and fundamentalism that imply new forms of exclusion as the promise of transnational flows of markets, technologies and labour dissipated when the world 'fractured' on 11 September 2001 (Obama, 2004, p. x). The gains made by the Civil Rights movement and the election of Barack Obama mean that the consideration of oppression requires reconfiguration in global terms, otherwise, in Obama's words, 'the hardening of lines, the embrace of fundamentalism and tribe, dooms us all' (Obama, 2004, p. xi). For Morrison, too, categories of religion, nation state and race can no longer affect the construction of meaningful identities or lasting political and social change. She turns instead to the universal category of love and thereby evokes James Baldwin's recognition of 'the torment and necessity of love' (Baldwin, 1963, p. 74) as the only source of redemption for America. In *The Fire Next Time* Baldwin responds to the separatist agenda of the Nation of Islam and anticipates Morrison's disquietude with nationalist ideologies when he claims that allegiances and groupings predicated on colour distinctions alone have 'nothing to do with love' (Baldwin, 1963, p. 71). The true, mutual recognition of love is painful but imperative for black and white Americans; a prerequisite for achieving political and social equality in a country that has refused to face the reality of its complex relationship with an African-American presence. For

Baldwin, 'Love takes off the masks that we fear we cannot live without and know we cannot live within', love here meaning a state of 'being' or 'grace – not in the infantile American sense of being made happy but in the tough and universal sense of quest and daring and growth' (Baldwin, 1963, pp. 81–2). In his novel *Another Country* (1962), love is the conduit for Baldwin's anguished exploration of race, class and sexual politics, his characters striving for love and self-realization amidst American constructions of racial and sexual codes. In this respect, 'another country' becomes Morrison's 'paradise' in which love and the confrontation of the past may affect 'the transcendence of the realities of colour, of nations, and of altars' (Baldwin, 1963, p. 72). Morrison, then, reconfigures Baldwin's idealism for the twenty-first century, her notions of love and home infused with ontological, ecological and universal dimensions to address a transnational, post-9/11, post-Obama world. In *A Mercy* (2008) she reaches back to seventeenth-century America and the founding of those structures by which possibilities for freedom became subsumed by stratifications of ownership, territory, race and religion. There are millennial possibilities for a post racial world, but *A Mercy* reveals how they are fragile and easily squandered.

As we have seen, Morrison has chartered African-American history in literary and critical work that has engaged variously with the concerns of diasporic experience – exclusion, the relationship between the individual and the community, the role of the ancestor and forced or voluntary migration. The very notion of diaspora of course evokes its opposite, namely the idea of 'home' and how it is to be defined and constructed in the terrain, often hostile, of a new continent. Morrison's delineation of African-American experience is distilled, in the second decade of the twenty-first century, into a novel, *Home* (2012), in which the concerns of her work as a whole are paradoxically explicit and yet oblique, sometimes lying beneath the surface of this slim volume. The novel may be seen as the apotheosis of Morrison's literary and critical aesthetic and as a significant intervention in the creation of twenty-first century American literature and its millennium concerns.

Love (2003)

That these concerns are global is clear in Morrison's 'The Dead of September 11', first published in *Vanity Fair* in November 2001, in which she speaks directly to those who died in the 9/11 attacks on America. For Morrison, 9/11 is more than an American tragedy, one of planetary reach in which the perished were 'children of ancestors born in every continent on the planet: Asia, Europe, Africa, the Americas, Australia; born of ancestors who wore kilts, obis, saris, gelees, wide straw hats, yarmulkes, goat-skin, wooden shoes, feathers and cloths to cover their hair' (Morrison, 2001, p. 154). She avoids the judgemental 'hyperbole' of the 'overheated heart' (Morrison, 2001, p. 154) and abandons the self-righteous rhetoric of the nation state, war and revenge because 'Speaking to the broken and the dead is too difficult for a mouth full of blood' (Morrison, 2001, p. 154). This is a form of cleansing through language, a 'freshening of the tongue' that offers, when the specificities of race are removed, redemptive possibilities on a wider, human scale. Language, always the site of contestation in Morrison's work, now assumes yet more transformative and spiritual significance after such a traumatic event. We can see, then, why in *Love*, Morrison's first novel of the twenty-first century, language is central to the recognition, realization and expression of love that crosses borders of generation, class, race and gender. On *Love* Morrison has said 'I'm thinking a lot in this book about the connection between love and language, and I wanted to have the narrator, the woman [L] who opens and closes the book, who intervenes in it, be a person who understands how precious language is' (Morrison intv. with Silverblatt, 2008, p. 217).

The ghost L, part narrator, commentator and chorus but who, when alive, actively participates in events through the forging of Bill Cosey's will, deploys ambiguous language to effect Christine and Heed's mutually dependent relationship and rivalry for the position of 'Sweet Cosey child' (*L*, p. 88). L's ghost is present at Christine and Heed's moment of recognition and remembrance of their loving innocence as children, the name L representative of the connection between language and love. As children they forge a friendship within their secret language 'idagay' that crosses the boundaries of colour separating the dark-skinned, lower class Heed from light-skinned, bourgeois Christine. Morrison takes these characters to their recognition of this original love after decades of mutual hatred fuelled by difference, but their reconciliation in Heed's last hours necessitates the realization that they have themselves been complicit in their enslavement to patriarchal structures. Christine tells Heed, 'we started out being sold, got free of it, then sold ourselves to the highest bidder' (*L*, p. 185), an admission that includes both Christine's sexual submission in the service of 1960s' black liberation and the patriarch Cosey's purchase of Heed as a child bride. Cosey is never present in the novel; his portrait, though, hangs above Heed's bed in the house at Monarch Street and is representative of the structures impeding love's progression to maturity. The focus of Morrison's critique is not Bill Cosey, whose point of view is never in fact established, but rather the structures that allow the purchase of an 11-year-old bride as an expression of power. L deconstructs Cosey, who she claims is, in the end, just 'an ordinary man' (*L*, p. 200) and Heed and Christine realize his 'Big Daddy' persona is merely a construction – 'We make him up?' they ask and reply 'He made himself up. We must have helped' (*L*, p. 189). It is the female ancestor rather than Cosey's status as patriarch that again presides at the novel's revelatory conclusion. The ghost of Bill Cosey's lover, the prostitute Celestial, sits astride his grave, obscuring the language on his gravestone, the lie 'Ideal Husband. Perfect Father' (*L*, p. 201), displacing Cosey from the centre of the story. Celestial is the ancestor Beloved in a red dress; both have been exploited under the economies of prostitution and slavery respectively and both bear the scars of their experiences. Beloved's scar appears, when remembered at the end of *Beloved* as the ghost of slavery, as 'the smile under her chin' (*B*, p. 275) and Celestial's becomes the mark of a 'sporting woman' (*L*, p. 188). Together, L and Celestial, in the last chapter, transform what has appeared to be a narrative of rivalry between Heed and Christine for Cosey's preference into an 'alternative world of meaning and value' (Wyatt, 2008, p. 195) as new connections across generation, gender, class and race become possible.

Junior, arriving at Monarch Street from Correctional and originating from a mixed race community, The Settlement, becomes the unlikely conduit for a love that is non-hierarchical or based on principles of primogeniture. Initially bent on exploiting Christine and Heed's rivalry over Cosey's will and in thrall to the image of him as her 'Good Man', Junior abandons the red suit borrowed from Heed and instead wears Cosey's undershorts in misplaced homage to his masculinity and power (*L*, p. 119). It is, however, Heed's old red suit that is her true inheritance. Resonating with Celestial's red dress, the red slip Heed wears when dancing rebelliously (*L*, p. 168), the red blanket signalling the beginning of Christine and Heed's friendship (*L*, p. 78) and the red suit, all constitute a network of imagery to indicate an alternative, non-linear, economy that both bypasses patriarchy and validates the transcendence of love.

Junior is invited to join Christine and the ghost of Heed in a triumvirate bound together by the salutation, 'Hey, Celestial' and their conversion of One Monarch Street into female space reminiscent of the playhouse they name Celestial Palace as children (*L*, p. 188). Romen's stability and feminine empathy awaken love within Junior, a moment that occurs, significantly, in water (*L*, p. 179). Like Sula's association with water and fluidity, female characters in *Love* search for themselves in water. Heed bathes in constant disavowal of 'sea life' (*L*, p. 71), L 'born straight into rain' (*L*, p. 64) and Celestial who, as ancestor, takes possession of the sea in an inversion of Beloved's memory of the traumatic Middle Passage. Celestial's dive into the water is a confident and free reclamation of the sea (*L*, p. 106).

These meditations on the fluidity and transcendent power of love are James Baldwin's literary bequest to Morrison. In her obituary for Baldwin in 1987, she writes of how Baldwin had given her three gifts; first a language that has 'made American English honest – genuinely international. . . . dialogic, representative, humane' (Morrison, 1987c, p. 91); second, 'courage' and third indefinable 'tenderness' (Morrison, 1987c, pp. 92–3). 'I loved your love' (Morrison, 1987c, p. 93), she writes to Baldwin, who in *Another Country* provided his own meditation on love – its possibilities and impossibilities in a racialized, gendered America. In Baldwin's novel there is a love based on dependence, need and desire between genders in a world where 'what men have "dreamed up" is all there is, the world they've dreamed up *is* the world' (Baldwin's italics, 1962, p. 112). The word 'love' is repeated incessantly in *Another Country* as his characters attempt to define and achieve it. Morrison, however, consciously omits the word until love is attained at the novel's conclusion.[1] For both Morrison and Baldwin language is crucially important, the impossibility of its true expression or the unspeakability of experience, but Baldwin's concern with the difficulty of achieving love in the context of America's construction of masculinity takes new form in Morrison's novel. Both provide critiques of patriarchy; Baldwin in the heightened racial consciousness of New York in the 1960s, Morrison in the confines of the house in Monarch Street and the relationships of the women who live there. Set in the 1990s, the imperative need for love is not to cure an America emerging into the Civil Rights era, as it was for Baldwin, but to heal a world in which class and gender divisions override those of race.

Baldwin takes one of his central characters, Vivaldo, who is in an interracial relationship with the singer, Ida from a position in which 'Love was a country he knew nothing about' (Baldwin, 1962, p. 291) to an epiphany in which 'something within him was breaking; he was, briefly and horribly, in a region where there were no definitions of any kind, neither of colour, nor of male and female. There was only the leap and the rending and the terror and the surrender' (Baldwin, 1962, p. 297). The nascent understanding of love unrestricted by 'definitions' is, for Vivaldo, never fully realized and in the end Baldwin has recourse to the

---

[1] Morrison has said that she went 'through the manuscript carefully after I finished it and knew what the title would be and removed every word every time "love" appeared so that it would be raw when the first time the women say it, is the only time they could say it' (Morrison intv. with Silverblatt, 2008, p. 220).

free expression of love in a transatlantic relationship between the American Eric and the Frenchman, Yves. For Morrison, however, writing with Baldwin's three gifts, love becomes limitless if the ancestor is valued. Baldwin's problematic relationship with the ancestor is resolved in *Love* and Morrison provides possibilities for mixed race identities in bringing Junior to a recognition of love that take her beyond the negative representation of the light-skinned Maureen Peal in *The Bluest Eye* (1970).

Morrison has described the structure of *Love* as crystalline, each narrative strand or point of view offering another dimension or layer of revelation and meaning. 'The meaning of the novel is in the structure' because of the complexity of a history encompassing civil rights, female emancipation and the sexual politics of the 1990s (Morrison intv. with Silverblatt, 2008, p. 218). The reader comes to an understanding of twentieth-century African-American history through a reading of L's posthumous first-person account and through the third-person extradiegetic narrations in which events are experienced or remembered by one character but then often re-narrated from the perspective of another. It is Morrison's manipulation of focalization and point of view that provide the crystal-like structure through which African-American experience is rendered as multifaceted and whereby the reader moves from misreading *Love* as '*a story made up to scare wicked females and correct unruly children*' (*L*, p. 10) to recognizing it as a '*cautionary lesson in black history*' (Morrison's italics, *L*, p. 201). As we saw in Chapter 3, gains made by the African-American community through Civil Rights were not without consequence for cohesion across generations and gender. May's paranoia arises from an anxiety about the Civil Rights movement that leads to the separation of Christine and Heed, their love sacrificed to class rivalries.

A Mercy (2008)

In *A Mercy* Morrison approaches another complex period of history, that encompassing the chaos involved in the construction of American identity and again the structure of the novel is crucial in 'summoning order out of this chaos' (Morrison intv. with Silverblatt, 2009). Set a century before the American Declaration of Independence in the 1680s and 1690s, *A Mercy* articulates, in Deleuze and Guattari's terms, an early form of capitalist expansion and its flows of deterritorilazation and reterritorialization that effect, in essence, a paradise lost, a utopia denied as artificial mappings of geography, law and race are superimposed upon nature, the 'lawless laws' 'authorizing chaos in defense of order' (*M*, p. 8).

Morrison's imagining of seventeenth-century America may be theorized as an aesthetic articulation of Deleuze and Guattari's concept of 'smooth space', a term they use to denote space without order that operates in contrast to 'striated space' that, in its reterritorializing mode, is structured by mapping, gridding and the instituting of state apparatus (Delueze and Guattari, 1980, pp. 474–500). As Brian Massumi explains:

> State space is 'striated', or gridded. Movement in it is confined as by gravity to a horizontal plane, and limited by the order of that plane to preset paths between fixed and identifiable points. Nomad space is 'smooth', or open-ended. One can rise up at any point and move to any other. (Massumi, 1992, p. 6)

America in the late seventeenth century is smooth space that has positive potential as 'Nomad space' but, 'the smooth itself can be drawn and occupied by diabolical powers of *organization*' (Deleuze and Guattari's italics, 1980, p. 480) and Morrison reveals in *A Mercy* the process by which existing circulations of capital, already transnational, occupy smooth space. It is the establishing of private property and laws against manumission that 'incite chaos' (Morrison intv. with Silverblatt, 2009), strictures that destroy any potential smooth space may possess for the creation of home in America. The utopian fog, a 'blinding gold' miasma at the forging of America (*M*, p. 8) and its liberating transnational flows as 'Atlantic and reeking of plant life' (*M*, p. 7) dissipates, consumed by the strictures of the ownership of human life and the construction of race through law. The orphan Jacob Vaark, a man in search of a home in a new continent, embodies the optimism of an early America only to be corrupted by association with the slave trade in Barbados. Despite his act of mercy in saving Florens from the sexual veracity of the slave owner, Vaark is exposed to the vicissitudes of an emerging capitalism, his efforts to create a home doomed to failure. Not content with his subsistence farmstead, Vaark constructs a house that never becomes home, his children die and the bountiful landscape is offset by the barren nature of his futile project. The serpents in the ironwork of his opulent gates belie the promise of Eden and Morrison invokes *Paradise Lost* (1667) in naming the Vaark settlement Milton.[2] The Native-American Lina recognizes the impracticality of

---

[2] Tessa Roynon, in 'Miltonic Journeys in *A Mercy*' argues that 'Miltonic journeys suffuse Morrison's representation of the "chaos" that was Virginia and New England in the late 1600s. At the same time, Morrison's richly allusive depiction of a world in flux highlights the ambiguities of many passages, both textual and physical, in Milton's work' (Roynon, 2011, pp. 45–6).

Vaark's folly: 'There was no need for a third [house]. Yet at the very moment when there were no children to occupy or inherit it, he meant to build another, bigger, double-storied, fenced and gated like the one he saw on his travels' (*M*, p. 41). Vaark's failure to bring nature under his control is the consequence of his inability to read the land and understand his place in it. He believes himself to be 'breathing the air of a world so new, almost alluring in newness and temptation', a landowner 'making a place out of no place' (*M*, p. 10) and yet who, in his self-satisfaction, forgets that his journey to the D'Ortega plantation is dependent upon the ancient Lenape Indian trail and that the geography of Algonquin and Sesquehanna is not 'his' (*M*, p. 11) to have.[3] As with Valerian Street in *Tar Baby*, Jacob Vaark's innocence is predicated on a false sense of entitlement, the belief that he can exploit land and people in a spirit of benign ownership. His investment in the Barbados rum trade, geographically removed from the slave system he so abhors in Maryland, nevertheless finances his grand scheme and belies his ignorance of the interdependent global economies of the black Atlantic. Professing his contempt for chattel slavery, Vaark needs order and his rationalization of the temptations the new world offers operates as a controlling impulse, itself the repression of the desire to succumb to such bounty. Already, his Utopia requires a fence, a boundary with gates and, unable to understand the rhythms and flows of the land, Vaark embarks on a form of ecological imperialism.

Without the patience necessary for successful farming, Vaark rejects Lina's knowledge of her own world and is unable to create home within a chaotic and unpredictable ecology that affronts his aesthetic sensibilities. Jacob 'ignored her warning of using alewives as fertilizer only to see his plots of tender vegetables torn up by foragers attracted by the smell. Nor would he plant squash among the corn. Though he allowed that the vines kept weeds away, he did not like the look of disorder' (*M*, p. 48). He becomes a moneylender investing in sugar and takes refuge in the preoccupations of European architecture, livestock and his English wife.

Having lost her family to smallpox, Lina retains elements of Native American practice that she blends with her newfound loyalty to a European master and mistress. A figure of hybridity and a survivor born out of dislocation, disease, domestic abuse and religious impositions, Lina represents one strand of what it

---

[3] James Braxton Peterson, in 'Eco-Critical Focal Points: Narrative Structure and Environmentalist Perspectives in *A Mercy*' points out the 'the narrator establishes a mild irony between the suggestion that Jacob owns (t)his geography and is moving through environments that are named according to the native peoples who were settled there long before the colonial forces that he represents set about the naming and claiming of the land' (Peterson, 2011, p. 13).

is to become American. 'Relying on memory and her own resources, she cobbled together neglected rites, merged Europe medicine with native, scripture with lore, and recalled or invented the meaning of things. Found, in other words, a way to be in the world' (*M*, p. 46).

Lina creates a cosmology of self-invention that is fluid enough to enable her survival as an exile in her own land. She exists in symbiosis with plants and animals, talking to them in a cosmology that does not recognize any hierarchical ordering of species, 'becoming one more thing that moved in the natural world. She cawed with birds, chatted with plants, spoke to squirrels, sang to the cow and opened her mouth to rain' (*M*, pp. 46–7). Jacob's very project, by contrast, is doomed because he does not ask the trees for permission, intent as he is on bending the environment to his folly (*M*, p. 42).

Vaark's rescue of Florens, a merciful act, reveals his species racism. Believing that Florens will be a replacement for his dead daughter Patrician, he makes a transaction in flesh to fill a void created, ironically, by his insatiable quest for a legacy as Patrician is kicked by a pull horse acquired for the construction of the new house (*M*, p. 87). Considered, in fact, as less than human, Florens is inscribed as the inferior replacement for Patrician, taken in lieu of a debt and without emotional connection; should she die 'her loss would not rock Rebekka so' (*M*, p. 24). In summarizing racism and speciesism in *Postcolonial Ecocriticism*, Graham Huggan and Helen Tiffin consider:

> The very ideology of colonisation is thus one where anthropocentrism and Eurocentrism are inseparable, with the anthropocentrism underlying Eurocentrism being used to justify those forms of European colonialism that see 'indigenous cultures as "primitive", less rational, and closer to children, animals and nature'. (Huggan and Tiffin, 2010, p. 5)

A Mercy is an intervention into ecocritical thinking as Morrison interrogates the distinctions between human, animal and nature. Her project necessitates a return to the imaginary, as land, indigenous peoples and animals have been overlaid by centuries of imperial control and internal colonization.[4] In this sense, the novel is positioned at the juncture of postcolonial and ecoenvironmental studies. The postcolonial ecocritical approach aims to combine a strand of postcolonialism, one that focuses on colonialism itself as

---

[4] Edward Said in *Culture and Imperialism* writes that imperialism 'is an act of geographical violence through which virtually every space in the world is explored, charted, and finally brought under control' and that '[b]ecause of the presence of the colonizing outsider, the land is recoverable at first only through imagination' (Said, 1993, p. 77).

its subject, with an examination of the environmental practices of imperialism (Huggan and Tiffin, 2010, p. 3). For the white settler, the unmapped is an open and clear space ready for exploitation, its inhabitants less than human and indistinguishable from its flora and fauna. Such an anthropocentric viewpoint, alongside hierarchies of classification and taxonomy, provides the justification for imperialist expansion. Writing on chaos in the context of a post 9/11 world in an essay, 'Peril', Morrison addresses the question of Enlightenment responses to the unknown and advocates a new kind of response, one of repose and stillness through art:

> When the chaos is simply the unknown, the naming can be accomplished effortlessly – a new species, star, formula, equation, prognosis. There is also mapping, charting, or devising proper nouns for un-named or stripped-of-names geography, landscape, or population. When chaos resists, either by reforming itself or by rebelling against imposed order, violence is understood to be the most frequent response and the most rational when confronting the unknown, the catastrophic, the wild, wanton, or incorrigible. Rational responses may be censure, incarceration in holding camps, prisons, or death, singly or in war. There is however a third response to chaos, which I have not heard about, which is stillness. Such stillness can be passivity and dumbfoundedness; it can be paralytic fear. But it can also be art. (Morrison, 2009, p. 3)

In *A Mercy* this stillness is the means for survival and the creation of home. Florens, for example, meets the threat of a bear with a stillness that allows her to complete both her physical journey to the blacksmith and her spiritual self-invention as wilderness (*M*, pp. 39–40). By contrast, Willard and Scully respond with violence to the threat from the wild, stabbing the bear in the eye (*M*, p. 145). Indentured servants themselves, Willard and Scully function to show how servitude and slavery are as yet not fully raced, but by the novel's end they are representative of another way to be American, as white paid labour responding violently to nature (*M*, p. 154). The blacksmith, Morrison's ancestral mythical figure, teaches Florens how to read the wilderness, warning her not to look bears in the eye because such mutual recognition is dangerous (*M*, p. 3). She must learn to read the landscape and its creatures, as literacy alone, though vital for the expression of her story on the walls and floor of her master's house, is not enough for survival and freedom. All the human senses are needed for reading the world; to write herself Florens must marshal her reading of nature's signs – the pea hen, the snake, the outline of a dog in the steam from a kettle – in a cosmology of imagery by which to create her own narrative (*M*, p. 1–2).

In relation to reading and misreading the world, Morrison's novelistic imagination conjures a world in which seeing and not seeing, religion, the land, the sea and animals are woven into a metaphorical design for her articulations of becoming. The eyes of bears, the moose gazing upon Rebekka as she bathes and its echo in the witch hunters' inspection of Florens for Devilish signs, the meeting of Jacob's and the blacksmith's eyes – all mark defining moments of realization. Rebekka, for example, becomes aware of her nakedness in paradise when watched by the moose, an inhabitant of Eden, a profound moment in her journey towards pious fundamentalism (*M*, p. 68). Florens's realization of her racial difference and its construction as a negative other occurs in Widow Ealing's version of Utopia as she faces the fact of her own blackness in yet another version of becoming (*M*, p. 113). As with all the projected Utopias in *A Mercy*, the Widow's settlement is already striated by the concerns of property, Daughter Jane condemned as a witch because the villagers want her pasture (*M*, p. 107). There are echoes here of Nathaniel Hawthorne's *The Scarlet Letter* (1850) in which we are told how Utopia necessitates a prison, 'the black flower of civilized society' (Hawthorne, 1850, p. 36).

A Mercy also contains a subset of imagery that includes trees, birds and their eggs. As we have seen, Lina communicates with trees, Jacob cuts them down as part of his nation-building activities and Rebekka finds in them cathedral-like qualities that presage her later piety. Florens takes to a tree that eventually yields to her, providing shelter. Florens is also associated with birds and flight and is told a story, by Lina, in which an eagle defends her eggs against the traveller's claims of ownership. The allegorical nature of the story is clear when Florens asks if the eggs hatch and the young survive and Lina replies 'We have' (*M*, p. 61). They all survive as orphans, even though America, the eagle, is forever falling in Morrison's allegory of the attack on the Twin Towers in September 2001 (Omry, 2011, p. 90).

Florens's reinvention of herself is articulated in terms of hatching and other bird imagery, as the feathered thing inside herself (*M*, p. 113). In embracing the wilderness, her dependence on the blacksmith and on Lina may end. Before her rebirth, the hatching of a new self, Florens must undergo spiritual and physical journeys on which her progress is marked by the significance of shoes. The high-heeled shoes she wears as a child, 'the shoes of a loose woman' (*M*, p. 164), signify her susceptibility to sexual violation in the eyes of her mother and her wearing of Jacob's boots, so necessary for her journey, prefigures Florens's occupancy of his house. Having taken possession of his boots, Florens appropriates the other tools of the master, namely writing and property, and shifts from dependence on others as a commodity to the ownership of herself as the wild, radical outlaw, 'I am become wilderness' (*M*, p. 159).

As a prequel to the historical periods Morrison has thus far uncovered in her work, *A Mercy* traces the beginnings of an African-American writing tradition through Florens's narrative, written with a nail and beyond the law in a transgressive act on the floor and walls of the house of America, the house that race built. Morrison, in her essay 'Home', claims that her literary endeavour is to 'transform this house completely', an effort that finds its fictional embodiment in Florens's scratchings on the fabric of the master's house. (Morrison, 1997, p. 4). The originary moment, late seventeenth-century America, serves as the site for Morrison's alternative creation myth in which identities are remade and reshaped. Florens comes to identify with the land through a narrative shaped for the immediacy and urgency of self-expression, the language of which situates Morrison as a postcolonial writer whereby 'the self-conscious process of renaming and revisioning is the subversion of the colonial language of taxonomy, discipline and control, and a key element in postcolonial literary production' (DeLoughrey and Handley, 2011, p. 11).

A question remains at the end of *A Mercy*, one of whether or not this wild zone is really a space offering possibilities for agency, the same question, in fact, addressed earlier (in Chapter 4) in relation to *Beloved*. Florens's words may simply talk to themselves or, with Lina, the lover of fire, she may burn down the master's house and release her words into the world as ash settling on the landscape, again evoking the collapse of the Twin Towers into hot dust (*M*, p. 159). Florens finally establishes her presence in the landscape, a presence absent from the dream in which she cannot see her face reflected in the turquoise lake. Her first-person narration, entirely in the present tense, merges memories of past events with the present in a story representing African-American experience as one in which the past continues to have a hold on the present.

If Florens is associated with land and Lina with fire, Sorrow's self-invention is connected to the sea. Her identity is fluid and split, having been raised as a boy at sea and engaged in dialogue with an imaginary friend. Found in water and giving birth in water to become Complete (*M*, p. 132), the ocean for Sorrow is regenerative, transnational and transgendered. For Rebekka, the sea is female space, associated with menstruation (*M*, p. 71) and emphasized by her friendship with the lawless women with whom she shares passage to the new world. The 'sea is a smooth space par excellence', itself open to territorializations and 'striation' but containing possibilities for a nomadic diasporic identity (Deleuze and Guattari, 1980, p. 479). Ultimately, however,

Rebekka rejects such possibilities for the construction of a community of women, turning instead to the wider society of Anabaptists she had once eschewed, self-invention restricted by her new and precarious status as Vaark's widow. Again, Hawthorne is evoked in the sense that Rebekka lacks Hester Prynne's radicalism in maintaining her position as outsider, necessary for the community but apart from it. Hawthorne's narrator informs the reader that for Hester, '[t]he world's law was no law' and that '[s]he assumed a freedom of speculation' that is compared to Cromwellian revolutionary spirit in the English Civil War (Hawthorne, 1850, p. 107). *The Scarlet Letter*, set in the seventeenth century, is in part Hawthorne's meditation on what freedom and identity may mean for his nineteenth-century reader. Morrison's evocation of the seventeenth-century narrative allows her, like Hawthorne, to consider the relationship between American individuals, their freedoms and their community in ways that are relevant for the contemporary reader. She returns to the suppressed stories of the early human negotiation of land and nature in order to recover a history that has been romanticized and to undermine easy appropriations of the idealized Native-American as the antidote to twenty-first century ecological crises.

Home (2012)

In her final novel to date Morrison returns to the concerns of *Paradise* (1998) and the 'endless work' (*P*, p. 318) involved in constructing 'home'. Moreover, there are autobiographical resonances in *Home* as Morrison writes back to her ancestral past, especially the migratory lives of her grandparents and her own experience of 1950s' America (Morrison, 1976, pp. 3–14). The novel is also a meditation on the significance of reading and writing as empowerment and on the importance of knowledge and understanding necessary for the negotiation of lives as lived through the Depression, migration, segregation and war. Morrison, as the privileged teller of this allegorical fairy tale, ameliorates detailed characterization and description and renders the segregated landscape of America, as experienced by Frank Money, in surrealist terms that subvert realist narrative and carry political intent. With Frank Money, unprotected and overwhelmed, Morrison confirms W.E.B. Du Bois's 1903 prophecy that 'The problem of the twentieth century is the problem of the color-line' (Du Bois, 1903, p. 9) as for Frank, in the middle of that century, 'whatever the world's the world's palette, his shame and its fury exploded' (*H*, p. 24).

The quest narratives of Greek myth and the fairy tale on the surface of *Home* are combined by Morrison to represent African-American experience through a defamiliarized realism, as the schematic allegorical mode gradually gives way to an account, through her omniscient narrator and Frank's interjections, of the underlying dissonance that distorts psychological development and a coherent sense of self. The realities of the Depression, migration, war and medical experimentation are offset by an allegorical mode in which trees, money, shoes, colour and animals take on significance beyond their physical description. Morrison deploys tropes of the fairy tale – the wicked witch, lost children, the damsel in distress and the hero's quest to rescue her – as structuring devices for a story rooted in the economics of a racialized society. Nevertheless, Morrison has recourse to the magical in the figure of the zoot-suited man, misread by Frank as 'comic' (*H*, p. 34), but who is in fact the guiding hand, the fairy godmother as the ancestor crucial for Frank's ascent from the subterranean to self-realization.

The presence of the ancestor uniting the trilogy of *Beloved* (1987), *Jazz* (1992) and *Paradise* finds new expression in *Home*, as does the interrogation of masculinity in *Song of Solomon* (1977), which Morrison now reconfigures against the realities of racial segregation in the South of the 1950s. Migration from the South, a perennial motif of Morrison's work, is similarly extended in *Home* to a concern with dislocation beyond the nation state, to Korea, as she picks up the thread of trauma that extends from her delineation of nineteenth-century slavery in *Beloved* to America's military adventure after the Second World War and its repercussions for Frank's struggle with manhood, shame and memory. Bringing together the strands of her work to date in what is, in effect, a novella, she evokes the complexities of African-American experience in condensed allegorical form and without the intricate structural devices employed throughout her earlier work. The innovation that has always characterized Morrison's work now takes form in an economy of prose, unadorned and yet rich in its association and encourages a deconstructionist reading to reveal a politics of reading and writing that is crucial for the reader's construction of the text. Call and response, as a literary strategy informed by African-American cultural practice, is less evident here than in, for example, *Jazz*, but is nevertheless significant in *Home*. Irony and the unreliable testimony of Frank Money mean that the reader must engage with an open narrative technique that may be said to possess the simplicity of a blues prose style for the expression of a jazz psychology, its nuances revealed in Morrison's speech, 'The Dancing Mind', as a 'dance of the open mind' – the participatory act of reading that, for Morrison, completes the act of writing

(Morrison, 1996a, pp. 187–90). In such an engagement the writer becomes an archivist and archaeologist of diasporic experience in all its fluidities of self-invention and creativity, of degradation and shame and, in *Home*, Morrison employs an economy of style that belies the complexities of exile.

A self-conscious authorial presence, an interrogation of how history is constructed and an intertextual approach including the use of the blues 'I' as being expressive of collective experience, are strategies that accentuate the fictionality Morrison deploys to match the fictionality underpinning America's racial and ideological strictures. To redress fictional constructions of race Morrison employs postmodern strategies in an approach that is neither ahistorical nor playful but rooted in a specific historical period and expressive of real, lived experience. Morrison raises questions of authorial responsibility and of the authenticity of experience as her characters misread central events in their lives, leaving space for informed understanding of their position in American society during the 1950s. The violence and displacement described in *Home*, together with Frank's interjections to the author, are corrective counterpoints to that version of American, post-second world war, history as a period of abundance and stability. The election of America's first black President in 2008 has somehow meant an aversion to revisit the fissures of the past, implying our capacity for empathy is exhausted, that the race story has been told and no longer bears repeating. In a review of *Home*, for example, Sarah Churchwell notes Morrison's depiction of 'history as a warehouse of horrors' (Churchwell, 2012, p. 6). We may want to celebrate globalization and the new individualisms promised by multiculturalism, consumerism and technology, or as Walter Goebel and Saskia Schabio put it, 'Transnational corporations, transnational flows of labour, money and data seem together to have accelerated the decline of the nation state and cosmopolitanism is once more on the agenda – boosted in the United States by the current Obama euphoria' (Goebel and Schabio, 2010, p. 1). Morrison, however, has written clearly on authorial responsibility in 'Peril' where she warns against the premature celebration of transnationalism:

> Certain kinds of trauma visited on peoples are so deep, so cruel, that unlike money, unlike vengeance, even unlike justice, or rights, or the good-will of others, only writers can translate such trauma and turn sorrow into meaning, sharpening the moral imagination. A writer's life and work are not a gift to mankind; they are its necessity. (Morrison, 2009, p. 4)

For Morrison, the enshrinement of equality in America's founding texts is not enough to assuage the oppression of its past or its legacies, and indeed it is the writer's responsibility to 'disturb the social oppression that functions like a coma on the population' (Morrison, 2009, p. 1).

Originally contracted to write a memoir, Morrison instead chooses to represent black experience in 1950s America in a novel that echoes twenty-first century, post 9/11 anxieties. Clearly, for Morrison at least, a novel interrogating America's past takes precedence over the individualism of the conventional autobiography. In her essay 'A Slow Walk of Trees (as Grandmother Would Say), Hopeless (as Grandfather Would Say)', she presents some of her most autobiographical writing, recording her family's experience of eviction in the South during the early part of the twentieth century. Here, Morrison defines her place in America in relation to the repetition of her grandparents' experiences as seen throughout her own lifetime. She writes of how her family can include herself, a literary artist, *and* a young man 'emotionally lobotomized by the reformatories and mental institutions specifically designed to serve him' (Morrison, 1976, p. 4). It is, however, the commonalities of African-American experience in Morrison's essay 'Rootedness' – 'the life of the tribe' – that are significant, not Morrison's personal trajectory towards the position of public intellectual, academic and author (Morrison, 1984, p. 57). Progress is indeed a 'slow walk' and for every flight there is the potential for the fall into the 'grotesque' eruptions of American history (Morrison, 1976, p. 8).

The euphoria of Barack Obama's election in 2008 has rapidly dissipated into an intensification of racially inflected politics as Republicans question Obama's identity as an American, and into new anxieties surrounding the killing of Trayvon Martin in 2012 that so clearly resonates with the murder of Emmett Till in Money, Mississippi in 1955. Writing against the backdrop of Obama's election, Morrison's impulse is to revisit the period of segregation, pre Civil Rights or notions of a radicalized racial consciousness, not so much to reopen old wounds but rather as a reminder of the slow pace of change and the exclusions that are always close at hand (Morrison intv. with Jian Ghomeshi, 2012). The allegorical nature of *Home* is clear as America continues to send men home from war, Morrison concerned to project the present onto imaginings of the past 'to yield up a kind of a truth' (Morrison, 1987a, p. 71). The war in Korea is remembered lest America slip further into amnesia or nostalgia for the prosperity of the Eisenhower years and *Home* is written to redress the ideological distortions of political discourse. In 'The Future of Time' she writes of how the 1950s

> has acquired a gloss of voluntary orderliness, of ethnic harmony, although it was a decade of outrageous political and ethnic persecution. And here one realises

that the dexterity of political language is stunning, stunning and shameless. It enshrines the fifties as a model decade peopled by model patriots while at the same time abandoning the patriots who lived through them to reduced, inferior or expensive healthcare; to gutted pensions; to choosing suicide or homelessness. (Morrison, 1996b, p. 175)

For Morrison, consumerism has profound implications for American society with Americans themselves mere taxpayers without any real sense of citizenship and prey to the banditry of the market. In returning to the past the writer is able to provide 'insightful examination' (Morrison, 1996b, p. 179) of such contemporary anxieties and at the same time gesture towards a 'redemptive future' (Morrison, 1996b, p. 185). The future, as articulated in *Home*, is home itself and to return there is not necessarily a retrograde step but can mean the amelioration of the individualistic impulse through a commitment to family and community. When forced to leave the family home – whether by landlord or the Klan – its significance intensifies. There are versions of home throughout the novel, but it is the prologue that evokes the house in darkness:

> Whose house is this?
> Whose night keeps out the light
> In here?
> Say, who owns this house?
> It's not mine.
> I dreamed another, sweeter, brighter
> With a view of lakes crossed in painted boats;
> Of fields wide as arms open for me.
> This house is strange.
> Its shadows lie.
> Say, tell me, why does its lock fit my key? (*H*, p. 1)

Unwelcome in the house of America, the voice of the prologue is that of the stranger imagining another place, one of redemption, of water and daylight. Evoking the Harlem Renaissance, poet Claude McKay's 'White Houses' in which he finds the door to America 'shut against my tightened face'(McKay, 1925, p. 134), the voice in Morrison's prologue now has possession of a key that fits, and McKay's rage is tempered, a position of refusal now replaced by one of enquiry. *Home* becomes, then, an investigation of how the unhomely house has been constructed, why the key fits the door to this gothic, mendacious nightmare and the suggestion is that there is no alternative to making this house into a home.

In an autobiographical collection of songs entitled *I'm New Here* (2010) the poet, musician and singer Gil Scott-Heron shares this mature, pragmatic reflection on the house of America in the contexts of migration, loss and the veneration of a sustaining maternal figure. At the end of his life, the home he left as a young man is the place to which he must return. 'New York is Killing Me' and 'On Coming from a Broken Home' (Parts 1 and 2) are meditations on the sustenance provided by the women in Scott-Heron's life that run counter to the construction of the African-American family as pathologically broken. Resonating with Morrison's testimony to the healing possibilities of home, Gil Scott-Heron speaks of how 'My life has been guided by women', how because of them he is a man and, in the same song, 'On Coming from a Broken Home' (Part 2), he writes about how his southern family life has been rendered as pathological, when in fact he and his family were engaged in the construction of meaningful lives and 'home'.

That strand in the male autobiographical narrative in which the struggle is to become a man thus continues as Scott-Heron returns not to the north, as in Frederick Douglass's nineteenth-century freedom narrative, but to his beginnings in the South and, like Morrison, deconstructs and reconstructs home, its regenerative powers and its deprivations. Although not writing an autobiography, Morrison, as a constructed author made self-consciously evident for the first time in her work, endeavours to answer her own question posed at the end of the prologue: 'Say, tell me, why its lock fits my key? (*H*, p. 1). The reconstruction of the past as a means to truth, self-acceptance and redemption is the writer's responsibility and it is in this sense that Morrison may be said to be employing strategies of autobiographical writing in *Home*. In telling the story of Frank Money the 'writer' engages in dialogue with Frank himself who, although hardly a reliable witness to his past, interjects to ensure that Morrison, as storyteller, accurately relays his experiences.

The telling of the story of Frank's journey home to Lotus alludes to the confessional mode of the slave narratives as dictated to the sympathetic, white abolitionist. Neither Frank, nor his sister Cee, can write their own story and Morrison's task, as responsible authorial voice, is complicated by Frank's confrontational interjections in which he interrogates the authority of a storyteller who is neither from the South or been to war: '*You never lived there so you don't know what it was like*' (all Frank's interjections in italics, *H*, p. 84). Frank wants the truth to be told and yet he has repressed the memory of the one event that is the true source of his struggle, his original trauma. He says of the burial he and his sister witness as children:

> Since you're set on telling my story, whatever you think and whatever you write down, know this: I really forgot about the burial. I only remembered the horses. (*H*, p. 5)

The memory of the burial emerges from beneath his exaltation of the horses, standing like men. Only at the end of Home does Frank recognize the authentic masculinity at the heart of this scene, the dead black man, shoeless and ignominiously kicked back into the grave. Frank's journey, ostensibly a quest to save the life of his sister in Lotus, culminates in a new understanding of what it can mean to be a man. Just as she proffers different versions of home, Morrison offers versions of manhood, some of which she deconstructs, such as Frank's versions of himself as brother and protector, the soldier, lover and provider. In each incarnation he abandons his charges and such constructions of masculinity are revealed to be fictions. He leaves Cee and Lotus to join the army and, traumatized by war and unable to hold down a job, cannot fulfil the roles of lover and provider to Lily. As each version of himself as a man breaks down, Frank's quest for masculinity is fulfilled only on his return to Lotus and the re-burial of the black man, this time standing upright, his name and dignity restored.

Given the ritual humiliations of segregation, masculinity has to be reconfigured as the conventions of being a brother, a lover and a soldier are meaningless distortions. Frank's conviction that to kill a Korean girl is preferable to succumbing to her sexual invitations only re-emphasizes his disorientation. He sacrifices this girl child to his masculinity and, as with the burial witnessed as a child, it is this incident, reluctantly revealed, and not the violent deaths of his friends in battle, that is the true source of his shame. Again, Frank addresses the writer directly:

> I have to tell the whole truth. I lied to you and I lied to me. I hid it from you because I hid it from me. I felt so proud grieving over my dead friends. How I loved them. How much I cared about them, missed them. My mourning was so thick it completely covered my shame. (*H*, p. 133)

And later,

> *I shot the Korean girl in her face.*
> *I am the one she touched.*
> *I am the one who saw her smile.*
> *I am the one she said 'Yum-yum' to.*
> *I am the one she aroused.*

A child. A wee little girl.
I didn't think. I didn't have to.
Better she should die.
How could I let her live after she took me down to a place I didn't know was in me?
(*H*, pp. 133–4)

We have here an allegory of the original sin, the rotting orange the girl reaches for the forbidden fruit, temptation in the theatre of war re-imagined as the means for a hungry girl's survival (*H*, p. 95). With Frank's revelation, Morrison unveils the atrocious truth of a war that has been forgotten by America, the truth of all wars, the slaughter of innocent civilians. The exposure of war crimes that have occurred from the Second World War through to Vietnam, Kosovo and the Middle East, provides a modern sensibility for Morrison to release the repressed trauma of the Korean War. Frank's return to Lotus enables the confrontation of his memories, 'sweet or shameful' (*H*, p. 8), and a realignment of his sense of manhood towards new revelations of self-knowledge. In saving his sister from the experiments of Dr Beau, Frank rescues himself and brother and sister are made anew at home, in Lotus. Having confronted the burial they saw as children, Frank and Cee are able to repeat the scene and re-bury the victim, this time as a known man, upright and shrouded in colour. Lotus itself is suffused with life's colour as they lower the quilted coffin beneath a crucifix like, split bay tree, damaged yet still alive. Like Frank and Cee, the two halves are no longer dependent upon each other and yet alive together, survivors heading for home.

The image of the split tree resonates with Frank's childhood experience of his community's eviction and Crawford's resistance, murder and burial beneath the magnolia tree that stands in his yard. The magnolia, a symbol of the South, stands as the oldest magnolia tree in the county, planted by Crawford's great grandmother and indicative of how the African-American presence is as old as America itself and, as such, how African Americans have valid expectations of the house as a home. The tree implies a rootedness and entitlement that proves fatal for Crawford, the victim of racial murder in Depression era America. This early experience of a man killed and buried beneath a tree finds more positive repetition at the novel's conclusion, this time as the redemptive burial of the past. Revealed almost as an aside, the murder of Crawford is nevertheless a defining moment in Frank's life and serves as the catalyst for other imagery; trees, burial – literally and as repression of memory and shame – seeing and not seeing and the significance of the shoes that are essential for Frank's life of flight and return.

Until Frank reaches Lotus his world loses all colour at moments of breakdown after Korea and his return home facilitates an Eden-like affirmation of life, light and nature. While evoking the film *The Wizard of Oz* (1939) in the use of inverted colour, the journey and notions of home, as well as the myth of Odysseus, Morrison alludes to that tradition in post-Second World War American writing dealing with the psychosis induced and institutionalized by America that includes J. D. Salinger's *Catcher in the Rye* (1951), Ken Kesey's *One Flew Over the Cuckoo's Nest* (1962), and Sylvia Plath's *The Bell Jar* (1963). Morrison is perhaps acknowledging how the individualist fantasy at the heart of American literature, namely to light out for the territory, always ends, in effect, with the return home. In *Home* it is the return home that demands courage, not the journey outward. Lacking self-knowledge, Frank sees Lotus as being 'worse than any battlefield' (*H*, p. 82) and implies that his true heroism lies not in his wartime experience but in his journey home to face whatever awaits him there. As in *Paradise*, creating home requires 'endless work' (*P*, p. 318) to transform traumas of the past into something useful and, as Frank comes to see, 'safe and demanding' (*H*, p. 132), upon which to construct the future. It is not simply a matter of recreating Eden but, as Ethel instinctively knows in *Home*, it is 'much more than that', unromanticized and messy but able to both nurture and repel the threat from outside (*H*, p. 130). The women of Lotus provide an alternative, practical system of care to counteract the institutionalization and incarceration offered by the American state to its sons of war. Morrison makes clear that America, the house, has failed in its duty of care to Frank the war veteran and to Cee, the victim of the 'medical industry' (*H*, p. 122). American healthcare sees Frank robbed by those entrusted with his care, leaving only his war medal, a worthless memento of his sacrifice, and the sacrifice of his friends, to the American dollar. Money itself is so elusive for Frank Money, despite his new wallet, and his journey starkly inverts the consumerist dream upon which America had embarked in the 1950s. Frank's lover Lily internalizes this dream and yet, despite her economic independence, she too is denied her own version of home, the modern suburban settlement, on grounds of racial origin (*H*, p. 73). For Frank and Cee's parents, making a home means working three jobs, leaving their children vulnerable to their grandmother Lenore, herself a woman embittered by the experience of forced migration during the Depression. Given such economic and racial strictures on the construction of home, peace for Frank and Cee lies in nascent creativity and work without alienation, not in the purchase of a Philco refrigerator.

Through use of the 'money' motif Morrison suggests a counterpoint to the monetization of American existence in the underground network Frank needs to get him back to Lotus and his sister. Emerging from the desegregated army, he experiences segregated civilian society in stark hallucinations that suggest madness or psychosis to be the only rational response to the world that surrounds him. The polarization into black and white of Frank's world-view becomes acute at moments of shameful dehumanization in a segregated landscape before the Civil Rights movement, notions of a black consciousness or the negritude sympathies of European intellectuals. Frank's rage remains inchoate without the knowledge that he is in fact struggling with the split in his consciousness engendered by America's racial system. He is unable to channel this duality to any advantage as Lotus, or so the writer is told, has bequeathed him nothing in the way of education, knowledge or stimulus. He is locked within a historical period, poised between a desegregated army and a segregated civil society, and without the insight proffered by the Du Boisian psychology of double consciousness, the radical counter narrative of racial pride articulated by the Harlem Renaissance movement or the later Pan-African consciousness. The racial dualities invented by America and deployed in its legislation, social practices and spatial, physical exclusions – the washroom, the bus and train, the lunch counter – have their origin in the binary opposition of black and white.

A few years before Frank Money's break down in the face of such oppositions, Jean-Paul Sartre, in his preface (also separately published) to Senghor's edition of Negritude poetry in French, *Black Orpheus* (1948), recognized hierarchical black/white binaries, 'the great Manichean division of the world into black and white' (Sartre, 1948, p. 19), but found redemptive possibilities for their destabilization in the politicized expressions of the Pan-African Negritude poetry movement. The 'hierarchic coupling' of 'black-white' in which 'black' has served the interests of colonialism dissolves in a celebration of blackness, an 'antiracist racism' that, despite its essentialism, will lead to the dissolution of 'all opposites' and 'a song of everyone of us and for everyone of us' (Sartre, 1948, p. 11).

The objective position of the white proletariat in capitalist society is inappropriate for understanding the status of the African without a developed racial consciousness. For Sartre, in his Marxist, humanist schema, a moment of essentialism coterminous with black consciousness is merely a stage towards the 'ultimate unity' of a global proletarian movement and, despite the heightened racial emphasis of the poets discussed in his preface, this artistic expression has universal potentialities.

That such an essentialist identity may be constructed to counteract the essentialisms of colonial and imperialist ideology serves to highlight the possibility that all identities are, in fact, constructions, whether deployed in the name of oppression or liberty. In the same sense that blackness is not an essence, masculinity is open to contestation and new forms of construction. Like the negritude poets, Morrison renders blackness in positive terms, although not through the characters in *Home*, who are never racially identified, but rather through descriptions of animals; a stallion of the deepest black, rising up like a man, and a beautiful black dog. The only clear reference to racial identity is the black foot shovelled into the grave, the burial of a man as yet unidentified but central to Frank's recognition of what manhood can be and to the novel's closure.

The ambiguity of identity carries into Morrison's introduction of the man wearing the zoot suit, fashionable in the 1940s. In his initial understanding of this ghostly but benign presence, Frank conflates essentialisms of masculinity and race as he contrasts this counter-cultural expression of urban America unfavourably with his own idea of what constitutes masculine, black authenticity. For Frank, at this point in his odyssey at least, masculinity means a romanticized, idealized version of the noble savage (*H*, p. 34), not the fluid identities being forged by modern, urbanized African Americans after the Second World War.

Before his encounter with the zoot-suited man, Frank's naïve misreading of his situation is clear when he reaches his first port of call having escaped from the hospital. This is the church of John Locke, the pragmatic Reverend very much attuned to the war veteran's vulnerability. Locke and his wife recognize Frank's condition and understand the connection between his experience in Korea and his state of mind, a connection Frank himself is reluctant to make as he thinks the 'army hadn't treated him so bad' (*H*, p. 18). This first stop on the 'underground railway', now inverted to run from north to south, provides Frank with the practicalities of money, shoes, food and advice about the realities of life in the north. This help comes from the wider community, a small flock that nevertheless allows him a duty of care that transcends affection and is necessary because Frank Money is just one more in the procession of lost men passing through Locke's church.

Without formal education but not without sensibilities, Frank is drawn to the sound of jazz erupting from a basement bar. Driving bebop is the only form of musical expression appropriate for his agitated state of mind and for the world after Hiroshima. A black musical sensibility is expressive, not just of Frank's surreal and chaotic experience, but also of the wider, planetary threat of nuclear weapons and the cataclysmic potential of the Cold War. 'After Hiroshima, the musicians understood as early as anyone that Truman's bomb changed everything and only scat and bebop could say how' (*H*, p. 108). Attuned to this postwar mode, the negritude poets, for Satre, deploy their percussive, rhythmical poetry in a 'dance of the soul: the poet turns like a dervish until he expires, he has installed in himself the times of his ancestors, he feels himself to flow away in spasmodic pulsations, and it is in this rhythmic flowing away that he hopes to refind himself' (Satre, 1948, p. 32). For Morrison, however, Frank must ascend from the essentialism of any surrender to the jazz rhythms in order to truly 'refind himself'.

A key moment in that quest is when Frank witnesses the jazz drummer's inability to control his performance at the jazz concert:

> The Drummer had lost control. The rhythm was in charge. After long minutes, the pianist stood and the trumpet player put down his horn. Both lifted the drummer from his seat and took him away, his sticks moving to a beat both intricate and silent'. (*H*, p. 109)

The performance ends with a scat singer to restore good cheer and to bring Frank and the audience to a condition of psychic stability. Frank can now find the serenity necessary for him to rescue Cee without recourse to the violence that has marked his journey so far. He begins to master the rhythms and repetitions of the black experience of exile and prejudice. Frank has, until this point, misread or misunderstood the knowledge available to him in Lotus, but realizes now that there are lessons to be learned in the music played in the bars of America. It is bebop that provides the catalyst for this epiphany and he now knows that to exploit the rhythm, rather than surrender blindly to its endless repetitions, will lead him back to Cee and towards self-realization. It is, then, a controlled rhythm that is necessary for the exorcism of trauma; without control the player is locked in and, unable to escape the repetitions of traumatic experience, becomes, in Ellison's words, 'dedicated to chaos' (Ellison, 1964, p. 203). If Morrison's work evokes a jazz aesthetic, it is one that may be said to avoid any essentialism of rhythm and in which she evokes the tones, chords or modes of jazz without attempting to imitate the 'riff' in literary form. We could, though, see the riff as an evocative metaphor for history itself, relentlessly and oppressively unmodulating, and around which the narrative of *Home* plays out as Morrison presents little more than the facts of Frank's life. Morrison's 'hero' is *Frank* Money, the novel an honest interrogation of the economics of American life in the 1950s. *Home* is in many ways a 'no money, no woman' blues and full of suffering, its profundity easily obscured by the simplicity of its execution.

The first line of a blues is often immediately repeated in knowing, sardonic reference to black experience, the second line serving as the response to the call of the first in an emphatic reiteration of life's tribulations. The communal characteristics of the work song are now embodied in the individual, free expression of one man or woman and the form takes on a significance beyond its origins to become a universal, post-racial sign of sufferance and longing that has been endlessly exploited. The blues are also of course expressive of new possibilities, post-reconstruction, for migratory movement and sexual relationships and therefore paradoxically a celebration of the freedom to love or be loved, to leave or to be left. This freedom, however, is striated by the blues form's preoccupation with the themes of money and sex, a concoction rarely imbued with direct political commentary. In 'Eisenhower Blues' (1954), however, blues motifs – shoes, money and women – are employed by J. B. Lenoir in a narrative of hardship that runs counter to the prevailing ideology of America in the 1950s. 'I'm only givin' you people the natural facts' he sings and, in his 'Korea Blues' (1954), he reminds America that it is in fact at war.

The scene witnessed by Frank and Cee at the beginning of the novel – the burial of a man forced to fight his son to the death – finds echo with the famous battle royal chapter in Ralph Ellison's *Invisible Man*, written in 1952, the year in which *Home* is set, the year Lloyd Price's 'Lawdy Miss Clawdy' plays over the radio as Frank takes his stricken sister from the car. There is an ironic disjunction between Cee's condition and this recording, a Rhythm and Blues hit that crossed over to reach a wider, white audience. The unequal and unfair nature of this exchange is clear as the struggle to save Cee's life plays out to what was, in 1952, a practically ubiquitous soundtrack of African-American expressive artistry and later recorded by Elvis Presley. In a song that itself has an intertextual relationship with the blues tradition, Price sings 'Lawdy, Miss Clawdy, you sure look good to me' and Frank and Cee's situation contrasts sharply with the evidently significant role that African-American expressivity plays in the cultural and commercial mainstream of American life.

In her opening scene, Morrison revisits a repetition of American life – men as beasts forced to fight one another for the entertainment of others. Towards the end of *Home* the truth of this event is revealed, its dehumanization transcended only by the very human act of self-sacrifice of the father for the son. The repetitions of America's racial past are revealed as Ellison's invisible man is hospitalized and medicated in ways that, again, reflect Frank's treatment on returning from Korea. Both Ellison's and Morrison's central characters experience false rebirths from the hospital bed, one in a racially conscious quest for identity, Frank in search of home.

Bibliography

Abel, Elizabeth (Spring 1993), 'Black Writing, White Reading: Race and the Politics of Feminist Interpretation'. *Critical Inquiry*, 19, 3, 470–98.
Allen, Samuel (1988), 'Review of *Song of Solomon*', in Nellie McKay (ed.), *Critical Essays on Toni Morrison*. Boston, MA: G.K. Hall and Co., pp. 30–2.
Appiah, Kwame Anthony (1986), 'The Uncompleted Argument: Du Bois and the Illusion of Race', in Henry Louis Gates, Jr. (ed.), *'Race', Writing, and Difference*. Chicago, IL: University of Chicago Press, pp. 21–37.
— (1992), *In My Father's House: Africa in the Philosophy of Culture*. London: Methuen.
Awkward, Michael (1995), *Negotiating Difference*. Chicago, IL: University of Chicago Press.
Baker, Houston A., Jr (1984), *Blues, Ideology, and Afro-American Literature: A Vernacular Theory*. Chicago, IL: University of Chicago Press.
— (1987), *Modernism and the Harlem Renaissance*. Chicago, IL: University of Chicago Press.
— (1993), 'When Lindbergh Sleeps with Bessie Smith: The Writing of Place in *Sula*', in Henry Louis Gates, Jr. and K. A. Appiah (eds), *Toni Morrison: Critical Perspectives Past and Present*. New York: Amistad, pp. 236–60.
Bakhtin, Mikhail (1981), *The Dialogical Imagination*. Michael Holquist (ed.), Caryl Emerson and Michael Holquist (trans.), Austin, TX: University of Texas Press.
Baldwin, James (1962), *Another Country* (2001 edn). London: Penguin.
— (1963), *The Fire Next Time* (1964 edn). London: Penguin.
— (1964), *Notes of a Native Son* (1995 edn). London: Penguin.
Baraka, Amiri Imamu (LeRoi Jones) and Amina Baraka (eds) (1983), *Confirmation: An Anthology of African American Women*. New York: Quill. See also Jones, LeRoi.
Bauman, Zygmunt (1991), *Modernity and Ambivalence* (1993 edn). Oxford: Polity Press.
Bell, Bernard W. (1987), *The Afro-American Novel and Its Tradition*. Amherst, MA: University of Massachusetts Press.
— (1996), 'Genealogical Shifts in Du Bois's Discourse on Double-Consciousness as the Sign of African American Difference', in Bell, Emily R. Grosholz and James B. Stewart (eds), *W.E.B. Du Bois on Race and Culture: Philosophy, Politics, and Poetics*. New York: Routledge, pp. 87–108.
Bell, Bernard W., Emily R. Grosholz and James B. Stewart (eds) (1996), *W.E.B. Du Bois on Race and Culture: Philosophy, Politics, and Poetics*. New York: Routledge.

Belles, Gilbert A. (1982), 'The Politics of Alain Locke', in Russell J. Linnemann (ed.), *Alain Locke: Reflections on a Modern Renaissance Man*. Baton Rouge, LA: Louisiana State University Press, pp. 50–62.

Benjamin, Andrew (ed.) (1989), *The Lyotard Reader*. Oxford: Blackwell.

Benjamin, Walter (Germany 1936), 'The Storyteller', in Hannah Arendt (ed.), Harry Zohn (trans.), *Illuminations* (1992 edn). London: Fontana, pp. 83–107.

Berman, Marshall (1981), *All that Is Solid Melts into Air: The Experience of Modernity*. (1983 edn). London: Verso.

Bhabha, Homi K. (1994), *The Location of Culture*. London: Routledge.

Blauner, Robert (1970), 'Black Culture: Myth or Reality?', in Norman E. Whitten and John F. Szwed (eds), *Afro-American Anthropology: Contemporary Perspectives*. New York: Free Press.

Bloom, Harold (ed.) (1990), *Toni Morrison: Modern Critical Views*. New York: Chelsea House.

Bluestein, Gene (1972), *The Voices of the Folk: Folklore and American Literary Theory*. Amherst, MA: University of Massachusetts Press.

Bogle, Donald (1989), *Toms, Coons, Mulattoes, Mammies and Bucks: An Interpretive History of Blacks in American Films*. New York: Continuum.

Bogue, Ronald (1989), *Deleuze and Guattari*. London: Routledge.

Bouson, J. Brooks (2000), *Quiet as It's Kept: Shame, Trauma, and Race in the Novels of Toni Morrison*. New York: State University of New York Press.

Boxhill, Bernard R. (1996), 'Du Bois on Cultural Pluralism', in Bernard W. Bell, Emily R. Grosholz and James B. Stewart (eds), *W.E.B. Du Bois on Race and Culture: Philosophy, Politics, and Poetics*. New York: Routledge, pp. 57–85.

Brenner, Gerry (1988), '*Song of Solomon*: Rejecting Rank's Monomyth and Feminism', in Nellie McKay (ed.), *Critical Essays on Toni Morrison*. Boston, MA: G.K. Hall and Co., pp. 114–24.

Brown, H. Rap (1969), *Die Nigger Die!* New York: Dial Press.

Butler-Evans, Elliott (1989), *Race, Gender, and Desire: Narrative Strategies in the Fiction of Toni Cade Bambara, Toni Morrison, and Alice Walker*. Philadelphia, PA: Temple University Press.

Butler, Judith (1990), *Gender Trouble: Feminism and the Subversion of Identity*. New York: Routledge.

— (1993), *Bodies that Matter: On the Discursive Limits of 'Sex'*. New York: Routledge.

— (1997), *Excitable Speech: A Politics of the Performative*. New York: Routledge.

Byerman, Keith (1985), *Fingering the Jagged Grain: Tradition and Form in Recent Black Fiction*. Athens, GA: University of Georgia Press.

— (1990), 'Beyond Realism: The Fictions of Toni Morrison', in Harold Bloom (ed.), *Toni Morrison: Modern Critical Views*. New York: Chelsea House, pp. 55–84.

Carby, Hazel V. (1987), *Reconstructing Womanhood: The Emergence of the Afro-American Woman Novelist*. New York: Oxford University Press.

— (1990), 'The Politics of Fiction, Anthropology and the Folk', in Michael Awkward (ed.), *New Essays on Their Eyes Were Watching God*. Cambridge, MA: Cambridge University Press, pp. 71-93.

— (1992), 'The Multicultural Wars', in Gina Dent (ed.), *Black Popular Culture*. Seattle: Bay Press, pp. 187-99.

Carr, Helen (1996), *Inventing the American Primitive: Politics, Gender and the Representation of Native American Literary Traditions, 1789-1936*. New York: New York University Press.

— (November 1998), 'Motherhood and Apple Pie', in Jan Montefiore (ed.), 'Maternity', an issue of *Paragraph*, 21, 3, 269-89.

Carson, Clayborne and Peter Holloran (eds) (1999), *A Knock at Midnight: The Great Sermons of Martin Luther King, Jr*. London: Little, Brown and Company.

Chartres, Ann (1990), 'Introduction' to Gertrude Stein *Three Lives*. Harmondsworth: Penguin Books, pp. vii-xx.

Christian, Barbara T. (1985), *Black Feminist Criticism: Perspectives on Black Women Writers*. New York: Pergamon Press.

— (1997), 'Layered Rhythms: Virginia Woolf and Toni Morrison', in Nancy J. Peterson (ed.), *Toni Morrison: Critical and Theoretical Approaches*. Baltimore, MD: Johns Hopkins University Press, pp. 19-36.

Churchwell, Sarah (1965), 'History as a Warehouse of Horrors', *The Guardian*, 28 April 2012, p. 6.

Clark, Kenneth B. (1965), *Dark Ghetto: Dilemmas of Social Power*. London: Victor Gollanz.

Clarke, Deborah L. (1993), '"What There Was before Language": Preliteracy in Toni Morrison's *Song of Solomon*', in Carol J. Singley and Susan Elizabeth Sweeney (eds), *Anxious Power: Reading, Writing, and Ambivalence in Narrative by Women*. New York: State University of New York Press, pp. 265-78.

Clarke, Graham (1990), 'Marking Out and Digging in: Language as Ritual in *Go Down, Moses*', in A. Robert Lee (ed.), *William Faulkner: The Yoknapatawpha Fiction*. London: Vision Press, pp. 147-64.

Cleaver, Eldridge (1969), *Soul on Ice*. London: Cape.

Clifford, James (1988), *The Predicament of Culture: Twentieth-Century Ethnography, Literature, and Art*. Cambridge, MA: Harvard University Press.

Collins, Patricia Hill (1991), *Black Feminist Thought: Knowledge, Consciousness, and the Politics of Empowerment*. New York: Routledge.

Cowart, David (2000), 'Faulkner and Joyce in Morrison's *Song of Solomon*', in David Middleton (ed.), *Toni Morrison's Fiction: Contemporary Criticism*. New York: Garland Publishing, pp. 95-108.

Crouch, Stanley (1990), *Notes of a Hanging Judge*. New York: Oxford University Press.

Croyden, Margaret (1994), 'Toni Morrison Tries Her Hand at Playwriting', in Danille Taylor-Guthrie (ed.), *Conversations with Toni Morrison*. Jackson, MS: University Press of Mississippi, pp. 218-22.

Cunard, Nancy (ed.) (1934), *Negro* (1969 edn). New York: Negro Universities Press.

Darling, Marsha (1994), 'In the Realm of Responsibility: A Conversation with Toni Morrison', in Danille Taylor-Guthrie (ed.), *Conversations with Toni Morrison*. Jackson, MS: University Press of Mississippi, pp. 246–54.

Davis, Cynthia A. (1990), 'Self, Society and Myth in Toni Morrison's Fiction', in Harold Bloom (ed.), *Modern Critical Views: Toni Morrison*. New York: Chelsea House, pp. 7–25.

Deleuze, Gilles (France 1968), *Difference and Repetition* (1994 edn, Paul Patton trans.). London: The Athlone Press.

Deleuze, Gilles and Félix Guattari (France 1972), *Anti-Oedipus: Capitalism and Schizophrenia* (1984 edn, Robert Hurley, Mark Seem and Helen R. Lane trans.), London: Athlone Press.

— (France 1975), *Kafka: Toward a Minor Literature* (1986 edn, Dana Polan trans.), Minneapolis, MN: University of Minnesota Press.

— (France 1980), *A Thousand Plateaus: Capitalism and Schizophrenia* (1988 edn, Brian Massumi trans.), London: Athlone Press.

DeLoughrey, Elizabeth and George B. Handley (2011), 'Introduction: Toward an Aesthetics of the Earth', in DeLoughrey and Handley (eds), *Postcolonial Ecologies: Literatures of the Environment*. New York: Oxford University Press, pp. 3–39.

Denard, Carolyn C. (2008a), 'Blacks, Modernism, and the American South: An Interview with Toni Morrison', in Denard (ed.), *Toni Morrison Conversations*. Jackson, MI: University Press of Mississippi, pp. 178–95.

— (ed.) (2008b), *Toni Morrison Conversations*. Jackson, MI: University Press of Mississippi.

Dennis, Rutledge M. (1982), 'Relativism and Pluralism in the Social Thought of Alain Locke', in Russell J. Linnemann (ed.), *Alain Locke: Reflections on a Modern Renaissance Man*. Baton Rouge, LA: Louisiana State University Press, pp. 29–49.

Dollard, John (1937), *Caste and Class in a Southern Town* (1957 edn). New York: Doubleday Anchor Books.

Douglass, Frederick (1845), *Narrative of the Life of Frederick Douglass, an American Slave, in Harriet Beecher Stowe: Uncle Tom's Cabin and Frederick Douglass: Narrative of the Life Frederick Douglass, an American Slave* (1993 edn). London: Everyman.

Du Bois, W.E.B. (1897), 'The Conservation of Races', in Eric J. Sundquist (ed.), *The Oxford W.E.B. Du Bois Reader* (1996 edn). New York: Oxford University Press, pp. 38–47.

— (1899), *The Philadelphia Negro: A Social Study* (1967 edn). New York: Schocken.

— (1903), *The Souls of Black Folk* (1994 edn). New York: Dover Publications.

— (1926a), 'Our Book Shelf'. *Crisis*, 31 January.

— (1926b), 'A Questionnaire'. *Crisis*, 31 February.

— (1926c), 'Criteria of Negro Art', in Angelyn Mitchell (ed.), *Within the Circle: An Anthology of African American Literary Criticism from the Harlem Renaissance to the Present* (1994 edn). Durham, NC: Duke University Press.

— (1968), *The Autobiography of W.E.B. Du Bois: A Soliloquy on Viewing My Life from the Last Decade of Its First Century*. New York: International Publishers.

— (1996), *The Oxford W.E.B. Du Bois Reader*, Eric J. Sundquist (ed.), New York: Oxford University Press.

Du Bois, W.E.B. and Alain Locke (1924), 'The Younger Literary Movement'. *Crisis*, 27 February.

Dyer, Richard (1997), *White*. London: Routledge.

Eliot, T. S. (1932), 'Tradition and the Individual Talent', in Eliot, *Selected Essays* (1972 edn). London: Faber and Faber, pp. 13–22.

Ellison, Ralph (1952), *Invisible Man* (1965 edn). Harmondsworth: Penguin.

— (1964), *Shadow and Act* (1994 edn). New York: Quality Paperback Book Club.

Fabre, Genevieve (1988), 'Genealogical Archaeology or the Quest for Legacy in Toni Morrison's *Song of Solomon*', in Nellie Mckay (ed.), *Critical Essays on Toni Morrison*. Boston, MA: G.K. Hall and Co., pp. 105–14.

Fanon, Frantz (France 1952), *Black Skin, White Masks* (1986 edn, Charles Lam Markmann trans.). London: Pluto.

— (France 1961), *The Wretched of the Earth* (1990 edn, Constance Farrington trans.). Harmondsworth: Penguin, 1990.

Faulkner, William (1942), *Go Down, Moses and Other Stories* (1960 edn). Harmondsworth: Penguin. 1960).

Favor, J. Martin (1999), *Authentic Blackness: The Folk in the New Negro Renaissance*. Durham, NC: Duke University Press.

Fox-Genovese, Elizabeth (1989), *Within the Plantation Household: Black and White Women of the Old South*. Chapel Hill, NC: University of North Carolina Press.

Freeman, Barbara Claire (1995), *The Feminine Sublime: Gender and Excess in Women's Fiction*. Berkeley, CA: University of California Press.

Freud, Sigmund (1957), 'On the History of the Psycho-Analytic Movement, Papers on Metapsychology and Other Works', James Strachey in collaboration with Anna Freud and assisted by Alix Strachey and Alan Tyson (trans.), *The Standard Edition of the Complete Psychological Works*, volume XIV, 1914–1916. London: The Hogarth Press.

Gates, Henry Louis, Jr (ed.) (1984), *Black Literature and Literary Theory*. New York: Methuen.

— (1984), 'Criticism in the Jungle', in Gates, Jr (ed.), *Black Literature and Literary Theory*. New York: Methuen, pp. 1–24.

— (ed.) (1986a), *'Race', Writing and Difference*. Chicago, IL: University of Chicago Press.

— (1986b), 'Writing "Race" and the Difference it Makes', in Gates, Jr (ed.), *'Race', Writing, and Difference*. Chicago, IL: University of Chicago Press, pp. 1–20.

— (1988), *The Signifying Monkey: A Theory of African-American Literary Criticism*. New York: Oxford University Press.

— (1989), *Figures in Black: Words, Signs, and the 'Racial' Self*. New York: Oxford University Press.

— (1997), 'Harlem on Our Minds', in Joanna Skipworth (ed.), *Rhapsodies in Black: Art of theHarlem Renaissance* (Exhibition Catalogue), London: Hayward Gallery; Institute of International Visual Arts; Berkeley, CA: University of California Press, pp. 162–7.

Gates, Henry Louis, Jr. and K. A. Appiah (eds) (1993a), *Langston Hughes: Critical Perspectives Past and Present*. New York: Amistad Press.

— (1993b), *Toni Morrison: Critical Perspectives Past and Present*. New York: Amistad Press.

Gayle, Addison, Jr (1976), *The Way of the New World: The Black Novel in America*. New York: Anchor Books.

Ghomeshi, Jian (2012), 'Interview with Toni Morrison: Toni Morrison on Her Two Selves' www.cbc.ca/q/blog/2012/05/24/toni-morrison-on-her-two-selves/ (last accessed on 4 February 2013).

Gibson, Donald (1993), 'Text and Countertext in *The Bluest Eye*', in Henry Louis Gates, Jr and K. A. Appiah (eds), *Toni Morrison: Critical Perspectives Past and Present*. New York: Amistad, pp. 159–74.

Gilroy, Paul (1993a), 'Living Memory: A Meeting with Toni Morrison', in Gilroy, *Small Acts*. London: Serpent's Tale, pp. 175–82.

— (1993b), *The Black Atlantic: Modernity and Double Consciousness*. London: Verso.

— (2000), *Between Camps: Race, Identity and Nationalism at the End of the Colour Line*. London: Allen Lane.

Glazer, Nathan and Daniel Patrick Moynihan (1963), *Beyond the Melting Pot: The Negroes, Puerto Ricans, Jews, Italians, and Irish of New York City*. (1964 edn) Cambridge, MA: The MIT Press.

Gobineau, Joseph Arthur, Count, de (France in 4 vols, 1853–5), *The Inequality of Human Races* [vol. I], (1915 edn, Adrian Collins trans.). London: Heinemann.

Goebel, Walter and Sakia Schabio (eds) (2010), *Locating Transnational Ideals*. New York: Routledge.

Gooding-Williams, Robert (1996), 'Outlaw, Appiah, and Du Bois's "The Conservation of the Races"', in Bernard W. Bell, Emily R. Grosholz and James B. Stewart (eds), *W.E.B. Du Bois on Race and Culture: Philosophy, Politics, and Poetics*. New York: Routledge, pp. 39–56.

Gordon, Deborah (1990), 'The Politics of Ethnographic Authority: Race and Writing in the Ethnography of Margaret Mead and Zora Neale Hurston', in Marc Manganaro (ed.), *Modernist Anthropology: From Fieldwork to Text*. Princeton, NJ: Princeton University Press, pp. 146–62.

Goulimari, Pelagia (2011), *Toni Morrison*. London: Routledge.

Grant, Robert (1988), 'Absence into Presence: The Thematics of Memory and "Missing" Subjects in Toni Morrison's *Sula*', in Nellie Y. McKay (ed.), *Critical Essays on Toni Morrison*. Boston MA: G.K. Hall & Co., pp. 90–103.

Gregson, Ian (2004), *Postmodern Literature*. London: Arnold.

Grisham, Therese (1991), 'Linguistics as an Indiscipline: Deleuze and Guattari's Pragmatics'. *SubStance*, 66, 36–54.

Haraway, Donna (1991), *Simians, Cyborgs, and Women: The Reinvention of Nature*. London: Free Association Books.

Harris, Leonard (1989), 'Introduction: Rendering the Text', in Harris (ed.), Alain Locke. *The Philosophy of Alain Locke: Harlem Renaissance and Beyond*. Philadelphia, PA: Temple University Press, pp. 3–27.

Harris, Norman (1985), 'The Black Universe in Contemporary Afro-American Fiction'. *College Language Association Journal*, 30, 1–13.

Harris, Trudier (1991), *Fiction and Folklore: The Novels of Toni Morrison* (1993 edn). Knoxville, TE: University of Tennessee Press.

Hawthorne, Nathaniel (1850), *The Scarlet Letter* (2005 edn). New York: Norton Critical Edition.

Hayes, Floyd W. (1996), 'Fanon, Oppression, and Resentment: The Black Experience in the United States', in Lewis R. Gordon, T. Denean Sharpley-Whiting and Renée T. White (eds), *Fanon: A Critical Reader*. Oxford: Blackwells, pp. 11–34.

Hemenway, Robert E. (1986), *Zora Neale Hurston: A Literary Biography*. London: Camden Press.

Henderson, Mae G. (1991), 'Toni Morrison's *Beloved*: Re-Membering the Body as Historical Text', in Hortense Spillers (ed.), *Comparative American Identities: Race, Sex and Nationality in the Modern Text*. New York: Routledge, pp. 62–86.

Higginbotham, Evelyn Brooks (1997), 'Rethinking Vernacular Culture', in Wahneema Lubiano (ed.), *The House that Race Built*. New York: Pantheon Books, pp. 157–77.

Hilfer, Anthony C. (1991), 'Critical Indeterminacies in Toni Morrison's Fiction'. *Texas Studies in Literature and Language*, 33, 1, 91–5.

Hill, Mike (ed.) (1997), *Whiteness: A Critical Reader*. New York: New York University Press.

Hirschkop, Ken (1989), 'Introduction: Bakhtin and Cultural Theory', in Hirschkop and David Shepherd (eds), *Bakhtin and Cultural Theory*. Manchester: Manchester University Press, pp. 1–38.

Hirschkop, Ken and David Shepherd (eds) (1989), *Bakhtin and Cultural Theory*. Manchester: Manchester University Press.

hooks, bell (Gloria Watkins) (1984), *Feminist Theory: From Margin to Center*. Boston MA: South End Press.

— (1991), *Yearning: Race, Gender, and Cultural Politics*. London: Turnaround.

Horsman, Reginald (1981), *Race and Manifest Destiny*. Cambridge, MA: Harvard University Press.

Houston, Pam (2008), 'Pam Houston Talks with Toni Morrison', in Denard (ed.), *Toni Morrison Conversations*. Jackson, MI: University Press of Mississippi, pp. 228–59.

Huggan, Graham and Helen Tiffin (2010), *Postcolonial Ecocriticism: Literature, Animals, Environment*. London: Routledge.

Huggins, Nathan (1971), *Harlem Renaissance*. New York: Oxford University Press.

Hughes, Langston (1926), 'The Negro Artist and the Racial Mountain', *The Nation*, 122, 3181, 692–4 (reprinted in Mithchell, 1994).

— (1930), *Not Without Laughter* (1998 edn). Edinburgh: Payback Press.
— (1994), Arnold Rampersad (ed.) and David Roessel (assoc ed.). *The Collected Poems of Langston Hughes*. (New York: Alfred Knopf).
Hurston, Zora Neale (1928), 'How It Feels to Be Colored Me', in Alice Walker (ed.), *I Love Myself When I Am Laughing... and Then Again When I Am Looking Mean and Impressive: A Zora Neale Hurston Reader* (1979 edn). New York: The Feminist Press, pp. 152–5.
— (1934a), 'Spirituals and Neo-Spirituals', in Nancy Cunard (ed.), *Negro* (1969 edn). New York: Negro Universities Press, pp. 359–61.
— (1934b), *Jonah's Gourd Vine* (1987 edn). London: Virago.
— (1935), *Mules and Men* (1990 edn). New York: Harper Perennial.
— (1937), *Their Eyes Were Watching God* (1986 edn). London: Virago.
— (1942), *Dust Tracks on a Road* (1986 edn). London: Virago.
Hutchinson, George (1995), *The Harlem Renaissance in Black and White*. Cambridge, MA: Belknap Press of Harvard University Press.
Johnson, Barbara (1984), 'Metaphor, Metonymy and Voice in Their Eyes Were Watching God', in Henry Louis Gates, Jr (ed.), *Black Literature and Literary Theory*. New York: Methuen, pp. 205–18.
— (1986), 'Thresholds of Difference: Structures of Address in Zora Neale Hurston', in Henry Louis Gates, Jr (ed.), *'Race', Writing, and Difference*. Chicago, IL: University of Chicago Press, pp. 317–28.
— (1998), *The Feminist Difference: Literature, Psychoanalysis, Race, and Gender*. Cambridge, MA: Harvard University Press.
Jones, Bessie (1983), 'Garden Metaphor and Christian Symbolism in Tar Baby', in Bessie Jones and Audrey L. Vinson, *The World of Toni Morrison*. Dubuque, IA: Kendall-Hunt, pp. 116–28.
Jones, Bessie and Audrey L. Vinson (1994), 'An Interview with Toni Morrison', in Danille Taylor-Guthrie (ed.), *Conversations with Toni Morrison*. Jackson, MS: University Press of Mississippi, pp. 171–87.
Jones, LeRoi (Amiri Imamu Baraka) (1962), 'The Myth of a "Negro Literature"', in Jones, *Home: Social Essays* (1968 edn). New York: Macgibbon and Kee, pp. 105–15.
— (1963), *Blues People: The Negro Experience in White America and the Music that Developed from It* (1995 edn). Edinburgh: Payback Press.
— (1965), 'American Sexual Reference: Black Male', in Jones, *Home: Social Essays* (1968 edn). New York: Macgibbon and Kee, pp. 216–33.
— (1968), 'The Changing Same (R & B and Black Music)', in Jones, *Black Music* (1998 edn). New York: Da Capo Press, pp. 180–211. See also Baraka, Amiri Immamu.
Kellner, Bruce (ed.) (1984), *The Harlem Renaissance: A Historical Dictionary for the Era*. New York: Methuen.
Kerouac, Jack (1957), *On the Road* (1972 edn). Harmonsworth: Penguin.
King, Martin Luther, Jr (1956), 'Paul's Letter to American Christians', in Clayborne Carson and Peter Holloran (eds), *A Knock at Midnight: The Great Sermons of Martin Luther King, Jr*. (1999 edn). London: Little, Brown and Company, pp. 25–36.

— (1957), 'Loving your Enemies', in Clayborne Carson and Peter Holloran (eds), *A Knock at Midnight: The Great Sermons of Martin Luther King, Jr* (1999 edn). London: Little, Brown and Company, pp. 41–60.

Kochman, Thomas (1977), 'Towards an Ethnography of Black American Speech Behaviour', in Norman E. Whitten Jr., and John F. Szwed (eds), *Afro-American Anthropology: Contemporary Perspectives*. New York: Macmillan, pp. 145–62.

Koenen, Anne (1994), 'The One Out of Sequence', in Danille Taylor-Guthrie (ed.), *Conversations with Toni Morrison*. Jackson, MS: University Press of Mississippi, pp. 67–83.

Krasny, Michael (1975) 'The Aesthetic Structure of Jean Toomer's *Cane*', *Negro American Literature Forum*, 9.2, 42–3.

Kristeva, Julia (France 1977), 'Stabat Mater', Léon S. Roudiez (trans.), in Toril Moi (ed.), *The Kristeva Reader* (1993 edn). Oxford: Blackwell, pp. 161–86.

— (France 1979), 'Women's Time', Alice Jardin and Harry Blake (trans.), in Toril Moi (ed.), *The Kristeva Reader* (1993 edn). Oxford: Blackwell, pp. 188–213.

Lawrence, David (2000), 'Fleshly Ghosts and Ghostly Flesh: The Word and the Body in *Beloved*', in David Middleton (ed.), *Toni Morrison's Fiction: Contemporary Criticism*. New York: Garland Publishing, pp. 231–46.

Lebsock, Susan (1984), *The Free Women of Petersburg: Status and Culture in a Southern Town, 1784–1860*. New York: Norton.

LeClair, Thomas (1994), 'The Language Must Not Sweat: A Conversation with Toni Morrison', in Danille Taylor-Guthrie (ed.), *Conversations with Toni Morrison*. Jackson, MS: University Press of Mississippi, pp. 119–28.

Lester, Rosemarie K. (1988), 'An Interview with Toni Morrison, Hessian Radio Network, Frankfurt, West Germany', in Nellie McKay (ed.), *Critical Essays on Toni Morrison*. Boston MA: G.K. Hall and Co., pp. 47–54.

Levering, Lewis David (1981), *When Harlem Was in Vogue*. New York: Alfred A. Knopf.

Levine, Lawrence W. (1977), *Black Culture and Black Consciousness: Afro-American Folk Thought from Slavery to Freedom*. New York: Oxford University Press.

Levy, Andrew (1991), 'Telling Beloved', *Texas Studies in Literature and Language*, 33, 1, 114–23.

Liebow, Elliot (1967), *Tally's Corner: A Study of Negro Streetcorner Men*. Boston, MA: Little, Brown and Co.

Linnemann, Russel J. (ed.) (1982), *Alain Locke: Reflections on a Modern Renaissance Man*. Baton Rouge, LA: Louisiana State University Press.

Lively, Adam (1998), *Masks: Blackness, Race and the Imagination* (1999 edn). London: Vintage.

Lloyd, David (1987), 'Genet's Genealogy: European Minorities and the Ends of the Canon', *Cultural Critique*, 8, 161–85.

Locke, Alain (1925a). 'The New Negro', in Alain Locke (ed.), *The New Negro: An Interpretation* (1997 edn). New York: Touchstone, pp. 3–16.

— (1925b), 'Negro Youth Speaks', in Alain Locke (ed.), *The New Negro: An Interpretation* (1997 edn). New York: Touchstone, Simon Schuster, pp. 47–84.

— (1925c), 'The Legacy of the Ancestral Arts', in Alain Locke (ed.), *The New Negro: An Interpretation* (1997 edn). New York: Touchstone, Simon Schuster, pp. 254–67.
— ed. (1925), *The New Negro: An Interpretation* (1997 edn). New York: Touchstone, Simon Schuster.
— (1942), 'Who and What is "Negro"?', in Leonard Harris (ed.), Locke, *The Philosophy of Alain Locke: Harlem Renaissance and beyond* (1989 edn). Philadelphia, PA: Temple University Press, pp. 209–26.
— (1969), *Negro Art: Past and Present*. New York: Arno Press.
Lott, Eric (1993), *Love and Theft: Blackface Minstrelsy and the American Working Class*. New York: Oxford University Press.
Lubiano, Wahneema (ed.) (1997), *The House that Race Built*. New York: Pantheon Books.
Lyotard, Jean-François (France 1982), 'Appendix: Answering the Question: What is Postmodernism?', (Régis Durand trans.), in Jean-François Lyotard, *The Postmodern Condition: A Report on Knowledge* (first published in France 1979 before the addition of Lyotard's appendix, Geoff Bennington and Brian Massumi trans., 1992 edn). Manchester: Manchester University Press, pp. 71–82.
— (1984), 'The Sublime and the Avant-Garde', Lisa Liebmann (trans.), in Andrew Benjamin (ed.), *The Lyotard Reader* (1989 edn). Oxford: Blackwell, pp. 196–207.
— (1989), 'Complexity and the Sublime', in Lisa Appignanesi (ed.), Geoff Bennington (trans.). *Postmodernism: ICA Documents 4 and 5*, London: Free Association Books, pp. 19–26.
Mailer, Norman (1957), 'The White Negro', in Mailer, *Advertisements for Myself* (1968 edn). London: Granada, pp. 270–89.
Malone, Ann Patton (1992), *Sweet Chariot*. Chapel Hill, NC: University of North Carolina Press.
Marcus, Jane (1995), 'Bonding and Bondage: Nancy Cunard and the Making of the *Negro* Anthology', in Mae G. Henderson (ed.), *Borders, Boundaries, and Frames: Essays in Cultural Criticism and Cultural Studies*. New York: Routledge, pp. 33–63.
Marriott, David (1996), 'Reading Black Masculinities', in Máirtín Mac an Ghaill (ed.), *Understanding Masculinities: Social Relations and Cultural Arenas*. Buckingham, PA: Open University Press, pp. 185–201.
Marshall, Paule (1983), 'The Making of a Writer: From the Poets in the Kitchen', in Marshall, *Merle: A Novella and Other Stories*. London: Virago, pp. 3–12.
Massumi, Brian (1992), *A User's Guide to Capitalism and Schizophrenia*. Cambridge, MA: The MIT Press.
Marx, Karl (1852), *The Eighteenth Brumaire of Louis Bonaparte* (1977 edn). Moscow: Progress Publishers.
Matus, Jill (1998), *Contemporary World Writers: Toni Morrison*. Manchester: Manchester University Press.
Mbalia, Doreatha D. (1991), *Toni Morrison's Developing Class Consciousness*. Cranbury, NJ: Associated University Presses.
McClintock, Anne (1995), *Imperial Leather: Race, Gender and Sexuality in the Colonial Contest*. New York: Routledge.

McDowell, Deborah E. (1989), 'Boundaries: Or Distant Relations and Close Kin', in Houston A. Baker and Patricia Redmond (eds), *Afro-American Literary Study in the 1990s*. Chicago, IL: University of Chicago Press, pp. 51-70.

McKay, Claude (1925), 'White Houses', in Locke (ed.), *The New Negro: An Interpretation* (1997 edn). New York: Simon & Schuster, p. 134.

McKay, Nellie, Y. (1984), *Jean Toomer Artist: A Study of His Literary Life and Work, 1894-1936*. Chapel Hill: University of North Carolina Press.

— (ed.) (1988), *Critical Essays on Toni Morrison*. Boston MA: G.K. Hall and Co.

— (1994), 'An Interview with Toni Morrison', in Danille Taylor-Guthrie (ed.), *Conversations with Toni Morrison*. Jackson, MS: University Press of Mississippi, pp. 138-55.

Middleton, David (ed.) (2000), *Toni Morrison's Fiction: Contemporary Criticism*. New York: Garland Publishing.

Mitchell, Angelyn (ed.) (1994), *Within the Circle: An Anthology of African American Literary Criticism from the Harlem Renaissance to the Present*. Durham, NC: Duke University Press.

Mobley, Marilyn Sanders (1991), 'Narrative Dilemma: Jadine as Cultural Orphan in Tar Baby', in Mobley, *Folk Roots and Mythic Wings in Sarah Orne Jewett and Toni Morrison: The Cultural Function of Narrative*. Baton Rouge, LA: Louisiana State University Press, pp. 134-67.

— (1993), 'A Different Remembering: Memory, History, and Meaning in *Beloved*', in Henry Louis Gates, Jr and K. A. Appiah (eds), *Toni Morrison: Critical Perspectives Past and Present*. New York: Amistad, pp. 356-65.

Mohanty, Chandra Talpade (1991), 'Under Western Eyes: Feminist Scholarship and Colonial Discourses', in Mohanty, Ann Russo and Lourdes Torres (eds), *Third World Women and the Politics of Feminism*. Bloomington IN: Indiana University Press, pp. 51-80.

Moi, Toril (ed.) (1993), *The Kristeva Reader*. Oxford: Blackwell.

Monson, Ingrid (1994), 'Doubleness and Jazz Improvisation: Irony, Parody, and Ethnomusicology', *Critical Inquiry*, 20, 2, 283-306.

Morrison, Toni (1970), *The Bluest Eye* (1990 edn). London: Picador.

— (1973), *Sula* (1991 edn). London: Picador.

— (1976), 'A Slow Walk of Trees' (as Grandmother Would Say), Hopeless (as Grandfather Would Say), in Carolyn C. Denard (ed.), *What Moves at the Margin: Selected Nonfiction of Toni Morrison*, (2008 edn). Jackson, MI, pp. 3-14.

— (1977), *Song of Solomon* (1998 edn). London: Vintage.

— (13 July 1980), 'Review of *Cane*', *New York Times Book Review*.

— (1981), *Tar Baby* (1991 edn). London: Picador.

— (1983), 'Recitatif', in Amiri Baraka (Le Roi Jones) and Amina Barka (eds), *Confirmation: An Anthology of African American Women*. New York: Quill, pp. 243-61.

— (1984), 'Rootedness: The Ancestor as Foundation', in Carolyn C. Denard (ed.), *What Moves at the Margin: Selected Nonfiction of Toni Morrison*, (2008 edn). Jackson, MI, pp. 56-64.

— (1987a), 'The Site of Memory', in Carolyn C. Denard (ed.), *What Moves at the Margin: Selected Nonfiction of Toni Morrison*, (2008 edn). Jackson, MI, pp. 65–80.
— (1987b), *Beloved* (1988 edn). London: Picador.
— (1987c), 'James Baldwin: His Voice Remembered; Life in His Language' in Carolyn C. Denard (ed), *What Moves at the Margin: Selected Nonfiction of Toni Morrison*, (2008 edn). Jackson, MI, pp. 90–94.
— (1989), 'Unspeakable Things Unspoken: The Afro-American Presence in American Literature', in Harold Bloom (ed.), *Modern Critical Views: Toni Morrison* (1990 edn). New York: Chelsea House, pp. 201–30.
— (1992a), 'Introduction: Friday on the Potamac', in Morrison (ed.), *Race-ing Justice, En-gendering Power: Essays on Anita Hill, Clarence Thomas, and the Construction of Social Reality*. London: Chatto & Windus, pp. viii–xxx.
— (1992b), *Jazz* (1993 edn). London: Picador.
— (1992c), *Playing in the Dark: Whiteness and the Literary Imagination* (1993 edn). London: Picador.
— (ed.) (1992), *Race-ing Justice, En-gendering Power: Essays on Anita Hill, Clarence Thomas, and the Construction of Social Reality*. London: Chatto & Windus.
— (1993), *The Nobel Lecture in Literature* (1994 edn). London: Chatto & Windus (reprinted in Denard, 2008).
— (1996a), 'The Dancing Mind: Speech upon Acceptance of the National Book Foundation for Distinguished Contribution to American Letters', in Carolyn C. Denard (ed.), *What Moves at the Margin: Selected Nonfiction of Toni Morrison*, (2008 edn). Jackson, MI, pp. 187–90.
— (1996b), 'The Future of Time: Literature and Diminished Expectations', in Carolyn C. Denard (ed.), *What Moves at the Margin: Selected Nonfiction of Toni Morrison*, (2008 edn). Jackson, MI, pp. 170–86.
— (1997), 'Home', in Wahneema Lubiano (ed.), *The House that Race Built: Black Americans, U.S. Terrain*. New York: Pantheon Books, pp. 4–12.
— (1998), *Paradise*. London: Vintage.
— (2001), 'The Dead of September 11', in Carolyn C. Denard (ed), *What Moves at the Margin: Selected Nonfiction of Toni Morrison* (2008 edn). Jackson, MI, pp. 154–5.
— (2003), *Love*. London: Chatto & Windus.
— (2008), *A Mercy*. London: Chatto & Windus.
— (2009), 'Peril', in Morrison (ed.), *Burn This Book: PEN Writers Speak Out on the Power of the Word*. New York: Harper Collins, pp. 1–4.
— (ed.) (2009), *Burn This Book: PEN Writers Speak Out on the Power of the Word*. New York: Harper Collins.
— (2012), *Home*. London: Chatto & Windus.
Moyers, Bill (1994), 'A Conversation with Toni Morrison', in Danille Taylor-Guthrie (ed.), *Conversations with Toni Morrison*. Jackson, MS: University Press of Mississippi, pp. 262–74.
Moynihan, Daniel (1965), *The Negro Family: The Case for National Action*. Washington: US Department of Labor.

Munton, Alan (1997), 'Misreading Morrison, Mishearing Jazz: A Response to Toni Morrison's Jazz Critics', *Journal of American Studies*, 31, 2, 235–51.

Naylor, Gloria (1994), 'A Conversation: Gloria Naylor and Toni Morrison', in Danille Taylor-Guthrie (ed.), *Conversations with Toni Morrison*. Jackson MS: University Press of Mississippi, pp. 188–217.

Neal, Larry (1968), 'The Black Arts Movement'. *The Drama Review*, 12.4, 29–39.

Nicholls, Peter (1996), 'The Belated Postmodern: History, Phantoms, and Toni Morrison', in Sue Vice (ed.), *Psychoanalytic Criticism: A Reader*. Oxford: Polity Press, pp. 50–74.

North, Michael (1994), *The Dialect of Modernism: Race, Language, and Twentieth-Century Literature*. New York: Oxford University Press.

Nott, Josiah and George Gliddon (1854), *Types of Mankind*. Cambridge, MA: Harvard University Press.

Obama, Barack (2004), 'Preface to the 2004 Edition', in Obama (1995), *Dreams from My Father* (2008 edn). Edinburgh: Canongate.

Omry, Keren (2011), 'Salt Roads to Mercy', in Shirley A. Stave and Justine Tally (eds), *Toni Morrison's A Mercy: Critical Approaches*. Newcastle: Cambridge Scholars Publishing, pp. 85–100.

Otten, Terry (1989), *The Crime of Innocence in the Fiction of Toni Morrison*. Columbia, MO: University of Missouri Press.

Outlaw, Lucius (1969), '"Conserve" Races?: In Defence of W.E.B. Du Bois', in Bernard W. Bell, Emily R. Grosholz and James B. Stewart (eds), *W.E.B. Du Bois on Race and Culture*. New York: Routledge, pp. 15–37.

Parry, Benita (1994), 'Signs of Our Times: A Discussion of Homi Bhabha's *The Location of Culture*'. *Third Text*, 38/39, 5–24.

Patterson, Orlando (1995), 'The Crisis of Gender Relations among African Americans', in Anita Faye Hill and Emma Coleman Jordan (eds), *Race, Gender, and Power in America: The Legacy of the Hill-Thomas Hearings*. New York: Oxford University Press, pp. 56–104.

Peach, Linden (2000), *Toni Morrison*. London: Macmillan.

Pechey, Graham (1989), 'On the Borders of Bakhtin: Dialogisation, Decolonisation', in Hirschkop and Shepherd (eds), *Bakhtin and Cultural Theory*. Manchester: Manchester University Press, pp. 39–67.

Peterson, James Braxton (2011), 'Eco-Critical Focal Points: Narrative Structure and Environmentalist Perspectives in Morrison's *A Mercy*', in Shirley A. Stave and Justine Tally (eds), *Toni Morrison's A Mercy: Critical Approaches*. Newcastle: Cambridge Scholars Publishing, pp. 9–21.

Peterson, Nancy J. (1997), 'Introduction: Reading Toni Morrison – From the Seventies to the Nineties', in Nancy J. Peterson (ed.), *Toni Morrison: Critical and Theoretical Approaches*. Baltimore, MD: John Hopkins University Press, pp. 1–15.

— (ed.) (1997), *Toni Morrison: Critical and Theoretical Approaches*, Baltimore, MD: John Hopkins University Press.

Posnock, Ross (1995), 'Black Intellectuals Past and Present', in David Murray (ed.), *American Cultural Critics*. Exeter: University of Exeter Press, pp. 246–69.

Pratt, Mary Louise (1992), *Imperial Eyes: Travel Writing and Transculturation*. London: Routledge.

Rainwater, Catherine (1991), 'Worthy Messengers: Narrative Voices in Toni Morrison's Novels'. *Texas Studies in Literature and Language*, 33, 1, 96–113.

Rampersad, Arnold (1976), *The Art and Imagination of W.E.B. Du Bois*. Cambridge, MA: Harvard University Press.

— (1993), 'Hughes's *Fine Clothes to the Jew*', in Henry Louis Gates, Jr and K. A. Appiah (eds), *Langston Hughes: Critical Perspectives Past and Present*. New York: Amistad, pp. 53–68.

Reed, Adolph L., Jr (1997), *W.E.B. Du Bois and American Political Thought: Fabianism and the Color Line*. New York: Oxford University Press.

Rice, Alan J. (1994), 'Jazzing It up a Storm: The Execution and Meaning of Toni Morrison's Jazzy Prose Style', *Journal of American Studies*, 28, 3, 423–32.

Richards, Phillip M. (1995), '*Sula* and the Discourse of the Folk in African-American Literature', in Warren Crichlow and Cameron McCarthy (eds), *Cultural Studies: Toni Morrison and the Curriculum*. London: Routledge, 9, 2, pp. 270–92.

Rodrigues, Eusebio L. (1997), 'Experiencing Jazz', in Nancy J. Peterson (ed.), *Toni Morrison: Critical and Theoretical Approaches*. Baltimore, MD: Johns Hopkins University Press, pp. 245–66.

Roynon, Tessa (2011), 'Miltonic Journeys in *A Mercy*', in Shirley A. Stave and Justine Tally (eds), *Toni Morrison's A Mercy: Critical Approaches*. Newcastle: Cambridge Scholars Publishing, pp. 45–61.

Ruas, Charles (1994), 'Toni Morrison', in Danille Taylor-Guthrie (ed.), *Conversations with Toni Morrison*. Jackson MI: University Press of Mississippi, pp. 93–118.

Rushdie, Salman (2008), 'An Interview with Toni Morrison', in Denard (ed.), *Toni Morrison Conversations*. Jackson, MI: University Press of Mississippi, pp. 51–61.

Said, Edward (1978), *Orientalism*. London: Routledge.

— (1993), *Culture and Imperialism*. London: Chatto & Windus.

Sartre, Jean-Paul (France 1948), *Black Orpheus* (1976 edn, S. W. Allen trans.) [Preface to L. S. Senghor (ed.), *Anthologie de la Nouvelle Poésie Nègre Malgache de Langue Française*]. Paris: Présence Africaine.

Sartwell, Crispin (1998), *Act Like You Know: African-American Autobiography and White Identity*, Chicago, IL: University of Chicago Press.

Scott, Patricia Bell, Beverley Guy-Sheftall and Jacqueline Jones Royster (1991), 'The Promise and Challenge of Black Women's Studies: A Report from the Spelman Conference, May 1990', *NWSA Journal*, 3, 282–8.

Segal, Lynne (1997), *Slow Motion: Changing Masculinities, Changing Men*, London: Virago.

Silverblatt, Michael (2008), 'Michael Silverblatt Talks with Toni Morrison about *Love*', in Denard (ed.), *Toni Morrison Conversations*. Jackson, MI: University Press of Mississippi, pp. 216–23.

— (2009), 'Toni Morrison, Part I' with Michael Silverblatt on Bookworm. KCRW, 22 January www.kcrw.com/etc/programs/bw/bw090122tonI_morrison_part_i (last accessed 3 April 2013).

Skipwith, Joanna (ed.) (1997), *Rhapsodies in Black: Art of the Harlem Renaissance*. (Exhibition Catalogue London: Hayward Gallery; Institute of International Visual Arts). Berkeley, CA: University of California Press.

Smith, Barbara (1977), 'Toward a Black Feminist Criticism', in Gloria T. Hull, Patricia BelScott and Barbara Smith (eds), *But Some of Us Are Brave: Black Women's Studies* (1982 edn). New York: The Feminist Press at the City University of New York, pp. 157–75.

Smitherman, Geneva (1998), 'Word from the Hood: The Lexicon of African-American Vernacular English', in Salikoko S. Mufwene, John R. Rickford, Guy Bailey and John Baugh (eds), *African-American English: Structure, History and Use*. New York: Routledge, pp. 203–25.

Snead, James A. (1984), 'Repetition as a Figure of Black Culture', in Henry Louis Gates, Jr (ed.), *Black Literature and Literary Theory*. New York: Routledge, 1984, pp. 59–79.

— (1986), *Figures of Division: William Faulkner's Major Novels*. New York: Methuen.

— (1994), *Colin MacCabe and Cornel West* (eds), [posthumously]. *White Screens / Black Images: Hollywood from the Dark Side*. New York: Routledge.

Spillers, Hortense J. (1990), 'A Hateful Passion, a Lost Love', in Harold Bloom (ed.), *Modern Critical Views: Toni Morrison*. New York: Chelsea House, pp. 27–54.

Stambolian, George (1979), 'A Liberation of Desire: An Interview with Félix Guattari', in Stambolian and Elaine Marks (eds), George Stambolian (trans.), *Homosexualities and French Literature*. Ithaca, NY: Cornell UP, pp. 56–69.

Staples, Robert (1970), 'The Myth of the Black Matriarchy', in Doris Y. Wilkinson and Ronald L. Taylor (eds), *The Black Male in America: Perspectives on His Status in Contemporary Society* (1977 edn), Chicago, IL: Nelson-Hall, pp. 174–87.

— (1971), 'The Myth of the Impotent Black Male', in Doris Y. Wilkinson and Ronald L. Taylor (eds), *The Black Male in America: Perspectives on His Status in Contemporary Society*. Chicago, IL: Nelson-Hall, pp. 133–45.

Stein, Gertrude (1909), *Three Lives* (1990 edn). Middlesex: Penguin.

— (1933), *Autobiography of Alice B. Toklas* (1933 edn). London: Bodley Head.

Stepto, Robert (1994), 'Intimate Things in Place: A Conversation with Toni Morrison', in Danille Taylor-Guthrie (ed.), *Conversations with Toni Morrison*. Jackson, MS: University Press of Mississipi, pp. 10–29.

Stewart, Jeffrey, C. (1997), 'Paul Robeson and the Problem of Modernism', in Joanna Skipworth (ed.), *Rhapsodies in Black: Art of the Harlem Renaissance* (Exhibition Catalogue). London: Hayward Gallery, Institute of International Visual Arts, Berkeley CA: University of California Press, pp. 90–101.

Sundquist Eric J. (1983), *Faulkner: The House Divided*. Baltimore: Johns Hopkins University Press.

— (1993), *To Wake the Nations: Race in the Making of American Literature*. Cambridge, MA: Belknap Press of Harvard University Press.

Tally, Justine (2007), 'The Morrison Trilogy', in Tally (ed.), *The Cambridge Companion to Toni Morrison*. Cambridge: Cambridge University Press, pp. 75–91.
— (ed.) (2007), *The Cambridge Companion to Toni Morrison*. Cambridge: Cambridge University Press.
Tate, Claudia (ed.) (1983), *Black Women Writers at Work: Conversations with Toni Morrison et al.* Harpenden: Oldcastle Books.
Taylor-Guthrie, Danille (ed.) (1994), *Conversations with Toni Morrison*. Jackson, MS: University Press of Mississippi.
Taylor, Ronald L. and Doris Y. Wilkinson (eds) (1977), *The Black Male in America: Perspectives on His Status in Contemporary Society*. Chicago, IL: Nelson-Hall.
Toomer, Jean (1923), *Cane* (1988 edn). Darwin T. Turner (ed.), [with backgrounds and criticism] New York: Norton, 1988.
Turner, Darwin T. (1988), 'Introduction to the 1975 Edition of *Cane*', in Jean Toomer. *Cane*, Darwin T. Turner (ed.), [with backgrounds and criticism]. New York: Norton, pp. 121–38.
Van Deburg, William L. (1992), *New Day in Babylon: The Black Power Movement and American Culture, 1965–1975* (1993 edn). Chicago, IL: University of Chicago Press.
Walker, Alice (ed.) (1979), *I Love Myself When I Am Laughing . . . and Then Again When I Am Looking Mean and Impressive: A Zora Neale Hurston Reader*. New York: The Feminist Press.
— (1983), *In Search of Our Mother's Gardens*. London: The Women's Press.
Walker, Melissa (1991), *Down from the Mountaintop: Black Women's Novels in the Wake of the Civil Rights Movement, 1966–1989*. New Haven: Yale University Press.
Wallace, Michelle (1978), *Black Macho and the Myth of the Superwoman* (1979 edn). London: John Calder.
Warren, Robert Penn (1966), 'Introduction: Faulkner: Past and Future', in Warren (ed.), *Faulkner: A Collection of Critical Essays*. Englewood Cliffs, NJ: Prentice-Hall, pp. 1–22.
Washington, Booker T. (1901), *Up from Slavery*, in Anthony Appiah (ed.), *Early African-American Classics* (1990 edn). New York: Bantam.
Watkins, Gloria. See hooks, bell.
Watkins, Mel (1994), 'Talk with Toni Morrison', in Danille Taylor-Guthrie (ed.), *Conversations with Toni Morrison*. Jackson, MS: University Press of Mississippi, pp. 43–7.
Weathers, Mary Ann (1970), 'An Argument for Black Women's Liberation as a Revolutionary Force', in Leslie B. Tanner (ed.), *Voices from Women's Liberation*. New York: New American Library.
Werner, Craig H. (1988), 'The Briar Patch as Modernist Myth: Morrison, Barthes and Tar Baby As-Is', in Nellie Y. McKay (ed.), *Critical Essays on Toni Morrison*. Boston, MA: G.K. Hall and Co., pp. 150–67.
— (1994), *Playing the Changes: From Afro-Modernism to the Jazz Impulse*. Urbana, IL: University of Illinois Press.

West, Cornel (1989), *The American Evasion of Philosophy*. London: Macmillan.
Whitten. Norman E. Jr and John F. Szwed (eds) (1977), *Afro-American Anthropology: Contemporary Perspectives*. New York: Macmillan, pp. 145–62.
Widdowson, Peter (2001), 'The American Dream Refashioned: History, Politics and Gender in Toni Morrison's *Paradise*'. *Journal of American Studies*, 35, 2, 313–35.
Willis, Susan (1987), *Specifying: Black Women Writing the American Experience* (1990 edn). London: Routledge.
Wintz, Cary D. (1988), *Black Culture and the Harlem Renaissance*. Houston, TX: Rice University Press.
Wright, Elizabeth (1987), *Psychoanalytic Criticism: Theory in Practice*. London: Routledge.
Wright, Richard (1937a), 'Between Laughter and Tears', *New Masses*, 5 October 1937.
— (1937b), 'Blueprint for Negro Writing', in Angelyn Mitchell, (ed.), *Within The Circle: An Anthology of African American Literary Criticism from the Harlem Renaissance to the Present* (1994 edn). Durham, NC: Duke University Press, pp. 97–106.
— (1940), *Native Son* (1995 edn). London: Picador.
Wyatt, Jean (2008), '*Love*'s Time and the Reader: Ethical Effects of *Nachträglichkeit* in Toni Morrison's *Love*'. *Narrative*, 16.2 (May), 193–21.
Young, Robert J. C. (1995), *Colonial Desire: Hybridity in Theory, Culture and Race*. London: Routledge.
— (1996), *Torn Halves: Political Conflict in Literary and Cultural Theory*. Manchester: Manchester University Press.
Zamir, Shamoon (1995), *Dark Voices: W.E.B. Du Bois and American Thought, 1888–1903*. Chicago, IL: University of Chicago Press.

Index

9/11 183–4

Anderson, Sherwood 18, 26–7, 31n
Appiah, Anthony Kwame 15n, 125
Awkward, Michael 96n, 107

Baker, Houston 5–7, 15, 21–2, 25, 72n, 76
Bakhtin, Mikhail 9, 31, 43, 49–57, 66–9, 89, 138, 142–3
Baldwin, James 100, 112, 116, 117, 133n, 133–5, 182–3, 186–7
Bauman, Zygmunt 18
  definition of modernity 28n, 174
Bell, Bernard 17n
Beloved (Toni Morrison) 51, 79, 106–8, 135, 137–40, 142–72, 161, 175, 185–6, 193, 195
  'Africanism' 139
  ancestor 138
  Bhabha, Homi context 140
  communally authored text 144–5
  community 146, 149, 150
  Deleuze, Gilles and Félix Guattari context 140–3
  Kristeva, Julia reading 152–4
  memory and the sublime 147–9
  motherhood 151
  postmodernism 149–51
  repetition 150–1, 153–4
  repression 138, 143–4, 146, 150
  slave narratives 143, 146–7
  storytelling 155
  time 150, 154
  trauma and unrepresentability 148, 150–1
  trilogy 137–9
  whiteness 139
Benjamin, Walter 'The Storyteller' 4
Berman, Marshall 149
Bhabha, Homi (*The Location of Culture*) 23–4, 52–3, 132, 140, 149–50, 150n
Black Aesthetic 43–9, 70

Black Arts *see* Black Aesthetic
Black Power 43–7, 63, 92, 110, 163
blues music 2, 3, 4, 6, 9, 39, 40, 44, 47–8, 65, 73–5, 79, 117, 187, 195–6, 205–6
Bluest Eye, The (Toni Morrison) 10, 41–2, 43–4, 48–9, 79, 92, 94–5, 102–3, 114, 117, 123, 137, 157, 163–5, 167, 187
  artistic potential of Cholly and Pauline 79
  Bakhtin, Mikhail context and readings of 49–57, 66–7, 69
  beauty myth 55, 57
  blues 67
  chorus and orality 68–70
  cinema 60–2
  community 76
  Fanon, Frantz and Black Power 62–5
  language and ideology 54–7, 65–8, 76
  nineteenth-century racial discourse 57–60
  signifying 49, 50–1, 57, 91
Boxhill, Bernard R. 15n
Butler, Judith 86, 122, 153, 164

call and response 47, 49, 195
  definition 48n
Carby, Hazel 82n, 86, 89n, 90, 135n
'changing same' 2–3
Chesnutt, Charles 22, 25
Christian, Barbara 82n, 95n
Clarke, Deborah 101–2, 131
Clifford, James 33
Collins, Patricia Hill 84
Crouch, Stanley 160
Cullen, Countee 22
Cunard, Nancy 35–6

'Dancing Mind' (Toni Morrison) 195
'Dead of September 11' (Toni Morrison) 183
Deleuze, Gilles and Félix Guattari 4–5, 8, 10, 56n, 119–25, 140–2, 160, 187–8, 193
Dollard, John 108–9

double consciousness 17–18, 28, 38, 41, 162, 177, 178
see also Du Bois, W. E. B.
Douglass, Frederick 97–9, 101, 143, 199
Du Bois, W.E.B. 9, 13–22, 26–7, 32, 34, 37–40, 77–8, 83, 98, 126, 133n, 139, 139n, 162, 177–8, 182, 194, 203

ecocriticism 190
Ellison, Ralph 2, 19, 23, 24, 44, 46, 47, 49, 99–104, 116, 116n, 139, 139n, 157n, 157–8, 161, 205–6

Fanon, Frantz 62–5, 113–16, 141n, 163, 165
Faulkner, William 95–100, 102–6, 120, 132, 157
Favor, Martin *(Authentic Blackness)* 7, 38n
female literary tradition 88–90
    Hurston and Morrison 90–2
feminism 83
    and the academy 83–4
    agency 85
    marginality 84–5
folk 2, 7, 9, 13–15, 17–23, 26–7, 30–4, 37–42, 43–8, 54, 65, 70–80, 88–91, 166
Frank, Waldo 18, 26
Freud, Sigmund 138, 139, 150
'Future of Time' (Toni Morrison) 197–8

Gates, Henry Louis, Jr. 5–7, 14, 23, 30–1, 33, 36, 50–1, 57, 89, 90n
Gayle, Addison *(The Way of the World)* 46
Gender relationships under slavery 107–9
    Song of Solomon 111–12, 118
Gilroy, Paul 2, 4–5, 18, 28–9, 87, 98n, 138n, 144, 149, 155, 162n, 162–3, 169–70, 170n, 172–4
Gobineau, Joseph Arthur 57–60
Gooding-Williams, Robert 15n
Gordon, Deborah 33

Haraway, Donna 162, 171, 171n, 172, 176, 179
Hawthorne, Nathaniel *(The Scarlet Letter)* 192, 194
Home (Toni Morrison) 183, 194–206
    allegorical mode 194–5

ancestor 195
autobiographical elements 197, 199
blues 206
female care 202
jazz 204–5
journey 199–200, 202
Korea 197, 201
masculinity 200–1
memory 199–200, 201
money motif 202
post-second world war writing 202
prologue 198
reading and misreading 195–6
Sartre, Jean Paul 203, 205
segregation 200, 203
shame 200, 201, 203
tree motif 201
'Home' (Toni Morrison) 161–3
hooks, bell (Gloria Watkins) 84–6
Horsman, Reginald 58–9
Huggins, Nathan 15n
Hughes, Langston 13, 19, 28, 32, 38, 40–1, 44–6, 63
Hurston, Zora Neale 13, 19–20, 32–41, 43, 45, 47, 77–9, 88–92, 109, 111, 123, 169
    community 91–2
    free indirect discourse 89
    folk identity 89–90
    orality 90–1
    signifying 91
Hutchinson, George 27–8

James, William 16, 25
'James Baldwin' (Toni Morrison) 182
Jazz (Toni Morrison) 10, 31, 137, 138, 155–68, 195
    community 161
    jazz motif 158
    and jazz readings of 155–9, 161
    repetition of history 156–9
    trauma 156–8
    whiteness 157, 161
Jazz 2, 4, 24, 40–1, 89, 95, 117, 124, 155–6, 161, 195, 204–5
Johnson, Barbara 83, 89
Johnson, James Weldon 18, 38
Jolson, Al *(The Jazz Singer)* 24
Jones, LeRoi (Amiri Baraka) 2–4, 6, 110

Kellner, Bruce 22–3
Kerouac, Jack *(On the Road)* 117
King, Martin Luther 74, 144, 170, 177, 178
Kristeva, Julia 152, 153–4

Lenoir, J.B. 'Eisenhower Blues' and 'Korea Blues' 206
Levering Lewis, David 15
Levy, Andrew 144–5, 148
Locke, Alain 9, 13–14, 20–2, 25–6, 32–5, 38–9
Lott, Eric *(Love and Theft)* 24
Love (Toni Morrison) 10, 181, 184
   ancestor 185
   Baldwin, James 186
   clothes 185
   language 184, 186–7
   nationalism 182
   patriarchy 184–5
   structure 187
   water motif 185–6
Lyotard, Jean-François 148n, 148–9

Mailer, Norman 116–17
Marshall, Paula 69
Marx, Karl 151
McKay, Claude 22, 25–7, 31
   'White Houses' 198
Mercy, A (Toni Morrison) 183, 187–93
   allegory 192
   ancestor 191
   chaos 188
   Deleuze, Gilles and Félix Guattari 'smooth space' 188, 193
   geography and ecological imperialism 189
   Hawthorne, Nathaniel 192, 194
   home 188–9, 191, 193
   hybridity 189
   Native Americans 189–90
   postcolonial ecocriticism 190–1
   reading and misreading 191–2
   seeing 192
   tree and bird imagery 192
   water motif 193
   wilderness 191–2
   writing 192–3
minstrelsy 13, 21–7
modernism 9, 13–15, 18–19, 24–9, 35–6
   Hurston, Zora Neale and modernism 88

Picasso, Pablo and Henri Matisse 25
Morrison, Toni on
   'Africanism' 93, 139, 139n
   diaspora and 'home' 163, 169
   Du Bois, W. E. B. 83, 178
   feminism 86, 129
   Garner, Margaret 138
   home and the academy 83–4
   jazz 89, 124, 155, 159
   King, Martin Luther 170
   language 122, 123
   music 3n, 4
   nationalism 124–5
   postmodernism 87, 149n, 162n
   romance form 93
   slave narratives 146–7
   universality 100
   the 'unknown' 191
   writing and folk 142

New Negro, The 13–14, 20–2, 26, 32, 34–5, 38–40
Nicholls, Peter 149, 149n, 150, 156
Nobel Lecture in Literature (Toni Morrison) 101, 164, 166–7
North, Michael *(The Dialect of Modernism)* 24–5

Obama, Barack 182–3
   Dreams from My Father 182
Outlaw, Lucius 15n

Paradise (Toni Morrison) 10, 114, 125, 138, 142, 145, 161, 164–80, 181, 182, 195, 202
   civic versions of paradise 169
   diasporic versions of paradise 171–2
   Du Bois, W. E. B. 177–8
   home 161–4, 169–71
   Hurston, Zora Neale 169
   King, Martin Luther 170, 178–9
   language 164–6, 167, 175–80
   nationalism 173
   postmodernism 162
   'Recitatif' 166–8
   religion 168, 170–1, 176–9
   stranger-hood 174–5
   trauma 168
   Washington, Booker T. 177–8
'Peril' (Toni Morrison) 191, 196

Playing in the Dark (Toni Morrison) 53–4, 93, 139, 140, 167
Price, Lloyd 'Lawdy Miss Clawdy' 206

Race-ing Justice, En-gendering Power (Toni Morrison) 111
Rampersad, Arnold on
    Du Bois, W. E. B. 19n
    Hughes, Langston 41n
'Recitatif' (Toni Morrison) 166–8
'Rootedness' (Toni Morrison) 47, 119, 163n

Sartre, Jean Paul 203
Scott-Heron, Gil 199
signifying 29, 31, 49–51, 57, 91
    definition 30, 30n
    Hurston, Zora Neale in *Their Eyes Were Watching God* 91
'Site of Memory' (Toni Morrison) 146
'Slow Walk of Trees. . . .' (Toni Morrison) 197
Song of Solomon (Toni Morrison) 10, 92, 93–114, 195
    ancestor 118–19
    ancestor and literary tradition 100–1, 116
    beauty myth 107
    community 106
    Douglass, Frederick and intertextuality 97–9
    Ellison, Ralph and intertextuality 102–3
    Faulkner, William 102
    Faulkner, William and *Go Down, Moses* 103–6
    flight motif 96, 101, 106–7, 119, 127
    intertextuality 98, 102–6
    Joyce, James 99–100
    language 101–2, 105
    love 107
    masculinity 96–7, 106–7, 111
    masculinity and Frantz Fanon on 113–14, 118
    migration 113–14, 119
    orality 97–8
    romance narrative 94–5
    sugar motif 133
    universality 99
    Woolf, Virginia 95
Stein, Gertrude 18, 25–7

sugar 133, 189
Sula (Toni Morrison) 10, 19, 35, 41, 43, 70, 71–5, 92, 94–7, 101, 118, 129, 130, 137, 143, 161, 163, 165, 169, 176, 185
    absence 81–2
    Black Power 71, 74
    community and marginality 70–6, 78–9, 80–1, 83
    female identity 82–3, 87
    folk 75, 80, 101
    folk and Zora Neale Hurston 77, 88
    folk and Philip Richards's reading 77–8
    masculinity 118
    migration 80–1, 84
    music 72–3, 75
    music and Douglass 76–7
    music and W. E. B. Du Bois and Zora Neale Hurston 77
    narrative form 81–2
    prologue 71–3
    Sula's individualism and artistic potential 79–80
    water motif 185
Sundquist, Eric *(To Wake the Nations)* 17n

Tar Baby (Toni Morrison) 10, 20, 41, 94, 107, 119, 125–35, 137, 143, 189
    ancestor 127, 128, 135
    Baldwin, James and 'innocence' 133, 189
    Deleuze Gilles and Félix Guattari context 119–26, 132
    Faulkner *(Go Down Moses)* 131
    female empowerment 129–30
    myth and orality 126–9, 130, 135
    naming 134–5
    postcolonial and ecocritical reading 131–3
    water motif 127, 131
    whiteness 135
Thomas, Clarence 111, 112
Toomer, Jean *(Cane)* 26–9, 31–2, 35, 38, 40, 44
transnationalism 182–3, 188, 193, 196

'Unspeakable Things Unspoken' (Toni Morrison) 8, 71, 82, 94, 99, 139

Van der Zee, James 138
vernacular theories of literature 5–8

Walker, Alice on Zora Neale Hurston 33
Wallace, Michelle *(Black Macho and the Myth of the Superwoman)* 109–11
Washington, Booker T. 18, 22, 25, 177, 182
West, Cornel 16
Williams, William Carlos 18
Willis, Susan 96n, 106

Woolf, Virginia 95
Wright, Richard 34–5, 44, 46, 63, 70, 100, 115–16

Young, Robert 28, 51–4, 56–8, 140–1, 151n

Zamir, Shamoon 15–16, 39n